SEARCHING FOR ASHOKA

NAYANJOT LAHIRI

Searching for Ashoka
Questing for a Buddhist King from India to Thailand

SUNY PRESS

First published by Permanent Black D-28 Oxford Apts, 11 IP Extension, Delhi 110092 INDIA, for the territory of SOUTH ASIA. First SUNY Press edition 2023.

Not for sale in South Asia.

Cover design by Anuradha Roy.

Published by State University of New York Press, Albany

© 2022 Nayanjot Lahiri

All rights reserved

Printed in the United States of America

No part of this book may be used or reproduced in any manner whatsoever without written permission. No part of this book may be stored in a retrieval system or transmitted in any form or by any means including electronic, electrostatic, magnetic tape, mechanical, photocopying, recording, or otherwise without the prior permission in writing of the publisher.

For information, contact State University of New York Press, Albany, NY
www.sunypress.edu

Library of Congress Cataloging-in-Publication Data

Names: Lahiri, Nayanjot, author
Title: Searching for Ashoka : questing for a Buddhist king from India to Thailand
Description: Albany : State University of New York Press, [2023] bibliographical references and index.
Identifiers: ISBN 9781438492858 (hardcover : alk. paper) | ISBN 9781438492865 (e-book) | ISBN 9781438492841 (paperback : alk. paper)
Further information is available at the Library of Congress.

10 9 8 7 6 5 4 3 2 1

for
Tarini
and in memory of her beloved
Dadi-Ma

Contents

	Preface and Acknowledgements	xi
	Introduction: Encountering Ashoka	1
1	Imaging Ashoka at Sanchi	20
2	Among Kings at Kanaganahalli	50
3	On the Edge of a Junagadh Lake	81
4	Looking Back at Barabar	101
5	Searching Siblings in Sri Lanka	119
6	Among Relics and Shrines in Myanmar	152
7	Ashokas in Thailand	177
8	Fabricating Remembrance	204
	Bibliography	217
	Index	227

PHOTOGRAPHS

(excluding Figs 5.8, 5.9, 6.5, and 6.6, all photos are by the author)

A.1	Ancient representation of the Sarnath pillar at Sanchi	9
A.2	Modern copy of the Sarnath pillar at Chiang Mai	10
1.1	Notice at Sanchi railway station	24

1.2	Remnant of the Ashokan pillar near the southern gate of the Great Stupa	32
1.3	Carved representation of the Sarnath pillar at Stupa 3	41
1.4	Ashoka's visit to the Ramagrama stupa	44
1.5.	A grieving Ashoka with his queen on his visit to the Bodhi tree	46
2.1	Kanaganahalli in 2010	54
2.2	Carved and engraved panel lying exposed on brown soil	55
2.3	Cracked sculpture of a dharmachakra crowned pillar	56
2.4	Another cracked slab of a Sarnath-inspired rendering of an Ashokan pillar	57
2.5	Chhimukha Satavahana with his queen	66
2.6	Ashoka with his queen	70
2.7	Ashoka as a pilgrim at Mahabodhi	74
2.8	Ashoka worshipping the Bodhi tree	75
2.9	Ramagrama stupa with Ashoka worshipping it	76
2.10	One face of Ashoka's Kanaganahalli edict stone	78
3.1	Building made over the Girnar rock	89
3.2	Girnar rock with Ashokan edicts visible on this face	91
3.3	Rudradaman inscription on the Girnar rock	96
4.1	An athletic-looking Varaha	106
4.2	A "loverly" Siva and Parvati among old images	107
4.3	Old images in a new structure of the Siddeshwarnath temple complex	107
4.4	Interior of the Sudama cave	111
4.5	Ashokan carved architrave on the exterior of the Lomasha Rishi cave	111

4.6	Anup Mukherjee's comments in the visitor book at Barabar	117
5.1	Sanghamitta carrying the Bodhi tree being received by the king	128
5.2	Model of the ship that carried Sanghamitta at Jambukola Pattuna	129
5.3	Small stupas at Kantarodai	132
5.4	Missaka mountain in Mihintale, with a line of visitors	136
5.5	Mihindu Seya	139
5.6	Brahmi epigraph at Mihintale	141
5.7	Brahmi epigraph at Vessagiriya	141
5.8	Epigraph at Rajagala. *Courtesy* Osmund Bopearachchi	144
5.9	Description of contents of Rajagala rock inscription. *Courtesy* Osmund Bopearachchi	146
6.1	Copies of epigraphs collected by King Bodawpaya	159
6.2	Mahabodhi temple in Bagan	165
6.3	View of the Shikhara of the Mahabodhi temple in Bagan	166
6.4	Kubyauk-Gyi temple	168
6.5	Mogaliputta Tissa performing miracles for Ashoka. *Courtesy* Amalesh Roy	170
6.6	Ashoka requesting that monks be told to hold the Uposatha festival. *Courtesy* Amalesh Roy	171
7.1	Dharmachakra with a couchant deer in front at the Bangkok National Museum	183
7.2	Dharmachakra in the Phrapathomchedi Museum, Nakhon Pathom	186

7.3	Wat Cedi Cet Yod in Chiang Mai that was apparently modelled on the Mahabodhi temple	197
7.4	Modern statue of Ashoka Dhamma-raja in Nakhon Si Thammarat	198
7.5	Modern statues of Dandakumar and Hemjala	200
8.1	Prime Minister Nehru at Sanchi with the Burmese premier U Nu, along with other dignitaries	215

Preface and Acknowledgements

THE EMPEROR ASHOKA first appeared in my professional life while I was exploring prehistoric sites in and around New Delhi in December 1985. I came face to face with his First Edict on a rocky outcrop in a South Delhi park behind the Kalkaji mandir. The edict captures his metamorphosis as a Buddhist. However, at that point in time Ashoka did not interest me as much as the stone tools I was searching for on slopes in the edict's vicinity, the relics of human beings who lived there many thousands of years before Ashoka's words were cut into rocks.

Yet this first experience with the emperor's words lay dormant within me and the fellow pounced into my head off and on over the years. Eventually, unable to keep him down, I began field work in 2011 for a biography, and in pursuit of source material I travelled to see his words *in situ* and imagine his presence on rocky paths and ridges in Buddhist holy sites, amidst high hills, cultivated fields, and sheltering forests. In such landscapes, *Ashoka in Ancient India* (2015) took shape.

That book is centrally concerned with the historical emperor's life and times. My travels had however also shown the intertwining of his life and memory in a variety of locations. So I found myself going back to the different ways in which Ashoka was remembered and trying to understand how memories of him had been shaped over time, accumulating and eroding like the slabs of rock on which he had left his words. I then decided to combine this aspect with the fun and feel of his forms in Thailand, Myanmar, and Sri Lanka.

As before in India and Nepal, it was a fascinating mixture of remembering and reinventing that I came to encounter and understand in my travels abroad to the East. This book is the outcome of those journeys. It is not a book about *all* things Ashokan; to tackle a subject as vast would have been impossible and I have not attempted it. Moreover, the world is full of countries with Buddhist hotspots and for financial and other reasons I could not have visited them all.

I owe a profound debt to Ashoka University, which made possible through annual faculty grants all the journeys I undertook in search of the emperor after whom the institution is named. After decades of coping with the red tape of government-aided institutions, the enabling environment at Ashoka University continues to surprise me. It has, above all, ensured that I have had the means and the leisure to carry out a large part of the work involved in writing this book.

The idea of travelling in search of Ashoka was first bounced off two close friends and colleagues, Rudrangshu Mukherjee and Upinder Singh. My decision to write this book has been stimulated by their friendship and encouragement. Several ideas that form the basic argument of this book were first articulated while teaching students at Ashoka University who had opted for my course on "History and Memory", and I owe a great deal to their insights, which helped me develop my ideas.

Many friends and scholars have helped my travels over the years, and I am specially indebted to Yashovardhan Sinha, Sudarshan Seneviratne, Krishnarajah Selliah, and Gautam Mukhopadhyaya.

I have thoroughly enjoyed the travels involving other friends as well because of the enthusiasm, conversations, and counsel of Ratna Raman in Karnataka and Sri Lanka, and Kishore Lahiri in Sri Lanka, Thailand, and Myanmar – where Kishore and I were joined by our children Karan and Vrinda.

Many other scholars and friends have provided references and feedback. Among these are Sanjukta Datta, Sudarshana Chanda,

Jairam Ramesh, Don Stadtner, and John Miksic. I want to specially mention Osmund Bopearachchi, who was enormously generous with wide-ranging reflections and comments which have substantially changed the chapter on Sri Lanka.

The material that I needed was provided in many instances by two remarkable librarians, Narendra Kumar (University of Delhi) and Bibhuti Nath Jha (Ashoka University). Without their unfailing help, it would not have been possible to access many of the library resources that I have drawn upon. The Siam Society Library in Bangkok was enormously helpful as well, providing hospitality and help with material. Its open shelving made it possible to spot all kinds of books that I read there and used when writing this book.

Searching for Ashoka is dedicated to my granddaughter Tarini, and to my mother. It was written entirely in the time of Covid and all credit for allowing it to happen must go to Tarini, who provided constant love and laughter. Seeing her play with her beloved Dadi-Ma – my late mother, Ajit Kaur Bassi – was a joy, especially in my mother's last few months at our home. Like Tarini, I continue to miss her intensely.

Rukun Advani has, as always, been my intellectual lodestar and editorial advisor over the making of this book.

January 2022   NAYANJOT LAHIRI

INTRODUCTION

Encountering Ashoka

> Oft of one wide expanse had I been told
> That deep-brow'd Homer ruled as his demesne;
> Yet did I never breathe its pure serene
> Till I heard Chapman speak out loud and bold:
> Then felt I like some watcher of the skies
> When a new planet swims into his ken . . .
>
> – Keats, "On First Looking Into Chapman's Homer"

THERE IS NO avoiding the figure of Ashoka (c. 304–232 BCE) in the Thai city of Nakhon Si Thammarat. He swam into my ken there, an unexpected planet. I had gone in chase of him, expecting little, but then seen enough to become a Keatsian watcher of the skies.

At first glance Ashoka's presence in southern Thailand may seem to the normal reader more than somewhat surprising. The third emperor of the Maurya dynasty of ancient India is, after all, separated from Thailand by his Indianness, several centuries, and the Indian Ocean. The first thing to do, it seemed to me, was to try working out why this very ancient Indian king was being remembered in this particular location so distant from modern Bihar, from where he had once ruled.

One aspect of the answer seemed to lie in geography: Nakhon Si Thammarat is a city in an isthmian region that partook of much that had happened in Asia between the South China Sea towards the east and the Bay of Bengal on the west. Its artefacts and antiquities, its oral legends and textual narratives, all reveal remarkable connections between Thailand and India. To discover them, though, one has to look beyond the city's modern façade.

Nakhon Si Thammarat is an urban centre with a provincial ambience. Nothing in its contemporary form – moderately sized clusters of restaurants and residences, hotels and movie theatres – specially stands out, and almost certainly no avatars of ancient Ashoka can be spotted within the uniform modernity that suffuses everything.

But only a short distance away, untroubled by new Nakhon, lies a charming historic hub where it is easier to see residual shadows and ghosts of things that once made up its history. It was these elements of a fascinating past, in fact, that had drawn me across the Malay peninsula to sojourn in Nakhon in the winter of 2017. The ambience of the old city owes much to its Buddhist *wats* (places of worship) and *wihaans* (image sanctuaries), representations of Hindu deities in temples and gardens, and those of the Buddha and Bodhisattvas (future Buddhas). There is, above all, the presence of kings with names that would ring a bell in the mind of more or less any Indian historian – appellations such as "Si Thammsok" or "Sri Dharmasokaraja", kings who ruled over territories here in the first half of the second millennium CE. The resonance of the earlier Indian Ashoka in these is almost a lesson in Thai political history, where the titles of rulers function emblematically. Thai dynasties sometimes sought to construct their history by invoking an ideal, even if that ideal was best conveyed by the name of a long dead Indian king.

Among all that is extraordinary about the presence of Ashoka in Nakhon Si Thammarat, the most remarkable and original is his representation in medieval chronicles composed around the city. These narratives centre on rulers who were described as having made Nakhon their capital – men who ruled there more than 1400 years after Ashoka. The texts speak of a letter carried to Thailand by a messenger from Sri Dharmasokaraja, who is described as a ruler of "Madhyadesha" – meaning "Middle

Country" – a term used in antiquity for a large part of North India.[1] This Indian king – a ruler of immense merit who could translate from the Pali language with the expertise of monks – is said in these texts to have built some 84,000 holy reliquaries in which to house relics of the Buddha. However, while he had all these reliquaries ready for the relics, he lacked the relics! Empty vessels make most noise, and so the reliquaries were, in a manner of speaking, crying out to be filled: the letter to the Thai ruler of the Nakhon region was one such cry. The Indian Ashoka needed the help of his Thai counterpart to send him relics of the Buddha to enshrine.

To the embarrassment of the Nakhon Ashoka, the location within his city where these relics were meant to have been buried was a mystery – or at least a mystery to him. A treasure hunt was called for. Eventually, the Thai king succeeded in getting the correct burial spot identified by a couple of people who were in the know about such antique matters. The story ends happily: the Thai Ashoka recovered the Buddhist relics within his territories and dispatched them to the Indian Ashoka, where they presumably alleviated the emptiness of 84,000 reliquaries awaiting fulfilment.

For nearly a millennium and a half, it would seem from stories such as these, old legends had grown and new ones been invented around Ashoka. And they had crept, filtered through, and made their way to distant lands – not just north to Tibet and China, but also east across an ocean. In their wake, six hundred or so years later, here I was on their tail, chasing tales.

By the time he came to be imagined in this part of Thailand, Ashoka's persona had undergone a transformation more or less absolute. As we know – and this is something I had narrated a couple of years earlier in my book titled *Ashoka in Ancient India*

---

[1] References will be cited and discussed at length later in the book, in the chapter on Thailand.

(2015) – during his rule the Indian emperor had issued many public communications, all inscribed on rocks that had been discovered scattered over Indian terrain from Afghanistan in the north-west to Karnataka in the far south. These edicts, as they are commonly called, are crowded around a few years in Ashoka's life – from around 261 to 243 BCE. In them Ashoka mentions several rulers and states to the west of his empire, from the Seleucid kingdom to Ptolemaic Egypt, from Antigonus II Gonatas of Macedon to Magas of Cyrene. But not a single ruler or region to the east of the Indian subcontinent – and not even in a generic sense – appears on these most antique intimations of lithography. It was clear to me that neither Thailand nor any other part of South East Asia ever swam into Ashoka's ken. Some of the texts about him that were put together centuries after his death – as for instance the Sanskrit legendary biography in Sanskrit called the *Ashokavadana* (c. second century CE) – did however associate Ashoka with the construction of stupas in which relics within earlier stupas were first exhumed and then reburied. In this part of Thailand, that ancient story had taken new shape: the Indian king was transformed into a supplicant seeking relics in a South East Asian region he very probably had no notion of. Ashoka, as he appears in medieval Nakhon Si Thammarat, is different in all but name from the kingly figure recorded in ancient South Asia.

This phenomenon, of making a historical figure visible while simultaneously reinventing him, and of adapting faint memories and echoes of him to new political or other purposes, has never ceased to amaze me across the many years that I have spent in the company of Emperor Ashoka. In this process of being transformed, of course, he is not exceptional. Poetry may emanate from emotion recollected in tranquillity, but history is more often political memory recollected in tumult; in both cases, the idea seems to be to transform what is being recalled. There is for instance Alexander, the fourth-century BCE Macedonian whose honorific "Great" rendered invisible the killings and pogroms in the trail of his conquests from Persia to India. And yet this ancient conqueror of Persia reappears as a Persian king in medieval texts.[2] Something similar happens to Sultan Saladin, founder of the Ayubbid dynasty, who recaptured Jerusalem from European Crusaders in 1187 CE. This Muslim sovereign was once turned into a Christian knight – supposedly through a genealogical link on his mother's side – and at another time into a convert to Christianity secretly baptising himself without his entourage being in the know.[3] In the world of art a most remarkable metamorphosis involves the black-haired Egyptian Queen Cleopatra being depicted by medieval and Renaissance artists as a "pale blonde because the pale blonde was their ideal of beauty".[4]

Human memory is notoriously selective. Psychologists have pointed out that what is played back is never an exact replica of events as they played out. Frederic Bartlett, famous for pioneering work on the character of remembrance, pointed out in *Remembering* (1932) that memory retains a "little outstanding detail" while the remainder is reconstructive. Changed contexts and alterations in outlook determine the nature of new images and perspectives on past figures and events. Historians have highlighted this phenomenon in relation to the hoary as well as the relatively recent past. Mahatma Gandhi, for instance, was selectively remembered even within his lifetime: people saw him as they wanted or needed to see him, and ideas of him were very quickly reworked in the popular imagination.[5] Within months of his visiting a particular area, what he said to his audience there – which is a matter of record – was a far cry from

---

[2] Romm, ed. (2012): Appendix L. For Alexander as a part of Persianite culture in India, see Cornwall (2020).

[3] A fascinating range of Saladin's avatars can be seen in Edde (2011), in the sixth segment of the book entitled "The Legend".

[4] Tyldesley (2008): 215.

[5] Amin (1988).

what many who heard him recalled him saying – which is also a matter of record. In such matters, obviously, time is *not* of the essence. Recollections manipulate and transform the image of a near contemporary, Gandhi, in much the way they do an ancient figure such as Ashoka.

Thinking about all these willed reincarnations and deliberate transformations made the Thai version of Ashoka seem to me part of a historical remembrance pattern. People remember what they please and as they please, and then a historian comes along to show what she sees as the original shape of a ruler, which is not exactly his original shape either, and she then follows up his distinctly differing manifestations in subsequent centuries and distant locations. An Indian Ashoka making an appearance as a new man altogether within a Thai relic redistribution saga was, you could say, almost de rigueur.

When I first plunged into the history of this emperor – whose knowable past I had, as I said, examined in my *Ashoka in Ancient India* – what had emerged from his epigraphs were eccentric political interventions and an exceptional ideology of governance. From all that he set down in stone he was, it seemed to me, the most powerful, prominent, and impressive king ever to rule ancient India, and quite possibly the most uniquely compassionate ruler anywhere.[6] His lifespan, as also that of the Maurya dynasty, was unfortunately finite. Some fifty years after he passed away, so did the dynasty of which he was the exemplar. In the ensuing centuries the core of what was known about the historical emperor became a casualty within many new conceptions of him. It is not that he was not remembered – on the contrary. But,

---

[6] I was naturally very far from being the first to show this: the history of his recognition as utterly extraordinary is a subject in itself and dates back to the time of the discovery of his existence in the mid-nineteenth century. Among the many who memorably extol Ashoka are H.G. Wells in his *Outline of History* (1919–20) and *A Short History of the World* (1922), and Jawaharlal Nehru in *The Discovery of India* (1946).

in the panorama of the past within which he was recalled, the jumble of images of him that came to circulate were largely those evident in religious iconography and texts rooted in Buddhism. The many avatars of this reified persona may not have been quite as dramatic as in Nakhon, but they did involve thoroughgoing reimaginings and redefinitions.

Searching for Ashoka follows these many reconceptualisations of the emperor. I encountered them in places to which I travelled in search of his traces. Several of the chapters that follow are about Ashoka in spots across India, from Jahanabad in Bihar to Kanaganahalli in Karnataka. Others emerge from sites and cities in Sri Lanka, Thailand, and Myanmar. Beyond a sense of curiosity about how Ashoka is remembered from South Asia to South East Asia, setting out on this trail helped me understand the nature and workings of historical memory.[7] And, I should add, also what might be termed historical forgetting. This subject – the memory and memorialisation of Ashoka – is vast and not limited to the collection of examples that I will offer. I have not engaged here with the Ashoka stupas in China, nor with the fate of Ashokan pillars in various parts of India and Nepal.[8] Nor does the range of representations from antiquity to modernity of any particular Ashokan artefact feature in this book except in an incidental way. The Sarnath pillar of Ashoka happens to be one of them: its memorialisation ranges from Sanchi in Central India during the late centuries BCE to Chiang Mai in Thailand in the

---

[7] Sumit Guha's *tour de force* (2019) looks at history and collective memory in admirable detail. He points to various modes of structuring and controlling memory, ranging from hagiographies to practices of commemoration. My book is limited to exploring the commemoration and memorialisation of one historical figure, Ashoka.

[8] Soper (1959) has extensive references to the Ashokan stupas and even Ashokan images. It is based on excerpts of the Japanese text of Omura Seigai. The afterlife of Ashoka's pillars in Nepal – from later epigraphs on them to the designation of a broken pillar at Gotihawa as Phuteshwar Mahadeva – is known to me from my own research there.

1960s (Figs A.1 and A.2). I am selective. I stop at historic sites and locales that I find fascinating and take some care to explain the historical traces of the emperor I see in them.

∼

Before I move on to recall what I saw over my journeys, I want to pause to pick out some threads that will make the tapestry of remembrance around Ashoka intelligible. Within his lifetime the emperor created images of himself through his own words, and I will often recall them here to evaluate what got filtered out and what remained. An issue I confronted each time I came upon memorialisations of Ashoka was: Has his image been added to or changed in relation to what I know to be true of his historical persona? This being a valid question, I reckon that for readers of this book it is first necessary to outline what I know about the man in his own lifetime.

The first thing to note about the historical Ashoka is that only a partial recall of his life is possible because, it turns out, this emperor, who is so communicatively expansive through his proclamatory edicts, said nothing at all about his birth, years as a prince, and early period as a ruler.[9] Nor do other contemporary records. So, for instance, if we do have a likely year for Ashoka's birth at the cusp of the fourth and third century BCE, this is a surmise arrived at by working back from the date when he was anointed emperor. His consecration figures persistently in the record and we do have a reasonably accurate date for it – 269/268 BCE. As with several other kings in ancient India whose lives were described in regnal years, Ashoka anchored various happenings during his reign in relation to this year. Dates start appearing once he starts feeling intensely enough about his ideas and innovations to want them inscribed on stone. And Ashoka's most intense feelings, as is well known, date from the aftermath of the

---

[9] This has been discussed in Lahiri (2015), esp. Chapters 1 and 12.

INTRODUCTION: ENCOUNTERING ASHOKA 9

Fig. A.1: Ancient representation of the Sarnath pillar at Sanchi

bloody Kalinga war. "Oh, from this time forth," says Hamlet in a moment of decisive reckoning, "My thoughts be bloody or be nothing worth": change "bloody" to "unbloody" and it exactly describes Ashoka after the Kalinga war. His monumentally famous remorse results in writings that make him as memorable as Marcus Aurelius, and in the Orient far more famous.

Fig. A.2: Modern copy of the Sarnath pillar at Chiang Mai

Ashoka's conversion to Buddhism is quite logically presumed to be on account of his change of heart following the Kalinga carnage. Rock surfaces and, later, pillars come to be inscribed with his words urging peace, goodwill, fellow feeling, compassion, and a great deal else. These have been found in some fifty-odd places across India, Pakistan, Nepal, and Afghanistan; there are likely to have been many more such that have either succumbed to time or remain undiscovered. The sheer geographical spread of these Ashokan edicts underlines an emperor who was not someone his subjects imagined ruling in a faraway capital, but rather someone real they encountered on a rock near paths where they lived, in the vicinity of where they worshipped, along routes they travelled. While I doubt that Ashoka himself visited all the places where his messages have been found, he is extraordinary in ensuring his presence across such a massive territorial expanse. In this he alone comes across as an emperor in the ancient world who desired communication with people in spaces that lay outside his comfort zone, far beyond the privileged royal surroundings where he himself was located.

Because he chose to speak in this way, we have an understanding of Ashoka's idea of kingship, aspects of his rule, his personality, the extent of his empire, and a few neighbouring rulers. From his reaching out we can at least assume it was of special importance to him that his subjects hear the singularity and sameness of his voice across the land he ruled: each message that he sent out to his administrators was in a form more or less identical with every other. Ashoka is singular as the communicator-king par excellence; copies of his communications were prepared and dispatched to his various provinces to ensure that his message of morality and related ideas of governance had a massive reach.

While he revealed very little by way of detail about his personal life, what little he did put down on stone shows a keenness to appear to posterity not as imperious but as a flesh-and-blood emperor. His first message gives a good sense of what he considered worthy of recounting to his subjects: not matters of state, but the state of his mind. He says he has become a Buddhist. His metamorphosis, he says, needs to be understood and emulated. The message is partly confessional, presenting his self-realisation as persuasion, and underlining the possibility that the new morality is open and available to all.[10]

[10] The Rupnath Edict in Hultzsch (1925): 166–9 is an example of this message.

A little later he records the big war he won at Kalinga as a disaster because of the slaughter, mostly collateral, that the victory involved.[11] He paints himself as the perpetrator of the carnage. This is, to put it mildly, mind-blowing. No other victorious ruler in history comes to mind who, after winning a huge war, sees himself as a defeated king. Images of the Oriental despot, the Mongol hordes, the Vandals and the Huns and the Goths, Genghis Khan and Timur have collectively coloured our notion of eastern monarchs as semi-savage warrior-kings. Humility and self-abnegation are the last virtues we associate in a colossally successful male monarch in Asia. In this respect, Ashoka is utterly singular.

Some years later he appears again, and again in an all-too-human way, publicly acceding to the desires of his queen, Karuvaki. She has gifted mango groves, gardens, and almshouses and wants them registered in her name.[12] The king informs his officers; the registration is done as she desires. All of this, for the average subject in Ashoka's time, may have been bewilderingly unlike anything that history had shown them as the day-to-day reality of royal rule. While kingship had a distinguished antiquity in large parts of Ashoka's empire, going back many centuries prior to the dynasty of the Mauryas, a king was not prone to confiding in his people about either the life-changing episodes of his career or the desires of his queen.

Ashoka went on to elaborate and disseminate information on what appear to be very novel modes of governance, as well as norms of public and personal conduct. Among his public messages the one which still resonates among liberals, secularists, and democrats – and no doubt sorely grates on majoritarians and religious fundamentalists – is addressed to all the sects of his day: it asks for a public culture in which every denomination honours

---

[11] Lines 36 and 37, Thirteenth Rock Edict, Kalsi version, ibid.: 44.
[12] This is known as the Queen's Edict. Ibid.: 159.

every other. This is the essence of the Ashokan ideal of political space drawn from dhamma/dharma – the new morality is extensively described in the commandment.[13] The king also vests enhanced spiritual responsibility in his officers, who are ordered, even while carrying out their routine duties, to do an inspection every five years and preach the dhamma.[14]

Enjoined on all are proper conduct towards the various classes of people and animal life, respect for parents and elders, and liberality with friends as well as those with differing religious inclinations. Ashoka himself undertook what were described as "dharma yatras" which involved "visiting Shramanas and Brahmanas and making gifts (to them), visiting the aged and supporting (them) with gold, visiting the people of the country, instructing (them) in morality, and questioning (them) about morality, as suitable for this (occasion)."[15] Alongside, the king made himself accessible at all times to ensure swiftness in the transaction of state business. His officials, he proclaimed, could come to him at any time, including in his harem or when he was dining. While the reality may well have been different, the message signalling his interest in the prompt dispatch of business indicates a new priority given to the common weal.[16]

In later messages engraved on pillars, Ashoka grappled with the question of how harsh punishments handed out by the state might be mitigated. He ordered an interlude of three days from the time punishment was pronounced by "rajukkas" – officials who were responsible for justice in the countryside – to when condemned prisoners were led to the gallows.[17] The respite was to allow relatives of prisoners on death row to appeal. Simultaneously,

---

[13] Twelfth Rock Edict, lines 3 and 4 of the Girnar version. Ibid.: 20.
[14] Third Rock Edict, lines 2 and 3, Erragudi version, Sircar (1979): 16.
[15] Eighth Rock Edict, line 23, Kalsi version, Hultzsch (1925): 36.
[16] Sixth Rock Edict, lines 1 and 2, Erragudi version, Sircar (1979): 17.
[17] Fourth Pillar Edict, lines 15 and 16, Delhi-Topra pillar, Hultzsch (1925): 123.

the hiatus might ensure a more dignified death by allowing the condemned man to prepare himself with fasting or bestowing gifts. On as many as twenty-five occasions from the time of his anointment, Ashoka released prisoners, and some of these were conceivably commutations.[18]

A slew of substantive injunctions against the killing of animals, birds, and fish constitute another exceptional dimension of the emperor's humane provisions. From the modern ecological perspective his Fifth Pillar Edict is without doubt the most copious royal message anywhere in the ancient world for the protection of living beings in general. The persona of Ashoka as a guardian of animals permeates his major rock edicts; they outline personal and public measures for a kind of proto-conservation. Sacrifices are proscribed, the slaughter of animals for consumption in the royal kitchen drastically reduced, veterinary hospices established, and provisions made for pack animals along roads. He elaborates at length on measures for protecting the habitat of such living creatures and preventing cruelty towards them. "Cocks must not be caponed," he says, and "husks containing living animals must not be burnt," nor forests uselessly razed as they destroy living beings. An emperor ordering his people not to kill pregnant and lactating she-goats and sows, and regulating animal castration, needs to say nothing else to appear extraordinary.[19] The success of this range of interventions on the ground is difficult to judge, but from this distance in time it seems enough that the effort was made and that its compassion is so staggering. Through his words Ashoka advances the notion of a fundamentally new kind of political and social community.

While still a young ruler, in words he first recorded in (what came to be known as) the Minor Rock Edicts – which were carved a little after 260 BCE – Ashoka offers a glimpse of himself, his move to Buddhism, and what that meant for him as a ruler

---

[18] Fifth Pillar Edict, lines 19 and 20, Delhi-Topra pillar, ibid.: 126.

[19] This, the Fifth Pillar Edict, is worth reading in its entirety. See Delhi-Topra pillar, ibid.: 125–8.

and his empire at large.[20] Very precise instructions were given on how he wanted his mission to be disseminated, and in many different places. Where these are found, as also in their hinterlands, there can have been no ambiguity in the minds of his readers and listeners that the king was publicly communicating as a Buddhist. His Buddhist persona was dramatically visible later as well. He travelled to Buddhist sacred places in the Nepal terai, such as Lumbini and Nigali Sagar; in the latter he had a stupa rebuilt, expanded, and dedicated to the Buddha Konakamana (or Konakamuni). Konakamuni was said to be an ancient Buddha (antedating the sixth-century BCE historical original), about whom we know very little. An emperor's pilgrimage to pay his respects would denote a revered deity. At Lumbini, the Buddha's birthplace, Ashoka inscribed a record of his pilgrimage on a pillar that he set up there. He also used the occasion to announce a reduction in taxes. At Sarnath and Kausambi in the Gangetic plains, and at Sanchi in Central India, he presented himself as a spiritual regulator and protector of Buddhist unity, opposing divisions ("samghabheda") among monks and nuns.[21]

All this takes Ashoka beyond the mere practice of supporting Buddhist Shramanas (monks) and erecting or enlarging holy places associated with the faith. Dampening dissension within the Sangha makes him sound like a Buddhist pontiff. He opposed factional breakaways and proposed punishing dissidents by forcing them to give up monastic robes and wear the white clothes of householders. At Bairat in Rajasthan he offered advice on the particular religious expositions he believed the monastic community needed to absorb. The confidence with which he suggested that they focus on listening and reflect on specific doctrinal messages would suggest he saw himself as the Buddha's preacher-successor.[22]

---

[20] Rupnath Edict, ibid.: 166–9.
[21] The Sarnath Edict exemplifies this well. Ibid.: 161–4.
[22] Bairat Edict, ibid.: 172–4.

Ashoka was obsessed with his ideas and interventions and dreaded their disappearance. He manifests an unusual degree of anxiety at the spectre of impermanence; it explains why he constantly urges his successors – his sons and his grandsons, and "the generations coming after them till the destruction of the world" – to continue his acts of merit, for "whosoever among them will abandon even a part of it will do an act of demerit." Hammering home the new moral message of dhamma, literally as well as metaphorically, by casting it in stone seems to have been the consequence of some nervousness over whether "his descendants may conform to it."

Did the Ashokan edicts also serve to relieve the emperor's angst about the future and the survival of his legacy with concrete remembrances of things past? If so, what did he find worth recall, and in what contexts? The form in which Ashoka invokes the past seems to me fairly similar to how others would later remember him. Dredging up an earlier event or persona, even his own self, and reshaping it in order to convey the creation of something new is the form he followed. It is writ large in his meditations on matters of the mind and the state.

The past features in Ashoka's words most often when he sets out the consequences of the new morality or dhamma that he is promoting, and sometimes in the slipstream of major episodes in his own life. So, for instance, in the first communiqué he sent off to his administrators his message presents the success of his mission and life with the assertion that whereas in preceding times humans and gods had not mingled, now in his empire – and he takes credit for this – such intermingling has been made possible.[23] Pointing to his own graduated progression as a Buddhist he says that though he became a lay worshipper two and a half

---

[23] Rupnath Edict, line 2, ibid.: 166.

years earlier, it was only a year or so ago that he became zealous on account of his interaction with the Buddhist Sangha (order). The past state of his kingdom, as also the past state of his own mind, are invoked to emphasise his transformation and mission to promote the same zeal in his subjects.

This juxtaposition of the features of a progressive present with memories of a less than edifying past is more dramatically clear in Ashoka's Major Rock Edicts, so called because they are more expansive than the Minor Rock Edicts – an earlier set of shorter messages. The practice of dhamma has altered the emperor and he is determined about its dissemination to make it universal. Whereas "many hundred thousands of living beings were formerly slaughtered" in the royal kitchen, now only three living creatures – two birds and one animal – are slaughtered.[24] Earlier, "for many hundreds of years, slaughter of lives, cruelty to living creatures, disrespect to Shramanas and Brahmans increased."[25] Now, what had increased "to a degree as was not possible to achieve for many hundreds of years in the past" was "abstention from the slaughter of life, absence of cruelty to living creatures, seemly behaviour to Shramanas and Brahmanas, obedience to mother and father [and] obedience to the aged."[26] Where war drums had once sounded, there was now the sound of morality ("bherighoso aho dhammaghoso").[27] While in the past martial music had accompanied armed battles – the beating of the "bheri" was a call to arms – there was now only the sound of dhamma being proclaimed.

Governance is described via similar contrasts between past shortcoming and present improvement. There was a time when no reports were submitted to the ruler, nor was the disposal of affairs speedy; now informers report the affairs of the people at

---

[24] First Rock Edict, lines 4 and 6, Erragudi version, Sircar (1979): 14.
[25] Fourth Rock Edict, lines 1 to 3, Erragudi version, ibid: 25.
[26] Fourth Rock Edict, lines 5 to 9, Erragudi version, ibid: 25–6.
[27] Fourth Rock Edict, lines 3 and 4, Erragudi version, ibid: 25.

any time and solutions are swift. In the past "kings set out on vihara yatras or pleasure tours", now the king's tours are morality missions ("dharma yatras"). In the Thirteenth Edict the emperor is at his most poignant, snatching defeat from the jaws of victory by remembering the life-changing war at Kalinga. In the eighth year following his consecration, the destructive consequences of his military victory there made him human. In part this painful past is invoked to appeal to a group of adversaries, the Atavikas (forest dwellers), to follow his example. He hopes they will do penitence, as he has done, so that they may spare themselves injury. A threat is being sent out, but in the language of cajolery.[28]

Memories of the past do not figure quite so often in the Pillar Edicts, but even in them he recalls past kings who, desiring men to make progress, promoted morality but failed. Their failure has made him consider the paths of success, and it has struck him that by issuing public proclamations and instructions, and giving muscle and teeth to his administration, he might succeed.[29]

Ashoka did not publicly remember his own background or events from his own past – neither his parents, nor his grandfather, nor even the circumstances which brought him to the throne. His reticence in personal matters is stark. When recounting the times and actions of past kings he does not mention them by name, nor says anything about their reigns that would help identify them. His references to them are abstract, they contrast generically in their morals and governance with him; the specificities of their states are not relevant to his purpose.

The more I looked at the words Ashoka chose to highlight the past so purposively, the more it became clear to me that he saw his calling as that of a missionary whose epiphanic Damascene moment happened on the road back from Kalinga. From this time forth the traces of the past that figure in his messages are

[28] Thirteenth Rock Edict, lines 18 and 20, Erragudi version, ibid.: 31.
[29] Seventh Pillar Edict, lines 17 to 22, Delhi-Topra pillar, Hultzsch (1925): 130.

those through which he seeks to highlight his willed departure towards what he had divined as superior. His dhammic zeal and agenda are burnished by these backward glances at a past comparably less glorious than the present being given shape by him. Even before I began to understand and uncover how Ashoka came to be reconfigured among a diversity of cultures in Asia, I had discovered how clearly his own memory is both constructive and reconstructive. By constructing a particular kind of past within the fabric of moral messages, the emperor was setting himself up as a watershed.

In this book I try to show how skilfully and selectively Ashoka was portrayed in later centuries. He may well have been annoyed by the Thai story in which he appears as a supplicant of a medieval ruler in South East Asia. But, given his own ability to recast the past, and given his powers of self-reflection, I doubt that he would have been surprised by the Thai attempt – and now my attempt – to tell a new story about him.

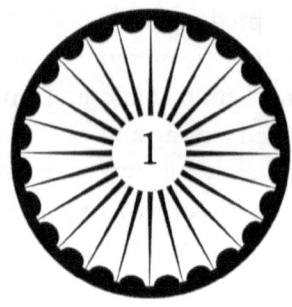

Imaging Ashoka at Sanchi

THE FIRST TIME I travelled to Bhopal was in a "Shatabdi" train which has wide-windowed coaches. Through them I was unexpectedly offered glimpses of the landscape of my childhood. As the train made its way across North India, the flat plains soon gave way to ravines, hill scarps, and plateaus. These dominate the "heart of India", an expression coined by a geographer to describe the area between the Gangetic plains and the Deccan plateau.[1] Here the train rattled through a couple of places where I'd grown up. One of them, a remote military cantonment town called Babina, was in the 1960s the most memorable hamlet of my growing-up years. In India, any settlement of 25,000 people or less must surely be counted a hamlet, and in the Babina of my recollection you had to peer for quite a while to see any Babinans at all. Our one regular link with the world outside Babina was with the medium-sized town of Jhansi, some thirty kilometres away, which had an imposing fort

[1] This was coined by O.H.K. Spate. See Spate and Learmouth (1967): 611.

and a long association with a valorous Rani, she of the flashing scimitar who, if our school history textbooks were to be believed, had nearly ended the British empire single-handed. St Francis Convent School at Jhansi was where many little girls from the Babina cantonment were brought up, all on piously nationalistic textbooks containing stories which made us all fervently patriotic for a time – before reasoning and learning entered our heads and eroded the fervour. I was carted to school and back in a novel mode of transport, a three-tonne army truck fitted with bus seats.

The Shatabdi that day halted at Jhansi junction, but the built-up city no longer provided a view of my old school and the rocks around it. We soon passed Babina. The train did not stop there, but it did go past bits of the cantonment. At the start of the journey I had begun Vikram Seth's novel *A Suitable Boy* (1993), in which the description of pistachio ice-creams and arrowroot biscuits took me back via food memories to Babina – of eating ice-cream made in an old-fashioned hand-crank freezer and ber (jujubes) picked from bushes in the scrubland surrounding the cantonment. The terror of trundling over the railway bridge was specially vivid as the train crossed the very bridge that had once spooked me with its fragility: every time I crossed that bridge, my heart popped into my mouth because of how certain I was the damn thing was going to collapse any minute under me. I was sure the Rani of Jhansi had never had to cross this bridge, else her valour would all have been in the river below. Other than these stray thoughts of childhood apocalypse that wandered into my head, the landscape of my remembrance of those childhood years showed me nothing much else – it was wholly bereft of archaeological relics and ruins, forts and memorials, the sort of stuff that I now know lies scattered there and which makes my innards positively swill with enthusiasm for ancient India.

The same, to begin with, was true of my engagement with Sanchi. When I first saw it, the ancient past of that historic space was not uppermost in my mind. I managed a glimpse of Sanchi on that journey which took me past Babina to Bhopal. Less than an hour before reaching Bhopal, we crossed Vidisha, an unremarkable town today whose most distinguished and ancient citizen in antiquity, Devi – one of the favourite spouses of the Emperor Ashoka – is known to have patronised the Sanchi monastic community more than 2000 years ago. Of course I had no idea where precisely the emperor caught sight of the contours of Devi, but the odd thing, if you happen to be a historian of times so utterly lost and remote, is that even the feeling of being in the proximity of people long dead who live in your mind sets you off on some imagined historical track which meanders and digresses. She had been around nearby, of that there was no doubt. Many years later there were just a few fragments of Devi that I was able to gather when writing about her husband, the very little there is about her in the historical record with which I'd pieced her together – she who was once vibrant and alive, now "a heap of broken images". In that biographical study of Ashoka, this is almost all I was able to say about her:

> In ancient narrations of Ashoka's life, romantic passion appears for the first time when the Pataliputra prince is sent to Malwa in Central India. Tellings of this intersect with him falling in love with a young woman who is known in the ancient Sri Lankan textual tradition as a Buddhist. Her name was Devi and the romance began in the city of Vidisha, where her father was a prominent merchant. Soon enough, Ashoka married Devi and moved on to Ujjayini.

That's about it. That's about all we know of this woman Devi, whose natal habitat I was passing that morning. I wanted to spend a few more minutes with her. She had come into my mind because of a train journey and might never cross my path again. Some fragments of her clung to my mind in connection with that ultimate celebration of a fragmented universe, Eliot's *The Waste Land*. It seems to me a poem addressed exclusively to archaeologists and historians who fix jigsaw-puzzled bits of the past into a seeming coherence. So many stray lines in that poem have a raw power that strike me as wasted on people who haven't spent their whole life seeing the world as a huge heap of shards and splinters that it's their life's purpose to piece together and then thread into a narrative suggesting seamlessness.

> What are the roots that clutch, what branches grow
> Out of this stony rubbish? . . .
> You cannot say, or guess, for you know only
>   A heap of broken images . . .

What else is this except the best possible description of my life's work? We are the clutchers of broken images, discovering in them the roots and branches that we nurse into our stories and histories. It's an art historians and raconteurs have perfected, peering for years at heaps of broken bones and fleeting images and threading them into books like this one, while knowing all along how much better at it the best poets have been. Sometimes they sum it all up in a single line that reverberates through the ages.

> Consider Phlebas, who was once handsome and tall as you.

This sounds even better if you're whizzing by Vidisha in a train and adapt it to immediate needs: "Consider Ashoka, who was once handsome and tall as you." If you're in the business of trying to resurrect the dead, there really doesn't seem any more to be said.

Soon, after crossing Vidisha's railway station, in the distance was the unmistakable egg-like hemispherical dome of Sanchi's largest stupa peeping out of a densely green hill covered with trees. The most abundant of these trees, I later learnt, was the evergreen khirni tree. Its little yellow fruit can in April be bought in the Sanchi market. There were also mahua trees with edible flowers used for making liquor – so memorably and lovingly described in Gopinath Mohanty's classic novel of Indian tribal life *Paraja* (1987) – and palash (Flame of the Forest) with clusters of deep orange blossoms. The Bhopal-bound train did not stop at Sanchi but it did slow down there, enough for me to notice that the station announced itself as a gateway to the monuments in an entirely charming way. Along with the Devanagari and Roman scripts, the name "Sanchi" was written in an ancient script which the notice helpfully identified as Ashokan Brahmi (Fig. 1.1). Travellers were encouraged to walk to the stupa and the museum by another notice which announced they were a mere fifteen minutes away. Until six years ago, when I last went to Sanchi, those notices were visible. Even though passengers who disembark

Fig. 1.1: Notice at Sanchi railway station in Devanagari and the Roman scripts, as also in Ashokan Brahmi

are usually people on a visit to the Buddhist complex, it doesn't harm to reassure them that they are only a short walk from their destination.

I recalled my first visit to this part of Madhya Pradesh, more than twenty years ago: it had had nothing to do with the antique past of Sanchi and everything to do with what had happened to Sanchi in modern times. The defining historical features of this location – specifically the story of how Ashoka had his presence built into the Buddhist community on its hill by constructing a pillar and stupa there – was embedded deep in my own absorption of ancient Indian history as a student. But over that trip twenty years ago I had been preoccupied with Sanchi's modern revival and conservation. I was trying to understand why Sanchi's monuments, which were in a remarkably good state of preservation when they were rediscovered in 1818, needed such urgent and extensive repair.

A man called Edward Fell was the first to leave an eyewitness account of Sanchi. He was a captain in the 10th Native Infantry and his account of Sanchi appeared in the *Journal of the Asiatic Society of Bengal* in 1819. The Great Stupa was in one piece at the time, or so his account says, though his opinion that its fine state of preservation was because of internal pillars and apartments supporting it was not the case at all. Notwithstanding his amateur reasoning, we owe an excellent description of the stupa to Fell: "On a table-land of a detached hill, distant from Bhilsa four miles and a half, in a south-westerly direction is an ancient fabric, of a hemispherical form, built of thin layers of freestone, in the nature of steps, without any cement, and to all appearances solid."[2]

The most stunning aspect of the Great Stupa happens to be its gorgeous gateways, and at the time of Fell's visit three of them were intact. A smaller stupa too, which was halfway down the

---

[2] Fell (1834): 490.

hill, was in "perfect repair". Fell was fascinated by the stories circulating around these stupas. They were known locally as *Saas bahu ka bitha*, i.e. "the mother-in-law and daughter-in-law mounds". Fell believed the mound of the daughter-in-law was located lower to maintain an appropriately respectful distance; she seemed to him to have been put very much below her husband's mother so that the old lady could lord it over the hill in solitary splendour.

Soon after Fell's visit the monuments came to be excavated and documented by British treasure hunters and archaeologists who, unlike Fell, substantially disfigured them by the means and circumstances of their work – resulting in two of the gateways falling down. The political agent at Bhopal, T.H. Maddock, and his assistant, a Captain Johnson, were a couple of such imperial vandals who in the 1820s, during their search for hidden antiquities (remembered in local memory as mining operations), destroyed substantial segments of the stupas. There was also, more surprisingly, Alexander Cunningham (1814–1893), who in 1871 went on to become the first director general of the Archaeological Survey of India. In the 1850s he, along with a fellow officer, F.C. Maisey, shafted the stupas in order to recover relic boxes and caskets and did not care to repair them.[3]

But there were saviours too – actually a star cast of saviours, ranging from an Indian ruler to the top archaeologist of the British Raj, John Marshall (1876–1958), who as director general of the Archaeological Survey of India planned and shepherded the restoration work at Sanchi. There was also Sultan Jahan Begum, the ruler of Bhopal in Marshall's day, who made his project possible by providing him the required money and men. The last in a dynasty of women rulers in that princely state, Sultan Jahan (1858–1930) is generally remembered for her pioneering work

---

[3] Cunningham (1854). For a masterly overview of Cunningham's life and world, Singh (2004) and Singh (2021).

on education and women's emancipation. Her involvement with Sanchi was to me a story both unfamiliar and fascinating: stories around Indian monuments in which the central character is a woman ruler are rare.[4] I was mesmerised by the Begum and what I had dug out on her in the National Archives of India at New Delhi. Her interventions in favour of archaeological work within her kingdom are well recorded. They had put me on the trail that first took me on a train to Bhopal, en route to Sanchi. I needed to know more about her. In that initial journey of discovery, Sanchi's antiquity had hardly figured in my mind. At the time, I was more interested in the modern history of Sanchi's stupas.

Some years later I began exploring ancient Sanchi, which was then known by a variety of names ranging from Kakanava/Kakanaya to Kakanada-bota/Bota-Sriparvatta. These names figure in epigraphs inscribed on Sanchi's gateways and railings, and on sculptures and walkways. The inscriptions, along with Sanchi's monumental and multilayered history, were documented in an immensely scholarly three-volume tome that Marshall put together many years after his work at this location.[5] It seems multiple stupas, chaityas, and viharas had been constructed at Sanchi and elaborated over a period of some fifteen hundred years, from the third century BCE onwards. The archaeological digs through which the evolving past of Sanchi had been reconstructed intrigued me specially, and soon enough an opportunity to see what lay beneath its façade presented itself.

In 2003 I managed a first-hand glimpse when I spent some weeks in an excavation conducted by the Archaeological Survey of India. The dig was directed by S.B. Ota, superintending ar-

[4] See Lahiri (2012a): 36–74.
[5] Marshall, Foucher, and Majumdar (1940): three volumes.

chaeologist of the Bhopal Circle of the Survey. I remember him as a bearded, bright-eyed, bushy-tailed man with a deep knowledge of and passion for Central Indian monuments.[6] The focus of his work at Sanchi was the high upper terrace on which, at one end, stood a large temple known in the literature as Temple 45. The origins of this temple were in the seventh–eighth centuries CE, its present structure having been arrived at a couple of hundred years later. It had been rebuilt when the original was destroyed in a fire.[7] While the platform where the temple had stood showed residual structures, the rest of the levelled area had evidently been filled up during conservation work. From below the one-metre-thick top deposit, early medieval remains, pottery, and antiquities slowly emerged – copper coins and iron objects, beads and fragments of sculpture, even a flake bearing a Brahmi inscription.

But more than this careful uncovering of buried remains, what the dig did for me was provide an opportunity to understand the character of the stupas in an unhurried and intimate way. The lofty platform which was being dug loomed over the main terrace where Ashoka's stupa, with its later additions and embellishments, stood. Consequently I was able to spend hours looking down at that most magnificent structure, marvelling at the architects who had conceptualised it and the sculptors who had exquisitely carved stories on its gateways.

Many mornings, we walked along a route from the Archaeological Survey colony where I lived. This meant passing another early stupa, known as Stupa 2 – the one described by Fell as *bahu bitha*. This stood halfway up the hill and its decorated ground

---

[6] It was there that I first met Dilip Khamari of the ASI and Ranbeer Singh Rajput who was then a trainee and is now a senior officer at the Bihar Museum, Patna. Over the years I have often requested them for help and picked their brains on all kinds of subjects. This would not have happened without that shared experience in the field.

[7] *Indian Archaeology – A Review* (2003–4): 154.

balustrade, which had conspicuous carvings, required a long halt allowing the onlooker to swoon with enchantment at the sheer beauty of it. A massive bowl at near-human height, probably meant for the communal distribution of food in ancient times, was situated a little higher up, a reminder of the large monastic community that had once lived here. A riot of shrubs and vines, bushes and trees surrounded the path leading to the Great Stupa, and poking out of the foliage were the ruins and foundations of shrines and monasteries. This conjured up in my head the kind of vegetation that must once have covered large parts of the hill before sections of it were tamed into the manicured lawns of a monumental complex.

The main terrace was built during the reign of Ashoka. On this terrace was constructed the Great Stupa and alongside it Ashoka put up a pillar carrying one of his edicts. The stupa itself shows no Ashokan epigraph, but we know it dates to his time since the level of the floor on which it stands is the same as that of the inscribed pillar.[8] Made of large burnt bricks, it was topped by a stone umbrella bearing the same kind of polish as on the pillar with Ashoka's message. And, as with most ancient monuments, the architects and workers remain anonymous.

Had Ashoka travelled here in person from his capital at Pataliputra when it was being constructed? We don't know for sure, but there is an even chance since he was the travelling sort. The distance from Pataliputra to Sanchi, roughly 1000 km southwest, wasn't much more than the distance from his throne to Kalinga in the south-east. We do know that Ashoka was much in the habit of visiting religious people and monasteries, and Sanchi is likely to have had a community of welcoming monks and nuns. His own epigraph from Panguraria, a little over a hundred km from Sanchi, constitutes a communication from him while on a march to one such monastery called Upunita-vihara.

---

[8] Mitra (2001): 16.

Why Ashoka chose to set up these monuments at Sanchi is worth pausing over. Unlike Sarnath and Vaishali, his presence here seems to have had nothing to do with the place's association with the Buddha. At Sarnath, just off Varanasi in Uttar Pradesh, the Buddha had preached his first sermon, while Vaishali in Bihar had a stupa in which was buried a share of the relics of the Buddha that were given to the Vajjis. These Vajjis were an oligarchy of some eight or nine clans that ruled in eastern India, north of the Ganga, in the sixth century BCE, with its capitial at Vaishali. The relics were part of what had been collected from the Buddha's funeral pyre at Kushinagara. His remains had been divided and ceremonially buried in eight places that lay within the territories of eight ancient states. Sanchi was not one of them.

Sanchi may, all the same, have been where the emperor got some relics of the Buddha *reinterred* two centuries or so after the first division of the holy spoils in Kushinagara. But why specifically Sanchi? The choice, if the Sri Lankan Buddhist chronicles are to be believed – and they offer the most detailed record available – had to do with his Buddhist spouse Devi, her father having been a prominent merchant in the town off my railway route.[9] Ashoka and Devi moved as a couple to Ujjayini, a distance of about 250 km to the south-west, where Prince Ashoka was headed as the viceroy of his emperor-father Bindusara. Devi soon became the mother of a boy named Mahinda, and a little later of a daughter, Sanghamitta. Sri Lanka's chroniclers were specially interested in these siblings because they are recorded as having introduced Buddhism to the island: Mahinda as the message bearer and Sanghamita as the bearer of the sacred Bodhi tree. At some point in time Mahinda, who had become a monk, is said to have come to meet his mother at the Vedisagiri vihara before leaving for Sri Lanka. The suffix "giri" – mountain in Sanskrit – attached to Vedisa, which is an alternative spelling of Vidisha, invokes a hill, so the conjecture is that a monastery

---

[9] For details, Lahiri (2015): 98–101.

near Vidisha was where the mother chose to take her monk-son and his companions. And that monastery could only have been the one at Sanchi.

From which it then becomes possible to surmise that because Ashoka had loved and lived with a Buddhist woman from Vidisha, he liked the idea, when he became emperor, of a hill not far from Vidisha on which a relic-rich stupa could be positioned. A stupa of any size and type, and more so the construction of a sizeable stupa, was a way for a Buddhist emperor to earn religious merit and ensure himself an even more lordly life in the hereafter. And since Buddhism is all about individual efforts to reach elevated levels of excellence via the acquisition of merit through good deeds such as building stupas, in Ashoka's case Sanchi may well represent the collateral construction resulting from some juicily meritorious nostalgia around the location of his early love life. In my mind's eye this possibility only added to the allure of Sanchi.

Some distance away from the southern entrance to the stupa's ceremonial path, Ashoka set up an imposing stone pillar. Its original appearance is somewhat difficult to visualise since it is now in a terribly broken state, with only part of the lower shaft intact (Fig. 1.2). As far as can be made out, its tapering tip had been surmounted by a bell-shaped capital with four magnificent lions, the animals all carved out of a single stone, much like those on the more famous Ashokan pillar at Sarnath. John Marshall was so struck by the similarities that he believed the original designs of the capitals at Sanchi and Sarnath were the work of the same artist, although, as he put it, "the difference in workmanship makes it virtually certain that the actual carving of the Sanchi capital was done by some less gifted assistant."[10] There is another more material difference: the Sarnath capital had a "dharmachakra" (Wheel of Law) above the lions which the Sanchi version did not have.

---

[10] Marshall, Foucher, and Majumdar (1940), I: 89.

Fig. 1.2: Remnant of the Ashokan pillar near the southern gate of the Great Stupa

Devi is not mentioned in Sanchi, nor anywhere else in his epigraphs, and all that scholars can do is suggest she may well have been part of the Samgha at Sanchi to which he addressed his message.

Ashoka's message carved at Sanchi is finger-waggingly stern. The ruler has assumed the mantle of spiritual regulator and protector of Buddhist unity to express his disapproval of divisions ("samghabheda") among monks and nuns. The monastic community is warned that "the monk or nun who shall break up the Samgha, must be caused to put on white robes and to reside in a non-residence."[11] White robes signified householders, and in the Buddhist hierarchy wearing them meant a demotion, and a demotion in this life in turn meant reduced circumstances in the life to come. The monks and nuns needed to watch out, they might end up as frogs' legs stewing in a witches' cauldron, as in the famous play about another king:

> Double, double toil and trouble;
> Fire burn and caldron bubble.
>
> . . .
>
> Eye of newt and toe of frog,
> Wool of bat and tongue of dog,
>
> . . .
>
> For a charm of powerful trouble,
> Like a hell-broth boil and bubble.

Ashoka added a line on the importance of monastic unity: "The Samgha both of monks and nuns is made united as long as (my) sons and great-grandsons (shall reign and) as long as the moon and sun (shall shine)." The monarch sounds positively papal here and the thought of having to wear white robes must surely have put the fear of the Buddha in the minds of the resident hermits. Sanchi shows the admonitory Ashoka. Here he sounds like a figure whose disciplinary powers within the monastic community are not in doubt.

Whichever way I looked at the royal programme of building over what are believed to be the Sakyamuni's relics, as well as the unsmiling Buddhistic ultramontanism of the inscription,

---

[11] This and the following quotation are from the translation of the edict in Hultzsch (1925): 161.

it is imperial authority that seems writ large all over Sanchi in the third century BCE. The monks and nuns to whom it was addressed remain entirely invisible, even as I imagined them quaking in non-white robes at the tone of their master's voice.

Although I learned a great deal about Sanchi from the description in Marshall's volumes, it was still a surprise for me to discover that in fact the stupa in front of my eyes was not the one Ashoka had built there. The original is nowhere to be seen because within a century or so after the emperor's passing it had to be completely reconstructed. The rebuilding became necessary in the second century BCE because of damage to what Ashoka's labourers had built. Most people think of the desecration of religious shrines as medieval and modern ransackings, but Sanchi is a reminder that humans have been vandals since antiquity. Who were these early thugs? Marshall infers their depredations "took place sometime after the downfall of the Mauryas, though necessarily before the addition of the outer envelope; it is a plausible conjecture, therefore, that it was done by the order of Pusyamitra, the first of the Sunga kings, who was notorious for his hostility to the Buddhists."[12]

Pushyamitra was the first of ten Shunga kings who came to power in c. 187 BCE, immediately after the Mauryas. He ruled from the same central Gangetic region and in Buddhist literature he generally appears as violently anti-Buddhist. He was in power for well over three decades and it seems very likely that his successors were no fonder of Buddhism than he. In fact several Buddhist stupas – at Taxila in Pakistan's Rawalpindi district and Deur Kuthar in Rewa district (Madhya Pradesh), for instance – also show signs of pyromaniacs and looters on the ram-

---

[12] Marshall, Foucher, and Majumdar (1940), I: 23–4.

page whom scholars have dated to broadly within the Shunga time frame. A colossal pillar had been built at Deur Kuthar in Mauryan times and then smashed into some fifty pieces. A fire set around it had caused it to collapse onto the flagstone floor.[13] The wreckage of the Sanchi structure seems to have been one part of a larger despoliation that struck many monumental sites across north and central India.

The hillside of Sanchi takes you clean away from this scenario of building, destruction, and reconstruction. Here along the hillside monarchs seem only part of the pageant of ancient people who have left their imprint. The more I looked at the Sanchi stupa from this other angle, the more I realised that from the time of the Shunga rulers the Buddhist establishment here had managed to grow and thrive in ways that actually had very little to do with kings.

The stupa's visible façade, for one, had metamorphosed into something that Ashoka could not have envisioned. The brick stupa was now practically double its initial size and was topped by its present dome shape. The massively enlarged structure was then encased in stone and coated with a plaster that entirely enveloped the Ashokan stupa to ensure the damaged core was no longer visible. Stairways and railings were added. And the top of the stupa came to be crowned with a balustrade and an umbrella.

Comparing the massive structure of this renovated stupa with the more modest Ashokan one that lay within it confirms the sense that the architect who designed the refurbishment ensured that the emperor's creation was both hidden and reincarnated as a higher and mightier form. No doubt he was a Buddhist applying doctrinal principles to a monument. Interestingly, it was also around this time that the idea of setting up pillars, inaugurated on some scale by Ashoka, came to be imitated. Unlike the

[13] Mishra (2001).

stupa, though, the new pillar was a pale imitation of the Ashokan creation. Its height, a mere six feet, seems that of a midget in the world of obelisks and monoliths. This dwarf pillar was set up on the main terrace and had a capital of the bell-shaped lotus type, resembling the Ashokan prototype. The crown part of it has disappeared. Guessing from the animal so greatly favoured in those days, it was probably a lion.[14]

Some time after the great Sanchi stupa assumed its impressive stone façade, a companion stupa, now known as Stupa 3, was built on the very same terrace, not far from the colossal column. It was modelled on the architectural lines of the larger structure, clad in stone, crowned by a single umbrella, and entombed the relics of Sariputra and Maudgalyayana – two of the Buddha's principal disciples: stone boxes in its relic chamber had lids inscribed with epigraphs saying they were resting within.

As regards Stupa 2, which lay some 300 metres down the hill slope, this stupa, which I had passed so often, was constructed towards the last quarter of the second century BCE. Like the others, it was built to house the relics of eminent Buddhist teachers of later times. Its location lower down the hill was again the application of a hierarchical principle: the relics of Buddhist monks it contained were lower in the pecking order, their position below the Great Master and his immediate disciples being indicated even by their relative lack of elevation in death. Ten teachers from three separate generations, presumably represented by fragments of their bones, lie in ossuaries inscribed with their names. It seems likely that portions of their relics were procured from various places and entombed in Stupa No. 2. This was an innovation: what had earlier been a cult of veneration around only the Buddha's remains – Ashoka constructed new stupas and expanded old ones – had been extended to take care of what might be called the analogues of Buddhist sainthood. The recipe

---

[14] Marshall, Foucher, and Majumdar (1940), I: 49.

Catholicism formulated for its expansion in the early period after Christ is anticipated by the Buddhists. The formula is straightforward and common to both: more saints = more relics = more sacred shrines = more worshippers.

The design and character of the sacred shrine had naturally to be modified to accommodate a more proactive Samgha, as also a wider spread of lay devotees who made donations. Those who lived on the hill, or even who merely visited, are likely to have marvelled at these large edifices having been built not at the instance of royal diktat or munificence but through an accretion of gifts by more ordinary folk – monks, nuns, lay worshippers, passing devotees.

There are some 250 records of gifts made by Buddhist nuns and monks, and teachers with titles like "Aya" and "Thera". As one scholar puts it, "[There] is something amazingly charming about the ways in which these pious men and women made their presence felt, the name-strewn architectural member/s on the stupas being the very ones that they gifted."[15] The names carved on stone around Buddhist stupas indicate parental preferences of the day in the naming of children. Buddharakhita (Buddharakshita) and Dharmarakhita (Dharmarakshita) are the mouthfuls that were particularly popular among monks. Several nuns had names derived from Yakshi, a folk deity, and there was even a monk called Yakhadina (Yakshadatta). Some nuns had names ending in "dasi", meaning "slave", such as Isidasi (Rishidasi), Yakhadasi (Yakshadasi), and Devadasi. We can be fairly sure that the names of these women indicate they were not merely socially or specifically enslaved to men – their names all showcase religious devotion and enslavement to their Heavenly Lord.[16]

---

[15] For a detailed analysis of the donors and their names, professions, and places of origin, Singh (1996). For monks and nuns specifically, ibid.: 15–18.

[16] The names mentioned here and below are from Marshall, Foucher, and Majumdar (1940): IV.

Where did all these nuns and monks come from? The inscriptions indicate a motley crew of arrivals ranging from Pushkara in Rajasthan to Mahishmati on the banks of the Narmada river. An overwhelming number of these places happen to be those in the Malwa region where Sanchi is located. Eight came in from Vidisha, all nuns of the Samgha like Devi, who is said to have joined the order after her years with Ashoka. Many nuns of Ujjayini also seem to have come in with donations for Sanchi's construction. The consequence of so many from the clergy is a carved babble of post-Ashokan voices that almost sideline that of the emperor.

This clamour also emanates from a few hundred tongues that are not monastic. The names of these pilgrims, inscribed on cross-bars and pillars, on railings and carvings, indicate their social identity. Sometimes what they are called originates in lunar constellations ("nakshatras") – e.g. Rohini and Asada; others are named after geographical regions – e.g. Kamboja and Gandhara – perhaps a way of remembering the family's origins in those territories. Religious beliefs figure most commonly in these donors' personal names. A few derive from Hindu deities like Vinhnumita (Vishnumitra) and Dhamasiva (Dharmashiva). Others reveal themselves as worshippers of Nagas and Yakshas – like Nagasena, a banker; Nagadata, the wife of a trooper; and one called Yakshadasi. Many more names show a Buddhist spin: Dhamagirika, Dhamarakshita, Dhammaka, Dhammamdasa, Dhamagiri, Dhamadina, Dhamapala, Dhamadata, and even a Buddha who proclaims herself as the sister of a man from Ujjayini.

Parents, it seems, were either not keen or were not encouraged to name their offspring after past royalty. Perhaps it was frowned on as pretension or lack of humility, or as a form of plebs getting too big for their boots. The several hundred names of donors carved within the precincts of Sanchi so seldom yield that of a dead ruler that this conclusion is plausible. There is just one carved name replicating the title that Ashoka is known to have used – Priyadarshi. This pilgrim was a second century BCE mason called Piyapasika (Priyadarshika) who records himself as the donor of a pavement slab. The only other instance that I've encountered of an ordinary person from the very ancient period assuming the exalted emperor's name is Ashokashrimitra: an ascetic described as being of unblemished character in a twelfth-century epigraph from Nalanda.[17] But he is not just rare, he is exceptional. As names, Ashoka and Ashok would have to wait for the twentieth century to become popular. Mahida or Mahinda, the name of Ashoka's son, manages to squeeze in among the names of Sanchi donors, as does Saghamita or Samghamitta, Ashoka's daughter: except that the Saghamita who records himself in Sanchi happens to be a man! This reminds me of a happily unlettered peasant woman I was told about in a remote Himalayan hill who named her two dogs Romu and Julie. She had heard of a famous play in which the hero and heroine were called by fancier versions of these and she liked the sound of this duo. She hadn't looked under her dogs when naming them. Her male dog answered to the name Julie, the female wagged her tail when called Romu.

In the first century BCE four stone-carved gateways were erected at the entrances of the Great Stupa. Breathtaking beauty that lasts forever lies beyond the descriptive capacities of a historian, specially as there's no beating this one-line summation of Cleopatra: "Age cannot wither her, nor custom stale her infinite variety." But Cleopatra went the way of Devi, both withered. The Sanchi gateways have not wilted for close on 2000 years. They're also a lot more substantial than the Egyptian queen, their enormous mass offset by minutely carved stories, these carvings contrasting so wonderfully with the plain stone dome of the stupa. There are epigraphs on the gateways too. They record the

---

[17] Verse 4 of the Nalanda inscription of Vipulasrimitra. Salomon (1998): 297–302.

patronage of gift-givers and, as in other areas of Sanchi, their discreet distance from rulers seems a separation of sculptural grandeur from imperial self-aggrandisement.

Ordinary folk had their names chiselled into Sanchi, but the carvings aren't only about visitors and donors. They also record powerful parables and pious characters. I'll get back to those later; for now, as someone in search of the various avatars of Ashoka, my first question, and the one that insistently came back again and again, was whether there was anything at all evoking the emperor on Sanchi's stone. Carved representations at stupas, and near monasteries where Buddhist monks and nuns lived, are quintessentially Ashokan: the emperor was the pioneer in this domain, he began the whole business of positioning carved lions and bulls, geese and horses on the capitals of decorative and commemorative pillars in the proximity of prominent sites. Within a century of his example, the Buddhist monastic community had decided to extend this practice to stones encountered while circumambulating or facing a major stupa. At Stupa 2 and Stupa 3 in Sanchi an extensive repertoire of sculpted reliefs, engraved in the last quarter of the second century BCE, did in fact allow me to spot carved representations of pillars that looked distinctly Ashokan: each pillar having been carved on the pillars of a balustrade or gateway.[18]

Why did these particular carvers consider Ashokan-inspired pillars so compelling? The answer may lie in the nature of the carvings. These pillars did not seem to me to reflect Ashoka's *Sanchi* pillar at all – several of them were surmounted by the Wheel of Law which crowns Ashoka's *Sarnath* pillar (Fig. 1.3). Carved dharmachakras, symbols of the Buddha's first sermon at Sarnath, are positioned nearby. So it seemed to me that these Sanchi

---

[18] Marshall, Foucher, and Majumdar (1940), I: 99–100.

Fig. 1.3: Carved representation of the Sarnath pillar at Stupa 3

sculptors had anchored their representations on Ashoka's *Sarnath* pillar as the most recognisable symbol of the Buddha's first sermon, making their pillars a manifestation of the Buddha more than homage to his follower Ashoka.

These "unfaithful" representations of Sanchi's Ashokan pillar in the heart of Sanchi betray Ashoka – in a manner of speaking –

in another way as well: they show a free play of imagination in their depiction of animals on the capitals. In one of them an elephant is set among the lions, in another the capital shows only elephants, and in a third the lions look like they have garlands hanging from their jaws! These ancient artists were having a field day carving animals just as they pleased with little respect for how Ashoka may have wanted them.

It gets worse: the Ashokan elements seem wholly marginal, if not absent, in a range of divinities and objects carved. There is an almighty sprouting of lotuses and trees, animals and birds, humans and hybrid creatures. It seems, as in the much later Khajuraho temples, a wild and almost crazy celebration of the plurality and diversity of human life – the variety that gets the goat of Hindu fanatics. People from different walks of life and places write themselves into the site; in much the same way the designers of the carvings on Stupa 2 put on display all kinds of living beings and subjects, Buddhist and non-Buddhist, and even un-Buddhist. There are representations not just of animals but of animals killing each other and men killing animals – and some of the animals slaughtered are those considered sacred in Buddhist iconography. A baby elephant being attacked by a lion looks unlikely to survive; a lion preying upon an antelope looks like the Buddha's urge to compassion is not remotely on his mind.[19] A lioness slayed by a man has her cub carried away by the fellow – indicating by this a very non-Buddhist savage.[20] Perhaps all this killing is meant to show a world full of the kind of barbarity that goes against the grain of Buddhist teachings and which Buddhism seeks to reform; it may also have something to do with the sorts of stories that Buddhist patrons preferred.

A nucleus of decorations more clearly relating to Buddhism are more easily palatable and recognisable. Foremost are those

---

[19] Volume 3, Plate 78, 24b and Plate 75, 8a.
[20] Volume 3, Plate 76, 14b.

relating to the Buddha's life – his departure from Kapilavastu, and the offering of "kheer" (rice pudding) to him by Sujata near the Bodhi tree. The assault of Mara, the Evil One, and Mara's defeat by the Buddha is also shown. So are the miracles he performed to impress would-be converts, such as the one in which he walks over the Niranjana river in flood.

Ashoka appears, but as merely one thread in the larger tapestry of Buddhist stories and events. Unlike the Buddha, or the monks and nuns who are all absent as individually identifiable people, Ashoka appears on the gateways on more than one occasion as a living being. No identifying epigraph accompanies these depictions – which is basically true of *all* the imagery in Sanchi. The identifications have been worked out on the basis of the subject matter of the reliefs, the visuals following quite definitely recognisable Buddhist textual narratives. Ashoka's presence is consequently clear from correlations made between sculpture and story.

He appears somewhat paunchy in appearance, decorated by a turban, ewer, and fly whisk – all royal insignia of his imperial status. He is most vividly memorialised on the richly carved gateway fronting the southern entrance to the Great Stupa.[21] This is not fortuitous. The southern gateway was the first to be set up and is the main entrance into the complex. No doubt Ashoka's lustrous stone pillar had been put up in its vicinity because it showed the main way in. This gateway enjoyed a bequest from the ivory carvers of Vidisha – and we know roughly why, given Ashoka's connection to the town via his spouse. Ironically, Devi herself is not to be seen on the gateway, having been displaced by another more colourful wife of the emperor.

Two different stories of Ashoka are told on the gateway. One shows us Ashoka's visit to the Ramagrama stupa, an event described in the legendary biography of the emperor, the *Ashokavadana*, written down only in the second century CE, several

---

[21] Marshall, Foucher, and Majumdar (1940), I: 215–16.

centuries after Ashoka. This work alludes to Ashoka's travel to Ramagrama, a place nearly 300 km distant from Pataliputra, to take possession of one of the original relic deposits of the Buddha (Fig. 1.4).[22] Ashoka is on a chariot, heading an impressive procession which includes infantry, cavalry, elephants, and chariots. The stupa that dominates the centre is meant to be the stupa at Ramagrama, though it resembles the Sanchi stupa, with many hooded Naga worshippers. These Nagas are shown with their families: the sculpted narrative juxtaposes military power represented by Ashoka with the power of piety symbolised by the Nagas. The text says as much:

> Today in Ramagrama the eighth stupa stands
> For in those days the nagas guarded it with devotion.
> The king did not take the relics from there
> But left them alone and, full of faith withdrew.[23]

This narrative representation is likely to have reminded pilgrims that the Nagas had resisted Ashoka and successfully

Fig. 1.4: Ashoka's visit to the Ramagrama Stupa

[22] Considering that the text was put down in a written form only by the second century CE, this is likely to have been based on an orally transmitted version (which, of course, matches the later composition fairly closely). Dehejia (1997): 130.

[23] Strong (1983): 219.

IMAGING ASHOKA AT SANCHI   45

circumvented his quest for relics. We do not generally associate Ashoka with failure: his uncommon success as the compassionate king has accustomed us to seeing him as the victor. This first of two stories on the Sanchi gateway reminds us that he was fallible. The *Ashokavadana* version of this story of Ashoka's travel to Ramagrama, after succeeding in gathering relics from seven stupas, is worth quoting:

> Then King Ashoka . . . went together with his fourfold army to the drona stupa that Ajatashatru had built. He broke it open, took out all the relics, and putting back a portion of them, set up a new stupa. He did the same with the second drona stupa and so on up to the seventh one, removing the relics from each of them and then setting up new stupas as tokens of his devotion. Then he proceeded to Ramagrama . . .

. . . where, as we know, he was unsuccessful.[24] The gateway narrative chose only to memorialise his Ramagrama fiasco, where apparently a tribe of Nagas "offered a courteous but implacable resistance to the imperial archaeologist's enterprise."[25]

The second Ashoka story is carved on the same gateway's western pillar: this one records his visit to the Bodhi tree. The king looks positively weepy, ready to faint and fall, but is stopped from keeling over by women – including a queen – who appear to be supporting him (Fig. 1.5). The sacred Bodhi tree was apparently withering because of the jealousy of one of Ashoka's queens (he had several), Tishyarakshita. Eventually, the Bodhi tree was saved by the intervention of the very sorceress whose handiwork had made it wither. In this story Ashoka is far from triumphant; he is in fact a figure of sorrow.[26]

This tale of woe continues on the eastern gateway's bottom architrave, where a chastened Queen Tishyarakshita is shown

[24] Ibid.
[25] Marshall, Foucher, and Majumdar (1940), I: 216.
[26] Strong (1983): 257.

Fig. 1.5: A grieving Ashoka with his queen on his visit to the Bodhi tree

twice over.[27] She is shown with Ashoka when he dismounts from an elephant, and then with him while paying homage to the Bodhi tree.

Spotting Ashoka on embellishments around a stupa whose core he himself had built gave me a good feeling. I had set out in search of his afterlife and found him in at least two clear reincarnations here in Sanchi. To most casual visitors he was hidden and hardly indistinguishable from the gremlins and demons and gargoyle-like dwarfs, but in plain sight to me as a historical figure by virtue of my having studied the Sri Lankan chronicles and the hagiography and the scholarship on the stories about his varied spreading of Buddhist ideas. Lying below all that learning it struck me that, in Sanchi, many of the events that had made Ashoka what he was in my head weren't really to be found in this location. Some of the stuff that elicits admiration for Ashoka in

[27] Dehejia (1997): 119.

the ancient Buddhist literature is what I'd written about in my own biography: of him there is, for instance, the Buddha's prophecy in one of Ashoka's earlier lives when, as a young boy called Jaya, his future greatness is forecast by the Great Sage himself:

> Here [in Buddhist literature], the Buddha is shown as having encountered an earlier avatar of Ashoka in the city of Rajagriha. Ashoka was, when thus encountered, a young boy, Jaya by name, who lived in this city, Rajagriha, which the sage had entered seeking alms. Walking along Rajagriha's main thoroughfare, the Buddha saw two young boys playing in the dirt. One of them, Jaya, on seeing the Buddha, decided to place a handful of dirt in his begging bowl. Typically, in such a story, the act of offering is accompanied by the formulation of a wish or statement of intent about the merit to be gained by the act. Jaya's statement is straightforward enough. By the good merit he might earn, he said, "I would become king and, after placing the earth under a single umbrella of sovereignty, I would pay homage to the blessed Buddha." Children usually have more modest aspirations, but Jaya was no ordinary child. The Buddha certainly believed so, as also that Jaya had the character and the resolve to achieve what he wanted. As he predicted, "the desired fruit would be obtained because of his field of merit." He therefore received the "proffered dirt", and thus "the seed of merit that was to ripen into Ashoka's kingship was planted." Soon thereafter the Buddha predicted to his disciple Ananda that a hundred years after his death "that boy will become a king named Ashoka in the city of Pataliputra. He will be a righteous dharmaraja, a chakravartin who rules over one of the four continents, and he will distribute my relics far and wide and build the eighty-four thousand dharmarajikas."

Well, given that this prediction had in fact come true, and that the great relic-gatherer had so handsomely honoured the Buddha, and that he had then gone on to show such extreme generosity towards the Samgha, why hadn't any of *this* been carved on stone? It's a perfectly good story for a chiseller to show off his artistry with.

While researching ancient Sanchi, this question has puzzled me continuously and no satisfactory solution has ever swum into my mind to resolve why Sanchi tells the unobvious Ashoka stories and omits those more clearly celebrated in Buddhist narratives. The logic of imperial statuary and related art suggests celebration and commemoration of the great donor. Why in Sanchi is Ashoka neither that, nor the man fated by the Almighty himself to be the greatest Buddhist emperor? It is how, for instance, he more or less is at Nagarjunakonda, where as Jaya he gifts earth to the Buddha. At Amaravati he is, equally, the Buddhist king of kings shown with the wheel on a pillar representing righteousness. The differences between what appears about Ashoka in Amaravati on the one hand and Sanchi's gateways on the other are confounding. What Sanchi highlights is an emperor of insufficient power: he cannot prevent near-disasters. The Bodhi tree withers and he is powerless; he marches to the Ramagrama stupa for relics but is stopped in his tracks and the riches he seeks elude him.

Why? Why would gateway carvings seek to represent fallibility in an emperor? One possibly plausible explanation which occurred to me is that Ashoka may have been seen not merely as the great disseminator of Buddhist ideas but also as the exceptional emperor who, after his pyrrhic Kalinga victory, had recognised his own failings and, in line with his rock edicts, positively wanted his frailties on display. To have carved him up as also prone to error and weakness may have been seen as in character, and therefore an enhancement on stone of his immense exceptionalism. Perhaps this seems like a retrospective over-reading of scanty evidence. But that then points to a problem fundamental for every historian who wants to time-travel into the very ancient world: rather a lot has to be inferred from circumstantial evidence. You read the larger context, you examine a large and layered sediment of stories, and from those you extract or construct a plausible story to explain mystifying data.

There is one other decent-looking explanation for the unusual character of Sanchi's Ashoka carvings: an emperor, even one as devout as this, was still not the ultimate Great Being who overcame all variety of misfortune and malevolence. Choosing to depict themes of fragility and deficiency was a way of showing the difference between the human and the divine – the difference between Ashoka and the Buddha. It was also a way of showing the limits of political power in general, and Ashoka's power in particular. His dynasty had, after all, passed and given way to another.

In his own lifetime, Ashoka had shaped Sanchi in the image he wanted. We know this from descriptions in the historical record of the stupa that he built and the pillar that he set up. We can also conjecture that he liked Sanchi's location because of its proximate association with the mother of two of his children. But Sanchi is much more than Ashoka. It made me understand that for the Buddhist Samgha, which flourished there for centuries after Ashoka, and for the pilgrims who visited it over several hundred years, Ashoka's persona was both qualitatively different and capable of more nuanced and imaginative interpretation than had happened at other locations. Looking at Sanchi offered me a somewhat new, slightly richer history of Ashoka.

Remembrance is never exact recall. Sanchi suggests there is always a twist in every tale of Ashoka.

Among Kings at Kanaganahalli

JOURNEYS TO MONUMENTS are usually via roads which allow visitors to reach them with ease and imbibe their environs at leisure. The roads leading to Ashokan sites in Karnataka, though, can sometimes pose difficulties and cause a lot of heavy sweating. Much like pilgrim paths, they involve disembarking from your vehicle, and then an arduous walk interspersed with some scrambling and stiff climbing over the Deccan plateau's boulder-strewn hills before you finally reach the precise spot where Ashoka positioned his messages. Typically, high perches full of picturesque boulders are where his presence is to be found engraved. His edict at Palkigundu, in Koppal District, which crowns a high and fairly inaccessible ridge, is only reached after negotiating a very steep elevation. In a similar setting, Jatinga-Rameshwara in the Chitradurga area is only made relatively easy today by several hundred steps. Buddhists of yore venturing up are likely to have felt they were ascending to some remote paradise in the heavens that they weren't likely to reach until their next life. The tracks show long usage with all kinds of markings on the older path – boulders with dramatic artistic bruisings and foot-worn crevices, and so on. All of this added to the romance of searching out the remaining signs of a remote emperor.

In November 2011 I went to Karnataka with two companions on what became a journey of discovery. Srinivas, a Hospet-based driver, was a master navigator who had spent much of his life travelling to archaeological sites and locations, and Ratna Raman, a friend and teaching colleague, shared my love for walking around countrysides cluttered with curious old relics. With Ratna my search for Ashoka also became a way of communing with nature. Walking in rolling landscapes of coconut trees and stretches of sunflowers, eating green tuvar dal (pigeon pea) from pods still on plants in the fields, and chewing on plucked tamarind fruit punctuated our convivial treks. Over that early winter season the sheer number of our sightings of Ashokan relics was extraordinary and the question I frequently asked myself was what I was learning by being in these places that I could not have elsewhere. Looking back, I think it was this on-site experience that convinced me of Ashoka being as much a king of the Indian South – certainly as far south as Karnataka – as of the North. It amazed me that while there are no surviving edicts of Ashoka in the entire stretch between the two capitals of ancient Magadha, Pataliputra and Rajagriha, sightings of the emperor here, in the shape of his rock inscriptions, were to be had on at least three occasions within some five kilometres of each other, and in one area thrice. The wanderings also left in me a sensation of understanding Ashoka through walking, and of an obscure and dimly felt connection with generations before me who had similarly wandered in search of signs of him. My sense of him in Karnataka grew into a memory map of old paths.

To my Ashoka-obsessed eye in those days the most elusive, and thus the most desired, of these sightings was in Kanaganahalli. This Buddhist stupa site, and its adjacent ancient city of Sannathi in Gulbarga District, are somewhat isolated and off the beaten track from Hospet, where we were based. After spending part of the day looking at the Ashokan edict at Maski, and the archaeological site of that name in the fields at some distance from the engraved rock, we reached the town of Lingasugur in the evening. It was the kind of place where one could get breakfast at a small eating place at half past six any morning, the sun barely visible on the horizon in the east. An early start is no bad idea when the prospect ahead is a longish traverse across fairly featureless black-cotton-soil country to reach the banks of the Bhima river. Not far from its banks stood the ancient locale of Kanaganahalli, named after a village of that name half a kilometre away.

Enough is now known to map the presence of Ashoka and the time of the Maurya dynasty in this part of the Bhima river valley. Three specific locations show signs of the emperor in this region – the city of Sannathi, the stupa at Kanaganahalli at some distance from the urban core, and an Ashokan epigraph – its surviving fragment being a locally found piece of the major edicts of the emperor. While these edicts were earlier in the Chandralamba temple, not far from the stupa site, at some point after 1999 they came to be placed within the stupa precincts.[1] Which was why we were headed to the stupa site. Other historic spots were known to exist in the area – ruins of stupas and a historic monastic complex, and more have since been discovered. But my gaze was monofocally on the Ashokan landscape.[2]

The Ashokan edict fragments are not the only ancient remnants discovered in the Chandralamba temple. In 1958 a scholar called Kapatral Krishna Rao chanced upon sculpted Buddhist remains in the temple, where he was a devotee. Within its precincts were relief slabs that had decorated the stupa, depicting the birth

---

[1] In 1999 the historian Harry Falk saw the edict stone at the back of the Chandralamba temple. Falk (2006): 130.

[2] For an enumeration of sites, newly discovered and those discovered earlier, Gupta, Rajani, and Menon (2019).

of the Buddha, the Great Sage's footprints, the Bodhi tree, and a great deal more. This came as further evidence of how a lot of ancient stuff manages to survive in India, where it is a common practice for sculptural relics to be collected and then worshipped in temples and folk shrines. An old object of worship is often integrated within a panoply of more modern religious icons. They are then chanced upon by scholars like Krishna Rao who confirm for us the existence of an ancient religious shrine preserved within an arena of modern worship, as here in the Chandralamba temple dedicated to a ferocious female deity.[3]

Soon thereafter Kanaganahalli, from where the Buddhist relics originally came, became the focus of exploration and then excavation.[4] To those familiar with the history of Indian archaeology, the trajectory of discovery here will seem both similar to and different from the field research of British colonial archaeologists like Alexander Cunningham and John Marshall. The excavations began in 1991 and were led by K.P. Poonacha who, like Cunningham and Marshall, was an officer of the Archaeological Survey of India (ASI). But unlike the detailed descriptions of new archaeological sites published in British India's annual ASI reports – the full reports were published subsequently – comprehensive preliminary write-ups of this variety did not appear on Kanaganahalli. The definitive excavation report on this Karnataka Buddhist site was published in 2011, all of twenty years after the excavation began. So, when I visited the place in 2010, I had

[3] It was an image of Kali that was installed on the edict stone. Kali is a fierce avatar of the goddess Durga. Chapter 9 in Lahiri (2017) cites a plethora of examples of such antiquarian practices across the Indian subcontinent.

[4] After Rao's discovery, M. Seshadri, Director of the Department of Archaeology and Museums, Karnataka, carried out an exploration. See Seshadri (1972). The first excavations were carried out in 1986–7 in the citadel area in a locality known as Ranamandala at Sannathi, and in the same year J.R. Howell, of the Society for South Asian Studies, excavated Anegutti, a stupa mound in Sannathi, with the Archaeological Survey. A summary of their work is available in Poonacha (2011): 7–9.

no precise pointer to its sculptures and their stories in the shape of published work.[5] The only way I could get to grips with its beautiful remnants was to visit and experience the place in person – perhaps the only happy outcome of a long-awaited report.

What remained of the original stupa appeared to be a fairly low mound, a little over two metres high, clearly visible that morning because the surrounding fields showed no standing crops. From a distance its original façade could not be recognised for the basic reason that its hemispherical dome – which is more or less what everyone thinks of when they think of stupa architecture – wasn't there at all (Fig. 2.1). I mean it just didn't exist any more. Nor did being at close quarters make any difference, my proximity to the stupa did not cause a hemisphere to float down on top and fulfil my expectations of a Buddhist shrine. What I was looking at was only the ghost of an edifice, a ruin showing some parts of a shell. This surviving shell and what surrounded

Fig. 2.1: Kanaganahalli in 2010

[5] The report is Poonacha (2011).

it were simultaneously stunning and sickening. Carved panels lay strewn around: these had originally surrounded the lower drum and upper terrace (or "medhi") of the dismembered stupa. Each carved segment contained two panels, one above the other, separated by a sculpted frieze. They were as striking as those of the richly carved gateways at Sanchi. Some, as we shall see, were unique to Kanaganahalli.

It horrified me to see that, notwithstanding their singularity and beauty, on site they were scattered like debris awaiting clearing over large parts of the bare brown soil within an area under an organisation, the ASI, which had been charged with protecting and preserving the country's heritage (Fig. 2.2). It made Kanaganahalli look pathetic, an abysmal contrast with well-preserved Sanchi. Railing pillars protruded at perilous angles and piles of carved structural supports lay like dismembered corpses heaped into an inhuman disarray. The general

Fig. 2.2: Carved and engraved panel lying exposed on the brown soil

state of disrepair was made worse by the sight of an alarmingly large number of cracked panels. The cracks were in fact sometimes as prominent as the exquisite carvings that told stories of the Buddha and long-dead rulers, of camels and winged lions, and of reliefs showing pillars crowned by the dharmachakra in allusions to the Ashokan prototype (Figs 2.3 and 2.4). Adding

Fig. 2.3: Cracked sculpture of a dharmachakra crowned pillar

Fig. 2.4: Another cracked slab of a Sarnath-inspired rendering of an Ashokan pillar

insult to architectural injury was that parts of this protected site had recently been ploughed over, even as priceless stone carvings lay forlorn along land which had been furrowed. Many of these cracked friezes had not been numbered and it was hideously clear that, when the restoration work began, the ASI would not know how to piece together such a gigantic jigsaw. One of the slabs with a representation of Ashoka had no number at all, almost as if the Survey had forgotten about it when it went about numbering the panels; in a recent book it has been designated "No. 00".[6] This miserable state of neglect, which was enough to make any archaeologist weep, had begun some fifteen years earlier, after Kanaganahalli had been entirely excavated, and continued largely unchanged till 2010! Looking at the state of

[6] Zin (2018a): 3.

desecration all around – and desecration is the right word for the apparent institutional vandalism – I imagined a time traveller called Mahmud of Ghazni moving in a reverse direction from mine, chancing upon this scene a thousand years into his future, and feeling he could have learnt a thing or two from the ASI.

Another comparative measure of the comprehensiveness with which the ASI had botched things up might be with the world's contemporary roughnecks – the US army in its ventures abroad to secure the world for "democracy". Around this time I happened to visit Vietnam and see the dramatic Hindu temples at My Son, many of them dedicated to the god Shiva. Decades after the end of the US–Vietnam war, that site was still littered with signs of the American bombing in 1969. If there was a monumental equivalent in India to a bombed-out historic site, it was Kanaganahalli in 2010. The fact is that a certain variety of Indian, who justifiably vilifies past Muslim marauders and contemporary neo-imperialists, also closes her eyes to the mindless and mind-boggling havoc against priceless indigenous artefacts for which Indian state institutions need to be held responsible.

I tried figuring out what it was that made Ashoka's character at Kanaganahalli and Sannathi different from what I had encountered of him elsewhere in Karnataka. A phenomenon that this area had not seen until the appearance in it of the Maurya ruler was a *historical* king – a monarch mentioned in texts. Ashoka's visibility in architecture here is the earliest instance of a ruler known to history being preserved in this region. There are of course archaeological pointers to earlier cultures, beginning with specialised hunter-gatherers who used microliths of all kinds. Later, an iron-using society with a black-and-red ware pottery, usually associated with megaliths in Karnataka, occupied the region. But their names and how they described their settlements remain hidden: nothing that has endured reveals them. Ashoka is the earliest singular and identifiable figure of the past in Karnataka. The historical character of Mauryan times overlies the iron-using horizon, and is far richer – not surprisingly, since there was a Mauryan urban centre at Sannathi.[7] Several features here resemble those at other Mauryan cities: burnt bricks were used, and there was that deluxe pottery called North Black Polished Ware which is so typical of historic sites across North and Central India. There were also antiquities here of Mauryan inspiration, such as a disc stone bearing a relief of standing goddesses flanked by palm trees and various animals. The raw materials used for manufacture were often exotic – beads of semi-precious stones, and of coral and lapis lazuli which would have come from afar. A threshold in the life of any site is when a fortification comes to be constructed around it, indicating that it needs to be defended. At Sannathi the first phase of fortifications – constructed by cutting a moat and heaping the earth to create walls – goes back to Mauryan times.

What explains the appearance here of the Mauryas? The gold resources of this region are a possibility. The area around Maski, some hours distant and, like Kanaganahalli, marked by an Ashokan epigraph, was rich in gold. Known to geologists as the main Maski band of the Dharwar series, a number of gold workings show that the deposits were exploited in pre-modern times. Given that gold objects of the first millennium BCE have been found at Maski, the auriferous veins here were very probably mined in ancient times. Ashoka's provincial capital in this region was known as Suvarnagiri (golden mountain) and may have been so named because of its control and regulation of gold. Going a step further, it seems possible to suggest that Sannathi was probably ancient Suvarnagiri, since it is by far the largest and most significant Mauryan urban centre of the region. Places

[7] Lahiri (2015): 215–17.

such as Maski and their resources would undoubtedly have been its hinterland. The beads found at Sannathi are like those used in ancient Maski, so both places were part of the same circuit, with subcontinental links to Afghanistan on the one hand and the coast on the other.

The Mauryan occupation was part of a larger prosperity not seen earlier – which does not necessarily mean Sannathi was *established* by Ashoka. The date of its urban centre cannot be precisely confirmed, but that it existed in the time of Ashoka seems fairly certain because of the edicts he put up there – the expansive major rock edicts that are also in Andhra and Uttarakhand, Gujarat, and Orissa. Unusually, at Sannathi these are inscribed on free-standing stone slabs with writing on both sides, leading to the inference that the slabs were set up vertically by the inscribers so that the inscriptions could be read by passersby. Ashoka's major rock edicts are therefore sometimes his major stone edicts.

This is not the only novel feature at Sannathi. The major rock edicts here do not include the famous thirteenth – on the Kalinga war and the consequent penitence.[8] Could it be that Ashoka did not want to proclaim conquest here because this part of Karnataka, like Kalinga, was conquered territory? The evidence is tenuous but worth considering: a scholarly suggestion has in fact been put forward that the reason Kalinga is so conspicuously not mentioned here is that Ashoka himself *did* conquer Karnataka.[9] What transpired in the Karnataka conquest was not comparable to Kalinga, but because this was a recently annexed region the emperor was being circumspect: warfare was likely to have been a hot potato in Sannathi.

A great deal has also been invested in the etymology of the name of a large eighty-hectare habitation mound here called

---

[8] For the edicts of Sannathi that have survived, Sarma and Rao (1993): 3–56.

[9] Veluthat (2000): 1085. For another interpretation which sees Sannathi as an extension of Kalinga: Majumdar, Ghosh, and Chatterjee (2019).

Ranamandala, meaning war territory (rana being war and mandala here being a territory). The name strongly suggests it was once a battlefield. Poonacha, the archaeologist who headed the Kanaganahalli excavations, says "the place may be the historic battlefield or site wherein the Mauryas subjugated the local Satavahanas in a battle."[10] This is speculation, not merely because no Ashokan message speaks of a conquest of Karnataka, but also because no evidence exists of such an early Satavahana political presence here.

What is not in dispute is that Ashoka had a stupa built at Kanaganahalli. We have no idea why: it was not a place with Buddhist connections, nor do we have evidence of any personal link between this location and Ashoka's life, as we do with Sanchi and Vidisha. So the greatest likelihood seems to be that stupas, like inscribed rocks, were Ashoka's signature tune. "When in doubt, build a stupa and inscribe a rock" might be called his motto, his insignia, his default thought when marking his territory. It was his way of spreading the Buddhist message into new areas, or perhaps giving visibility to a nascent Buddhist community for the first time in this part of his kingdom.

The Mauryan stupa that was discovered here has been described, in phrasings typical of archaeology, as a "simple earthen tumulus raised by piling up alternate layers of medium to small-size boulders, pebbles and limestone blocks and black cotton soil around a pit of loose ashy soil."[11] So the Ashokan original was an unprepossessing and humble structure in relation to what was built there later. Like the stupa at Sanchi, the later construction had a pillar by its side, of which now only a stump remnant survives. The excavator surmises it was crowned by a lion capital made from fairly coarse sandstone of a variety not found in this region. Remnants of the lion, substantially mutilated, have been found in the shape of tufts of its mane: the animal has been

---

[10] Poonacha (2011): 14.
[11] Ibid.: 625.

identified by this fragment, as well as its polished and lustrous finish – a characteristic of Mauryan sculptural relics.

Around the first century BCE a political ruling family known in history as the Satavahana line appeared at Kanaganahalli. By then the stupa was called the Adhaloka Chaitya or the Mahachaitya. The Satavahanas ruled till the third century CE across large parts of Karnataka, Maharashtra, and Andhra, and for considerably longer than the much-better-known Mauryas. The longevity of Satavahana reign – nearly five centuries – provides a sense of the vast consolidation and success of this dynasty's state machinery.[12]

The Satavahanas were an ancient lineage about which I knew much less than either the Maurya, the Kushana, or the Gupta dynasties. My fascination from 2011 onwards with Kanaganahalli made me think hard, even obsess, about my ignorance, and for many reasons. An important reason was that during my undergraduate days the unusually enthusiastic man who taught us antiquity tended to get so immersed in what he thought his students would want to chew the cud over that, by the time he began to hold forth on the Satavahana dynasty, only a couple of weeks of teaching remained.[13] So our batch of students, I think, ended up knowing very little about the Andhra and Karnataka regions between roughly the second century BCE and the third century CE. This was also true for the Kushana dynasty, about which, however, I knew a great deal more because one of its political capitals was Mathura, much visited because of its proximity to New Delhi, where I lived. In the Mathura Museum I had

---

[12] For the political history and administration of the Satavahanas: Chattopadhyay (2014).

[13] I do wish here to briefly honour this teacher of mine, P.S. ("Sagar") Dwivedi, because of how thoroughly he managed to infect so many students with his always deep and often eccentric enthusiasm for things ancient.

seen statues of the Kushana rulers, including a striking one of the headless Kanishka fulsomely attired in his boots and his sword and with nothing at all missing except merely his head. His somewhat handicapped state in the Mathura Museum had made me feel more than mildly aghast. It was so out of character for a king to be put on display beheaded, and the Mathura Museum Kanishka remains deeply etched in my mind as an image of possibly the only man in the world who managed to be king from the neck down.[14] The kings and the capitals and the places where the Satavahanas had held sway yielded no image as startling as the decapitated Kanishka; that, plus the fact that they had lorded it over distant Andhra, far from my Punjabi roots and Delhi residence, made them continue in a rather remote region of my mind.

Later, once I was researching and writing about the history of Indian archaeology, I realised that the Satavahanas had also occupied no more than a corner of my consciousness because they had been equally relegated to the margins of Indian history by the bulk of the Orientalists and historians who had first discovered them. One reason for their relative neglect had been that decipherment of the scripts and languages in which the political monologues of great rulers like Ashoka and Samudragupta were inscribed had cornered the historical attention of the pioneers. The discovery of the personal voice of individually distinguishable kings had taken precedence over the abstraction of a lineage within which no one seemed as identifiably singular as Ashoka.

It was not as if Satavahana inscriptions had remained unknown. Three of them at Nanaghat in the Western Ghats had first been published by a colonial enthusiast, Colonel W.H. Sykes, in 1837. This Sykes was a naturalist who served with the military and wrote extensively on Buddhism: so the "Boodh"

[14] Another majestic figure in the Mathura Museum, also headless, is a Kushana king shown seated on a chair-like throne. He may be Wima Kadphises, Kanishka's predecessor.

associations of such places interested him deeply.[15] The Satavahanas *per se* are not even mentioned in his account, nor the fact that the place where he found the inscriptions, Nanaghat, had strong associations with that dynasty as well as Hinduism. It was only much later, in the latter part of the nineteenth century, that reputed scholars like Bhagvanlal Indraji and R.G. Bhandarkar edited and wrote about diverse source materials – from coins and epigraphs to ancient cave and stupa sites – relating to this dynasty.[16] But not even then – after their unearthing had made them more concrete via material evidence – did any historian choose to write a book centred around a Satavahana king. One of the kings in this line, Gautamiputra Satakarni, the most famous of the Satavahana rulers, probably has enough going for him to make a short book, but there isn't one yet. For the moment, these kings largely figure in general histories of the Deccan as rulers of a significant and long-lived regional dynasty.

So I was surprised and delighted to chance upon Kanaganahalli, where I came face to face with Satavahana rulers for the first time in the field, seeing their presence etched into a place by religious imagery. By their time, it seemed apparent to me, the humble Ashokan stupa had undergone a dramatic transformation. It had been expanded and encased in stone. Of the sculpted stone reliefs on it, the most unusual were several large carved portraits of kings, often with their spouses, each fairly different from the other. These form only part of Kanaganahalli's iconographic agenda, which, like Sanchi's, is largely devoted to scenes from the Buddha's life story and Jataka folk tales. Buddhist subjects of this sort are commonly found in the visual programme of most Buddhist sites. But what makes Kanaganahalli's depictions astonishing is that simultaneously, and for the first time, reliefs of historical Satavahana kings occupy a prominent place within a sculptural saga at a Buddhist religious site.

[15] Sykes (1837): 287–8.
[16] For an excellent account of Indraji's work on western India: Dharamsey (2012); Bhandarkar (1928, third edn).

Before looking at this regal portraiture, it is helpful to understand its distinction in relation to how Ashoka imaged himself in his own lifetime. At Kanaganahalli Ashoka's political authority was expressed in the form of edicts along with a stupa and pillar. He did not institute a physical representation of himself – neither at Kanaganahalli nor elsewhere do we find Ashokan imperial portraits on sculpture or coins. The friezes showing Satavahana rulers, on the other hand, depict them as human beings; they are portrayed with family and friends, and sometimes they and their entourage serve to illustrate existing stories about them that were in circulation.

So here we find Simukha, the founder of the dynasty, who reigned for some twenty-three years over a kingdom stretching from Andhra to Karnataka. Several places have yielded coins bearing his titular name stamped on them – *Rajno Chchimukha Satavahana*. His son, Satakarni I, is shown as married to Naganika, the daughter of a chieftain of Naga lineage called Maharathi Tranakayira. This was a diplomatic alliance strengthening the father's position in a fight against the last Kanva king, Susrman, whose vassal he was; in fact Simukha had become king by overthrowing Susrman. His alliance with the Nagas is recorded sculpturally at Kanaganahalli. A broad-chested monarch sits with his queen, who looks on approvingly, as though happy to have finally become queen (Fig. 2.5). They are in an elaborate pavilion with women courtiers bringing up their rear. The epigraph mentions the king, and that he is a friend of Nagaraya. The king's rather grander full title is given as Raja Siri Chhimukha Sadavahano Nagaraya Sakhavapi.[17] The friend is seated in the lower panel, attended by a woman holding a bowl with flowers. The depiction is of a strategic political friendship.

In these kingly representations we see quite a variety of folk, and despite gracing a stupa they do not appear remotely pious. The only ruler who seems to be doing something positively Buddhist

[17] Zin (2018a): 52–3.

Fig. 2.5: Chhimukha Satavahana with his queen

is Satakarni I, Simukha's successor, who is said to be gifting lotus flowers to a couple of Buddhist monks: the epigraph says this is what he is doing, whereas what the king is in fact doing is pouring water from a pitcher – suggesting an offering – into the hands of one of several monks. The elaborately dressed king, wearing many more jewels than Chhimukha in the previous panel, looks impressively regal; the monks wear plain robes.

Many kings are accompanied by their queens, and in charmingly different ways. Matalaka and his queen, for example, seemed to me to be having a jolly good time over a drink together, cavorting and pleasuring each other in front of what is presumably their palace. Matalaka holds a stemmed glass of wine in his right hand while his left knee supports the queen's hips. She seems in need of his amorous support because she "has embraced the king with her right hand and her left hand is placed over a left thigh and she wears a loosened (disturbed) pitambara and the kati-bandha which slips on to her hips." Her intoxication is suggested by her "almost closed eyes and pouted lips".[18] The pose struck by King Sundara Satakarni is also positively un-Buddhist, his queen being seated on the "right lap of the thigh", while his right hand rests deliciously above her bosom. It is obvious that India's ancient royalty, and no doubt its plebs as well, had all the right ideas about what men and women should get up to after a swig or two. Modern Indians, with their notions of sexuality distorted by a poisonous mix of social repression, religious strictures, and a prolonged Victorian hangover, are attuned to dismissing as vulgar what is in fact a happily hedonistic celebration of sexual energy. The sculptors of these carved curves intended the onlooker to relish and empathise, not judge or condemn, and the voice of an Indian poet, many centuries later, probably had such portraitures in mind when recounting passion enhanced by "a beaker full of the warm South" equally colourfully:

> Still I recall her flushed with love and wine,
> Great eyes in which the darting pupils swim,
> On a ground of Kashmir saffron every limb
> With figures in black deer-musk ornamented;
> Her mouth with camphor and with betel scented . . .
>
> Still I recall how when I had grown drunk
> Upon the wine with which her mouth was filled
> Into her rounded breast I pressed my nails
> And left a mark at which her body thrilled . . .
>
> – Bilhana's *Chaurapanchashika*[19]

I thought the most unusual of all the royal portrayals was the rendering of the Satavahana ruler King Pulumayi (probably Pulumayi II), who here bequeaths the city of Ujjayini to an

---

[18] This description of the queen is from Poonacha (2011): 300.

[19] For a full translation of this titled "Fifty Stanzas of a Thief", Bailey and Gombrich (2005): 291ff.

adversary, Ajayata (which literally means "undefeatable"). The label mentions this most concretely. Both kings are shown as equals, elaborately dressed, with three men standing behind each of them. This alludes to territorial surrender. It must be, I imagine, the only representation in ancient India of a ruler capitulating. It was not an act that any monarch could possibly have relished celebrating on sculpture, and I could not help wondering why, of all that happened in Pulumayi's life, it was this that came to be imaged here. It seemed vaguely reminiscent of Ashoka's declaration of remorse after Kalinga, a very uncommonly human confession of failure and weakness, though the thought connecting the two kings is possibly only a stray connection that happened to cross my mind.

The very next question which came to mind about the entire line of portraits is not at all stray: Why do kings of this dynasty occupy such a prominent place in a shrine? They were not themselves the donors, nor are there any other kinds of epigraphic dedications showing their connection to the edifice. The donors are a diverse lot – nuns and monks, lay worshippers, artisans and commercial men ("gahapatis"), a minister, and many who describe themselves as daughters, daughters-in-law, wives; there is even one who calls herself a housewife ("gharaniya"); there are mothers, sons, and brothers. A Toda family that gave gifts here is represented on a carved slab.[20] Occasionally, the donors mention the reigning king at the time of making their donation.[21] But the epigraphs are silent on any gifts made by the Satavahanas themselves.

What I inferred about their presence here had therefore to do with what had transpired elsewhere. It was during the time of the Satavahanas that many Buddhist sanctuaries flourished, especially Amaravati in Andhra. In Nasik (Maharashtra), too, epigraphic imprints show that members of the Satavahana family financed

---

[20] Hnuber (2018): 358.
[21] Poonacha (2011): 464. No. 101.

the creation of a cave and provided its resident Buddhist monks with land to pay for the upkeep of their sanctuary. So, possibly, the creators of this sculptural programme at Kanaganahalli were keen to show their gratitude by depicting them in a larger-than-life artistic form. It was, after all, the duty of kings to provide support to all religious groups, so sculpting them into a religious landscape was one way in which beneficiaries reciprocated their recognition by a king; they were making visible the fact that they had received his support. This meant creating a royal spectacle which was also a spectacular display of faith.

I wondered how others before me had perceived this strange group. From the point of view of ancient pilgrims and donors, visiting a stupa was a religious experience, and in such moments the royals arrayed there would have been seen as protectors and supporters of Buddhism. But here they may well have been seen as oddities, or as strange, or as bewildering, because a royal couple in their cups, and another sealing strategic political relationships, were not evident in other Buddhist places of worship. Ancient visitors who had been to other places on the Buddhist pilgrim circuit may well have wondered why so much effort and riches had been squandered sculpting kings in dalliance with their wives, and what any of all this revelry had to do with the Great Sage to whose memory the Kanaganahalli stupa is primarily devoted. It may all have seemed rather peculiar and politically incorrect to the "woke" among the devoted in ancient Karnataka.

Which loops me back to representations of Ashoka. As against the Satavahana kings, the responses of ancient pilgrims to him would have been different, and not only because his fame as the pre-eminent Buddhist king was widespread. The reason is that his carefully crafted presence here is made to fit into stories that allude to what was held sacred in relation to the Buddha. This is something that would have made sense to the spiritually inclined and given much satisfaction to the ancient "woke".

At first glance Ashoka appears here – much like the Satavahana kings – with his queen. The royal couple are surrounded by others including female "chauri" (fly-whisk) bearers and a female umbrella bearer (Fig. 2.6). The couple seem to be sharing a tender moment: Ashoka's face is turned towards his queen while she looks at him adoringly. The portrait is labelled "Raya Asoko" to enable recognition. The queen is unnamed. Practically all kingly

Fig. 2.6: Ashoka with his queen

portraits at Kanaganahalli are similarly labelled, rubbing it into our faces that only the male in the couple matters. As far as the name of this male goes, it is in line with an epigraph several centuries old at Maski: Ashoka's own epigraph has it there in much the same lettering.

This depiction made me think of two entirely different elements. The first concerns an odd aspect of this specific sculptural rendering of Ashoka: he wears what looks like a sacred thread across his right shoulder (a "yajnopavita"). Why? The conventional fallback answer would be that the designer and sculptor represented him as a Brahman. The truth, though, is that while we know very little about his family background, no ancient text has ever claimed Ashoka was a Brahman. The caste background should not matter in any case, because after Kalinga Ashoka is a Buddhist and only remembered as a Buddhist, and as far as we know Buddhists and Brahmans seldom saw eye to eye. This representation of Ashoka is therefore incommensurate with our knowledge of the historical emperor. Possibly, like art in more contemporary times, ancient art has more to do with the personal vision and predilections of the artist, and the work of artists can seem quite anachronistic to later historians who are interested in matching their art with what is historically verifiable.

The second element relates to the Satavahana kings shown here, and those who conceived the designs of these carvings. Why did they decide to include Ashoka in their litany of kings? It seemed to me a possibility that Ashoka was specifically chosen to connect Simukha and other Satavahana kings with the most renowned and illustrious emperor of the past. The usefulness of palimpsest techniques in art and overlayering in sculpture are established methods for creating a lineage or indicating the continuity of a hallowed tradition. The decorative friezes sculpted with stories were very possibly also made for the same reason – they were links enhancing present monarchical status with irrefutable past grandeur. If the founder of the Satavahana line of kings had in fact patronised Buddhism, it would have made sense for them to pay spatial homage to the Buddhist ruler who had first built the stupa. A kind of parity between Ashoka and these later rulers was being proclaimed here via adornment in stone.

From my point of view, if this idea of attempted parity is credible, it might suggest a catholicity of outlook among the Satavahanas, who were far from being avowed Buddhists. In fact the difference between them and Ashoka was quite major: the Mauryan emperor was the prime mover and shaker of Buddhism as a personal faith whereas the Satavahana dynastic line was Hindu and provided support to Brahmans.[22] Their provision of patronage to Buddhists was conceivably in line with a more general and widespread anti-fundamentalist or broadly tolerant conception of worship. A monarch and his successors, while themselves preferring a particular faith and its doctrines, did not as a reflex consider other deities and alternative forms of devotion anathema. This contrasts with the Roman empire's suppression of Christians at roughly the same period. Christianity went underground and its dimensions grew into those of a resistance movement. Confrontation and suppression seemed warranted as the imperial response because of a perception of threat to traditional religion. Buddhism in the Indian South was quite different. The Buddha may, like Jesus, have emphasised peace and compassion and non-violence, but at no point in the Indian South was Buddhism so rampant and so powerful that local Hindu rulers felt they might soon be swamped. Sanity is likely to have dictated coexistence and conciliatory attitudes to sects such as Buddhism in their territories. It was probably part of the public function of a Satavahana ruler to look with magnanimity at diverse forms of prayer.

However, as we saw earlier, the themes by which the sculptors of their time chose to recall Ashoka had nothing to do with his

---

[22] Fynes (1995): 44–7.

generous patronage of Buddhism. On the contrary, as in the Sanchi representation on the southern gateway pillar, he is seen here with his queen and a crowd of women. It is as if this was the Buddhist brand image of Ashoka, proactively pushed by those who designed such sculpture, and since the Sanchi gateway was built in the first century BCE, well before Kanaganahalli, it is entirely possible that the inspiration for his representation in Karnataka came from the same source. The question, then, is why Ashoka at Kanaganahalli gazes so tenderly at his queen. In the Sanchi panel he is grief-stricken because his queen has been machinating to ensure that the Bodhi tree withers; the location of his portraiture is worth mulling over, and in fact it has been well mulled over by a scholar, Monika Zin. The depiction of Ashoka at Kanaganahalli was apparently located among "four other slabs, which have a rather unique character. These slabs depict important Buddhist symbols: the *cakra*, the *stupas*, the tree, and the lion pillar." If this was indeed their original location, Ashoka and his queen were positioned among symbols with which he had a personal association: the dharmachakra was widely imitated and was atop the pillar he had installed in Sarnath; the stupas that he built and expanded extended from the north-west to Karnataka; the Bodhi tree – so often depicted with a throne beneath it – was the gift that he had placed there in honour of the Buddha; and the lion pillar is what he had put up at places like Vaishali and Kanaganahalli. All the same, Ashoka in the midst of these symbols is, in Zin's opinion, incongruous, and his representation, if there is a story being told here, belongs elsewhere. She suggests a compositional unity would become apparent if the slab were located in relation to the Bodhi tree. There would then be a narrative event, because the "king faces the tree: the two panels thus depict Ashoka's visit to the *Bodhi* tree in Bodhgaya."[23] The queen, however, does not look in the

---

[23] Zin (2018b): 545–6. Also see Zin (2019).

direction that Ashoka does; she looks at him, which perhaps puts this hypothesis in doubt. Many such questions arise because the original placement of several of the slabs remains uncertain, making possible multiple interpretations of this old art as a narration of an even older past.

There is no doubt, though, about the second representation of Ashoka: he is meant to be seen in relation to the Bodhi tree, and the artist's rendering follows the Buddhist texts, including Ashoka's legendary biography. The king is shown as a pilgrim in the midst of other pilgrims. The focus of obeisance is a throne and footmarks, representing the Buddha, around which the group is seated (Fig. 2.7). The same throne in the lower register is shown with more landscaping around it. Ashoka, hands folded, worships the tree (Fig. 2.8). The footmarks resemble the earlier ones which show five swastika signs around the chakra.

Fig. 2.7: Ashoka as a pilgrim at Mahabodhi

Fig. 2.8: Ashoka worshipping the Bodhi tree

There is possibly yet another representation of Ashoka at Kanaganahalli, this time – as at Sanchi – showing his connection with the Ramagrama stupa. We can't be a hundred per cent sure that this is Ashoka, because no label survives saying it is him. Assuming it is Ashoka, his depiction here is unlike that in the Sanchi panel of the same theme: in the Sanchi version there are soldiers and multiple Nagas, with Ashoka himself on a chariot; in the Kanaganahalli rendering the focus is the stupa. Several Nagas are shown entwining it while the figure on the pilaster venerating it is quite possibly Ashoka (Fig. 2.9). The emphasis seems to be on the powerful Nagas, entirely confident of their authority over the stupa; unlike at Sanchi, Ashoka does not matter here: it is the Nagas who occupy centre stage.

My search for signs of Ashoka's afterlife may leave the impression that most of the stonework in Karnataka I visited is about a king, or kings among whom Ashoka is one. This is not so. In fact monarchs form neither the sole nor even the main

Fig. 2.9: The Ramagrama stupa with Ashoka worshipping it

subject matter at Kanaganahalli. The Buddha's life, and those of all kinds of souls connected with him, jostle with Nagas and Yakshis, musicians with instruments, archers drawing bowstrings, and palaces as well as places of worship. There is also a singular series of animals – winged lions, elephants, camels, deer, and bulls – moving in one direction, as if circumabulating the sacred shrine. Their abundance is extraordinary. My reason for highlighting the presence of monarchs and Ashoka within this plenitude is that stupas do not usually commemorate royalty, and certainly not in this way. Ashoka within a panorama is something of an oddity in that his visibility is being enhanced within a location where he himself had inaugurated a stupa. This larger spectacle into which he finds himself incorporated is quite unique because, before Kanaganahalli, monarchs do not occupy this kind of spatial prominence within a religious shrine.

Nor did this grow into a motif in sculptural habit subsequently. Kanaganahalli seems a sea of exceptional artists and patrons doing what nobody before them had done, moving beyond the norms of artistic tradition to render rulers in a new way. Were these artists pushing the envelope on norms deemed suitable in religious embellishment? Or is their art primarily an acknowledgement of the patronage that Buddhism enjoyed under the Satavahana rulers? It is possible to speculate endlessly.

What of the afterlife of the Ashokan stone edict in the Chandralamba temple? And the slabs strewn so despicably on ground that had been ploughed? And to the dilapidated state of Ashoka and his queen as I found them there?

I had first encountered this Ashokan slab immediately upon reaching the stupa site. It was the time of morning when the angle of light was most conducive to fine photography. The stone slab I was photographing had not been abandoned and buried in the way that the stupa had. The stupa had gone into oblivion because, as far as I knew, Kanaganahalli's floruit in the third century CE ended once royal patronage to the shrine dried up. The sacred site having lost the funds required for its upkeep, the stupa there eventually collapsed. But the stone on which Ashoka's edicts had been carved was, unlike the stupa, not an immoveable object; it proved useful at another location in the centuries that followed, being repositioned in the Chandralamba temple complex at Sannathi as a base for the image of the deity (Fig. 2.10). Some decades ago, when this "base usage" – in both senses – seemed in need of cleaning, the archaic lettering on it was discovered on both its front and back. The removal of this

Fig. 2.10: One face of Ashoka's Kanaganahalli edict stone. The rectangular hollow is where the image of the deity in the Chandralamba temple was placed

base slab was fortuitous: scrubbing it free of dirt was part of a renovation planned for the temple as a whole. The old image of Mahakali (a version of Durga) within the temple was badly broken, so a proposal to reconsecrate the shrine with a new image of the deity involved the removal of loose stones, pillars, and beams.²⁴ During this process of clearing and cleaning, the epigraph on the pedestal stone happened to be noticed.

The Ashokan stone with its edict as the pedestal base for Kali can be seen symbolically as a rather concrete and material fusion of Buddhism with an older form of worship. Postmodernists could have a field day interpreting this image: the large rectangular hole cut into an Ashokan edict stone to make it serve as a pedestal for the most revered Hindu goddess of destruction and doomsday could be interpreted as the obeisance of Buddhism to Hinduism. You could also choose to see it as an image of the hole cut into the heart of Buddhism by resurgent Hinduism, causing Buddhism to flee to places such as Nakhon Si Thammarat. With a "deconstructed" edict, the interpretive possibilities for a deconstructionist are legion!

As for the sculpted avatar of Ashoka with his queen, soon after photographing the Ashokan edicts I managed a glimpse of the couple on a frieze that had been placed under a tree. There they were, cracks and all, with smatterings of mud accumulated in the depressions and crevices on the slab. My precious king had survived centuries of wear and tear under soil and debris, but now a fate worse than burial awaited him – his discoverers were the standard cack-handed employees in a Kanaganahallian manifestation of a colossally inept ASI. The state of Ashoka's queen on the panel was even worse than Ashoka's, he was lucky in being dead and not seeing what had been done to her in the course of the ASI "repairing" her. Her head had been defaced with a resin lump by an ASI vandal employed as a conservator. Ashoka seemed to be gazing at his rani in stupefaction, wanting to ask her how she had managed to get herself into such a state!

Worse was to come. In 2011 the ASI celebrated its 150th anniversary, and among the things that it chose to do was bring out a book. For the book jacket, and as their publicity image, they

---

²⁴ Sarma and Rao (1993): 6.

used the Kanaganahalli representation depicting Ashoka and his queen.[25] The photograph was no doubt meant to highlight all that the organisation had discovered in post-Independence India. An exhibition was organised at the National Museum in New Delhi, where this book was released as a kind of accompanying catalogue.

The Ashokan jacket image looked stunning, but the printed glamour had been manufactured at considerable cost – the heaviest price being paid by the real state of the sculpture on the grounds of Kanaganahalli. Ashoka and his queen had been powdered and prettified to appear on a book, even as they were being powdered back into the dust at the location where his messages had long been positioned.

The strange saga of Kanaganahalli revealed to me that in our own time the institutional guardians of India's heritage have been as profoundly destructive with ancient paraphernalia as the Huns, the Vandals, and the marauding hordes of medieval times. I was left with the ironic thought that the modern keepers of ancient material and its memorialisation can be as culpable for making Indian history bite the dust as the Muslim invaders whom we more routinely blame.

---

[25] See the cover of *Rediscovering India 1961–2011* (2012).

On the Edge
of a Junagadh Lake

I WAS DRAWN TO Junagadh in Gujarat by an impression about the place in the nineteenth century, when it was meant to have had several residents with an antiquarian curiosity that had inspired them to uncover its past. One such Junagadh resident was Bhagwanlal Indraji, born in 1839 into a family of Ayurvedic medical practitioners. As a boy he had studied Sanskrit in a traditional school and by the age of fourteen had taught himself to read the ancient scripts inscribed on the massive Girnar rock on the edge of his town. Unlike James Prinsep (1799–1840), the colonial administrator-savant who had pored over facsimiles of such inscriptions sent to him in Calcutta and there brilliantly deciphered Ashokan Brahmi, Bhagwanlal spent many days by the rock itself and deciphered words and phrases by examining them *in situ*. For me, his distinction in being the first Indian to have extensively travelled with Ashoka also mattered: he seemed a kindred spirit because his research, like mine, had made him cross the length and breadth of India to many of the sites imprinted with the emperor's words. He had discovered Ashoka's Sopara edicts in Maharashtra as well as his Bairat edicts in Rajasthan. Unlike his contemporary Alexander Cunningham, who did his fieldwork in the winter season, Bhagwanlal spent five years – over which he travelled all year round – deciphering epigraphs, excavating sites, and producing a range of photographs of ancient places and antiquities. There had to be something about the ambience of Junagadh that produced a self-trained scholar like him, and I knew that when the possibility arose I would go to his birthplace and pay homage.[1]

Bhagwanlal spent long hours navigating the meanings encoded in the epigraphs on the Girnar rock.[2] One of these is a vivid description of an environmental disaster in antiquity.[3] In 456 CE or so, on a wet and stormy monsoon night, a lake in the hills there had breached its embankment. Known as the Sudarshana Lake, on that fateful night the earth-and-stone bank that enclosed it keeled over after a dangerous build-up of water. There had been a ceaseless downpour, and as the rivers that fed the lake coursed down the slopes around the mightiest mountain in the vicinity – then known as Urajayat and now as Girnar – the

---

[1] The biography of Bhagwanlal Indraji by Virchand Dharamsey (2012) points to several impressively learned Junagadh residents of the nineteenth century. One of the best known is Ranchodaji Amarji (1768–1841), the Dewan of Junagadh, who was greatly interested in the Girnar rock: "He had the Girnar inscriptions copied, and engaged in discussions about them with Sanskrit pandits and other scholarly inclined people, even before the visit of Colonel James Tod." Dharamsey (2012): 36. There was also Haridatt Karunashankar, Indraji's nephew, trained by him, who helped Vallabhji Acharya and Manilbhai Kilkani – both from Junagadh – to read a few epigraphs for their work on the Kathiawad gazetteer.

[2] Bhagwanlal actually tried to locate the dam, although, as we now know, his identification was off the mark. Indraji and Buhler (1878).

[3] For the Skandagupta epigraph, Bhandarkar, Chhabra, and Gai (1981): 296–305.

lake could take no more. The deluge came with such fury that it forced a rupture in the dam and washed away homes, trees, and fields. The river waters, sweeping across the plains, joined those of the Arabian Sea. An image of a watery hand stretching from the hills to the ocean appears in the inscription of the Gupta monarch Skandagupta (455–467 CE), poetically capturing the event: "[N]oticing the great bewilderment caused by the advent of the rains, the mountain Urajayat, wishing to do a good turn to the great ocean, stretched forth, as it were, a hand, consisting of the River Palasini, decorated with the numerous powers that grew on the edges of its banks." Looking back from the vantage point of some 1500 years, this description of the rains seemed so evocative because it made the terrain of ancient India seem much the same as ours. Skandagupta's epigraph seemed to me an additional good reason to visit Junagadh, since flood narratives, vaguely reminiscent of Biblical diluvian disasters in the Book of Genesis, are quite rare in our context.

It was much before the monsoons, in the summer of 2011, that I set off to see Junagadh for myself. This was some days after the anti-corruption social activist Anna Hazare began a hunger strike, on 5th April that year, in the heart of Delhi. The swelling support for him and consequent traffic jams made it difficult to move around to libraries in the city. It seemed an opportune moment to decamp to Saurashtra and get a sense of the material reality of the lake that lapped in my imagination – an urge that called to mind how a poet had (as always) put my feeling in words that I myself could never have found:

> I will arise and go now, for always night and day
> I hear lake water lapping with low sounds by the shore;
> While I stand on the roadway, or on the pavements grey,
> I hear it in the deep heart's core.[4]

---

[4] From W.B. Yeats' "The Lake Isle of Innisfree".

But there was more than just the urge to see the archaeological remnants of a lake. The very rock where the words of Skandagupta were engraved had first been used as a tablet by Ashoka, seven hundred or so years earlier. Since in my mind all roads *had* to lead to Ashoka, this particular rock held an almost supernatural and larger-than-life presence because, after Ashoka yet another ruler, this time in the second century CE – a Saka Kshatrapa king of the Kardamaka family called Rudradaman (r. 130–50 CE) – had had a long epigraph carved on it.[5] One stone, three kings! Ashoka, Rudradaman, Skandagupta.

Kings and leaders have of course been connected with rocks and rock formations, perhaps the most famous in antiquity being the Ten Commandments of Moses, which are believed to have been inscribed on stone tablets; and in our own time the best known is of course the controversial Mount Rushmore in South Dakota, USA, snatched from Native Americans to carve up four of the country's famous presidents. The Bayon temple in Cambodia shows the serene face of the Buddha hewn magnificently out of rock slabs in medieval times. Christ, "king of the Jews" – the bedrock of Christianity – is often conceived of quite specifically as a rock of stability, most famously in that lovely and deeply moving eighteenth-century Anglican hymn "Rock of Ages", with its powerful image of Christ as a rock that bled compassion:

> Rock of Ages, cleft for me,
> Let me hide myself in Thee.
> Let the water and the blood,
> From Thy riven side which flowed
> . . .
>
> While I draw this fleeting breath,
> When mine eyes shall close in death,

[5] This is the Junagadh rock inscription of Rudradaman. Kielhorn (1905–6).

When I soar to worlds unknown,
See thee on thy judgment throne,
Rock of Ages, cleft for me,
Let me hide myself in thee.

Rocks, when used as memorials or as tablets are, in brief, not as stony-hearted as ordinary rocks. They resonate with voices from the past. It struck me frequently during my hankerings after Ashoka's long-lost voice that other voices had mingled with his on a single rock, and that they were all now mingled – often mangled – in my head, all of them culturally and religiously remote from the Buddhist emperor's own.

As I left Rajkot and journeyed towards Junagadh – the places are some two hours from each other – at some point a faint line of hills with multiple peaks in the distance became visible. Then the road seemed to be going towards mountains whose ridges and scarps, with shadows in the hollows of slopes, remained a constant presence as we moved in their direction. The great rugged Girnar was made up of many peaks and, as I later learnt, its Goraknath peak, at a thousand-odd metres above sea level, is possibly the highest point in all of Gujarat.

On reaching, my first port of call was the Archaeological Survey of India. One of my oldest friends in the ASI, Kishan Nauriyal, was then the superintending archaeologist of the Vadodara Circle of the Survey and had nudged me towards their Junagadh office. Nauriyal himself was very keen to sustain Junagadh's heritage; his wish list included mapping its buried features, revisiting all the archaeological discoveries made there, and making a digital recording of how they had happened. Like many who worked in the government, he was up to his neck in administrative work and I have no idea now if he ever managed to turn all his fine dreams into reality.

The man I met at Junagadh was J.P. Bhatt, an old Survey hand in charge of the monuments there who would help me locate the places I wanted to visit. As we talked, he insisted that I meet his brother, a man called Rasik Bhatt, who was meant to know oodles about archaeological remnants in forested areas around the district. I soon learnt why.

This sprightly 70-year-old was a well-known and respected Junagadh environmentalist who had retired as an agricultural scientist. He had been following the trails that converged around the Girnar region and beyond; in fact he had spent a lifetime walking this area. He had seen the landscape at close quarters, spotting pre-modern brick-and-stone remnants, mounds, and hero stones, along with medicinal plants and Asiatic lions, during his traverses. Bhatt's passion for treks made him seem much younger than he was. Practically all the knowledge I gained of the material past in this part of Saurashtra was informed by his experience and understanding of the region. This was wonderful for me because, to my Ashoka-filled eye, it meant encountering and absorbing the character of this hilly and forest-girted area of Junagadh in order to make sense of the presence of the Maurya dynasty in this region of Gujarat.

To properly understand the Ashokan presence in Junagadh it is first necessary to get a sense of signature signs of his grandfather, Chandragupta (r. 324/321–297 BCE), the first monarch of the Maurya dynasty. His presence here took shape as the construction of the dam because of which the Sudarshana Lake was created: Chandragupta's provincial governor in the region had been asked to have it constructed. How may we comprehend the administrative presence in Junagadh of this pan-Indian Magadha-based empire? And if its provincial governor was based here, why was the Mauryan provincial capital in Junagadh rather than elsewhere in Saurashtra?

One reason is likely to have been the defensive possibilites that are evident from Junagadh's hilly location: this will have made it relatively secure. It is also no doubt why, over the centuries, a number of towns developed in these hilly parts, ranging from Adityana and Mendarda to Talala and Visavadar.[6] Junagadh's accessibility to the sea coast will have been another important factor. Its distance from the coast is less than eighty kilometres, and in fact nineteenth-century observers frequently say that from the Girnar Hills a glimpse could be had of the forests and low hills that ran in one continuous sweep to the sea. The famous James Tod of the *Annals and Antiquities of Rajasthan* was one of these observers who, having ascended the summit of the seven-peaked Girnar, marvelled at having seen "the ocean lighted up by the sun's last rays, while silence ruled over the remains of fading glory."[7] Tod, as an army antiquarian of the British East India Company, had travelled over many places in western India and has left us some superb descriptions of its ancient treasures.

The other aspect of Junagadh which comes alive via inscriptional allusions to the construction of a dam by the Mauryan state in the time of Chandragupta – the dam continued to receive royal attention during the reign of Ashoka – is the availability of water. So, was there a large town around here? Where was it located? And why did the administration decide to build an embankment rather than, for instance, dig wells?

The ancient town's exact situation is not entirely clear. It is likely to have been in the area of the modern Chamunda locality, where the accumulation of habitation deposits in a mound-like formation is visible over the hillside in its vicinity, and on the outer edge of the fortifications in what is known as Uparkot. Walking around the Chamunda area, we were told by residents that it was common to find sculptural relics, pottery, stone artefacts, and even skeletons in the vicinity.[8] The area is not far from what must have been one edge of the lake that came to

---

[6] Rajyagor (1975): 8.

[7] Tod (1839): 401.

[8] Lahiri (2011) for this, and other field observations mentioned in this chapter as part of my work there.

be formed behind the dam. The reason for the embankment here was the availability of a large bowl-like space – you could imagine looking down at it from space and seeing a hill-encircled basin, its only possible exit being the Sonarekha river (sometimes called Suvarnarekha). The embankment for water storage had to do with the limitations of well technology in those times: they didn't have the wherewithal to dig deep enough to reach the water table. We know that, in the late-nineteenth century, wells in other parts of Junagadh never exceeded a depth of fifteen metres or so, the exception being Junagadh city, where water was found at a much greater depth. For this reason it is pocked by many elaborate "vavs" (wells) which go down deep, all of them being constructions dating to the medieval centuries.

If the town was situated not far from the lake, another edge of the watery reservoir was in the rough proximity of the Girnar rock. Today, this part of the lake has a road which winds around hills and allows access to the base of the rock – from where one can move on to the valley around the Girnar mountain; and from thence Hindu and Jain pilgrims regularly pass on to their temples located in the vicinity.

But there are also Buddhists who come to Junagadh, and mainly to look at the Girnar rock. As I finished examining the word-filled rock on my first visit there, I saw a Japanese woman paying obeisance to it with folded hands. Only after this brief worship did she feel able to ascend the steps for a "darshan" of what she regarded as wholly sacred. The massive boulder, minutely inscribed, associated with the spread of Buddhism, inscribed by Hindu monarchs, and an obvious "rock of ages" that seems to have defied time and the forces of erosion, draws in all kinds of people and every kind of worship, from spiritual supplicants to scholars.

The rock itself is covered with a canopy meant to safeguard it. This obscures its sheer majesty and I have no doubt that in antiquity it looked far more magnificent than it does today (Fig. 3.1).

Fig. 3.1: Building made over the Girnar rock

Certainly, when Bhagwanlal devoted his teenage years to the words on this rock, it made a spectacular impression on him. While ancient inhabitants too must have marvelled at it, no description of those times has survived. The most beautifully worded account is Tod's early-nineteenth-century impression of a visit to Girnar in 1822:

> Let me describe what to the antiquary will appear the noblest monument of Saurashtra, a monument speaking in an unknown tongue of other times . . . The memorial in question, and evidently of some great conqueror is a huge hemispherical mass of dark granite,

which, like a wart upon the body, has protruded the crust of mother earth, without fissure or inequality, and which, by the aid of the "iron pen", has been converted into a book. The measurement of its arc is nearly ninety feet; its surface is divided into compartments or parallelograms, within which are inscriptions in the usual antique character... I may well call it a book; for the rock is covered with these characters, so uniform in execution, that we may safely pronounce all those of the most ancient class, which I designate the "Pandu character," to be the work of one man.[9]

Tod's response to Girnar was written before the Brahmi script had been deciphered; possibly, had his visit there been after the script had been unlocked by Prinsep in 1837, he would have realised that the rock was not a memorial to a conquering king. Prinsep's efforts revealed that Ashoka was interacting with the citizens of the area on an entirely different plane – by publicly inscribing his message of dhamma on a large rock face. Standing in front of his words, it was evident that there was a significant difference between the elevation where the edicts were inscribed and the general lay of the land towards the lake's edge. So, some specially designated official very likely communicated the message to the man inscribing it while standing somewhere near the rock.

More unusual than the mode of communication is the missive itself.[10] An emperor with his capital in Pataliputra was commanding his subjects in Girnar to follow a moral path (Fig. 3.2). His morality was expansive, ranging from non-violence towards animals (Edict 3) to proactive measures for providing nurture and medical care for them (Edict 2). A whole way of life was recommended, including obedience to parents, liberality to Brahmanas and Shramanas (renunciants), and a "middle path" of moderation in relation to expenditure and possessions (Edict 3).

[9] Tod (1839): 370–1.
[10] The version of the Ashokan Girnar edicts I use is from Hultzsch (1925).

Fig. 3.2: The Girnar rock with Ashokan edicts visible on its face

Even more intriguing is to see Ashoka fleshing himself out as all too human, revealing his failings and flaws to his subjects. Even as he asks that no living thing be killed as sacrifice, he has the candour to admit that two peacocks and a deer continue to be cooked daily in the royal kitchen (Edict 1). In Edict 13 he describes the dimensions of slaughter, death, and deportation during and as a consequence of his conquest of Kalinga: the edict seems calculated to shock, given that the emperor acknowledges Brahmanas and Shramanas, as also householders who had led moral lives, having been among his victims. This tale of bloody triumph concludes in remorse – a sentiment expressed more bitterly and regretfully by another king who, after a bloody victory, realises the futility of a success which lays waste to what was once so meaningfully alive. The terrible world that Macbeth faces after his murderous road to power is summarised by his response to the news that his wife is dead. The situations of Ashoka and

Macbeth are widely removed across time and geography but the circumstances are not as entirely dissimilar as they might seem at first sight. Ashoka's state of mind, as suggested by his Thirteenth Edict, could quite conceivably have had this as its coda:

> To-morrow, and to-morrow, and to-morrow,
> Creeps in this petty pace from day to day,
> To the last syllable of recorded time;
> And all our yesterdays have lighted fools
> The way to dusty death. Out, out, brief candle!
> Life's but a walking shadow, a poor player
> That struts and frets his hour upon the stage
> And then is heard no more. It is a tale
> Told by an idiot, full of sound and fury,
> Signifying nothing.

Or, well, I suppose he would have preferred deleting those last two words since, unlike Macbeth, he did not perish, he flourished, and had the freedom and good fortune to assert that what he was signifying through his rock edicts was more or less *everything*. Reform and welfare measures came to be proactively pushed in his kingdom. Life improved for him, and perhaps a little for his subjects. And once his own brief candle went out, it wasn't as if his afterlife was extinguished; in fact, "to the last syllable of recorded time" is about as accurate a poetic description as it is possible to get in relation to the recorded reign of any emperor of such antiquity. And I – if it was the last thing I did – was intent on getting to every last syllable of his recorded time.

Interestingly, while Junagadh had a lineage of connections going back to Chandragupta, Ashoka neither mentioned him nor spoke about what he himself had added to the lake that his grandfather had constructed; that bit, as we have noted, figures in epigraphs some centuries later. When trying to understand the emperor's silence on this, my sense is that Ashoka recorded only what was of central importance to him. There was unlikely to have been a shortage of stationery and writing materials, such as stones and chisels, to carve thoughts and prescriptions with: most of India is littered with enough large rocks to keep even a prolix emperor happy. But the reading habit hadn't quite picked up, and the populace had to be asked to consider only as much as seemed strictly necessary to the remoulding of their lives and a new kind of state based on dhamma. Informing them of the Sudarshana Lake and the dam and what he had done towards their upkeep was, for Ashoka's regnal purposes, superfluous information doomed never to make it into an epigraph.

What Ashoka chose to omit was in a way something like standard practice among rulers. Sultan Jahan Begum was of the same ilk. We know she was the chief benefactor in the restoration of the stupas at Sanchi, but in her memoir, *An Account of My Life*, she did not think her munificence stellar enough to seem worthy of mention.[11] Sanchi had figured in her public life on many occasions – she had hosted viceroys, military commanders, and members of Indian princely families there. Was she just being impeccably modest about what the place had cost her to prettify? Or was the size of her purse so enormous that the restoration expenses had seemed trifling? The most likely explanation, however, lies in her temperament and predilections. What really got her firing on all cylinders, in the way that the dhamma did Ashoka, was her work on education and women's emancipation. Her good deeds in those areas were the main things for her, and those were what she thought worth remembering.

In *As You Like It* the malcontent Jacques tells the protagonist Orlando that he does not like the name of Orlando's beloved, Rosalind, to which Orlando retorts with a devastating one-line put-down: "There was no thought of pleasing you when she was christened." My point here is that people set down what they consider important, and there can be no anticipating what

[11] Begum (1922 and 1927): 233f., 272 (vol. II), and 203 (vol. III).

scholars are going to be looking for later in the day: Ashoka and Sultan Jahan Begum clearly seem to have had no thought of pleasing me when they wrote their edicts and memoirs!

Why did the creation of the dam and Ashoka's addition to the hydraulic structure merit mention hundreds of years later, in the second century CE? The reason has to do with repairs: Rudradaman was overhauling and stretching the dam and, rather unusually, also decided to record the creation and expansion of the dam by the Mauryas. His epigraph provides a vivid account of the lake and bund, as of some of Junagadh's natural and cultural features. From it we also learn the ancient name of the town – Girinagara; and of the majestic Girnar – the Urjayat mountain. The names of the streams flowing there sound similar to their modern names, Sonarekha and Palasini; these were the Suvarnasikata and Palasini earlier. Modern gazetteers mention freak cloudbursts in Junagadh, where a few hundred mm of rain can fall in the course of a day. The Rudradaman epigraph provides the earliest recorded instance of this phenomenon in October–November 150 CE, when, in a storm "with the clouds pouring with rain the earth had been converted as it were into one ocean." The swollen flood waters of the rivers and streams "tore town hill-tops, trees, banks, turrets, upper storeys, gates and raised places of shelter." As the waters escaped, the lake, says this poetic rendering, from being "Sudarshana" became "durdarshana".[12]

The earlier history of the lake is provided at this point: a line in the epigraph says it was "ordered to be made by the Vaishya Pushyagupta, the provincial governor of the Maurya king Chandragupta adorned with conduits for Ashoka the Maurya by the Yavana king Tushaspha."[13] The description is sparse but

[12] Lines 6 and 7 are extremely evocative and are quoted here. Kielhorn (1905–6): 46–7.

[13] Line 8 of the epigraph.

the purpose it served in its time was to remind people of the two Maurya monarchs who were part of the historically remembered landscape of Junagadh in the early centuries CE. The remembrance is exceptional: it is perhaps the only instance of Ashoka being connected to the construction and expansion of an edifice that was not religious. Like his grandfather, he is likely to have made many such interventions in various parts of the empire, but such instances were either entirely forgotten or have not survived. I remember thinking, looking at the Girnar rock, that the Ashokan connection with the dam and lake near it was not one that the emperor himself was remotely interested in, else he would surely have had it carved on this specific stone.

The other odd thing in relation to Rudradaman's epigraph is that rulers of later dynasties had almost never drawn attention to the construction work of previous dynasts; they were quite reasonably preoccupied with blowing their own trumpets. The epigraphist of the second century CE follows this template in waxing eloquent on the exploits of the ruler who had commissioned his work while allowing previous history to squeeze in as incidental mention.

In the fifth century CE, during the reign of Skandagupta, the embankment was again breached and renovated. The epigraphic record of this does not concern itself with antecedent history. All the same, between them the two epigraphs make it possible to chart the progress of an ancient dam over some thousand years or so, which is remarkable enough to give historians of ancient India a lot to think about (Fig. 3.3).

The two epigraphs that were inscribed after Ashoka are careful not to obliterate the earlier message. Ashoka's edicts occupy the north-east boulder. The twenty lines of Rudradaman's inscription are on the western side, near the top, while the Gupta epigraph is on the north-west face. Other surfaces of Ashokan epigraphs also found Gupta companions. The Allahabad inscription of Samudragupta is one of these and happens to be on a pillar

Fig. 3.3: Rudradaman's inscription on the Girnar rock

that bears several Ashokan epigraphs – not merely the six Pillar Edicts but also a couple of other short epigraphs – as well as a sixteenth-century inscription of the Mughal emperor Jahangir. Apart from the fact that all three are general significations of royal power, they have nothing in common. The narration of the travails of the Sudarshana Lake are, unusually, on the very rock which contains the Ashokan edicts. Possibly the later engravers believed that the Ashokan message on the rock was also about the lake and the embankment, and that they were only continuing the narration of a story that he had begun.

What about the archaeological remnants of the lake and dam? At the time of my second visit I met Parimal Rupani, Junagadh's premier collector, a keen amateur historian. During a conversation with him I learnt that these had been identified in the late-nineteenth century by Khan Bahadur Ardeseer Jamsedjee. A local resident, Jamsedjee was the Naib Dewan of the princely state of Junagadh. On reading a paper written by him – provided to me by Rupani – I saw how he had explored these remnants. Following a conversation with J.M. Campbell, an officer of the Bombay Civil Service and compiler of the Bombay gazetteer, he had begun to search the banks of the Sonarekha for traces of a dam. Eventually, this helped him identify relics made of earth and stone. While one arm of the embankment was found near the city wall, another was recognised across the river towards the Jogiana Hill, along with masonry blocks in the bed of the river.[14] This discovery dates to 1888. Amazingly, the remains of the high earthen embankment that Jamsedjee first described are still visible and traceable.

These were remnants of the dam constructed in the reign of Rudradaman. Chandragupta's dam, to which Ashoka had added, was according to Jamsedjee "older and shorter" and located further upstream. This first dam he sought to identify with blocks of masonry in the bed of the Sonarekha river near the sacred Triveni, which is close to the Dharagir gate and in whose vicinity there are mounds. He also tried to identify the conduits or sluices mentioned in Rudradaman's inscription as a feature of Ashoka's renovation.

Beyond the Girnar rock, archaeological sites and structures of the late centuries BCE and early centuries CE in and around Junagadh city and beyond in the forests continue to show attenuated signs of Ashoka. One of these is the stupa of Bhoria, also called the Lakha Medi stupa. Located in the thick wooded range of the Girnar Reserve Sanctuary, this is the most impressive early Buddhist structural relic of the area. The stupa is built on a rocky knoll about seven km to the east of Junagadh, in a delightfully secluded valley from where the grand Girnar and the Datar Hill can be seen. Because it is a protected area, the landscape

---

[14] Jamsedjee (1890–4): 51.

remains much as in an 1891 account by the archaeologist Henry Cousens:

> The great rugged sides of Girnar, with its everlasting rocks, kissed by the lingering rays of the rosy sunset, and begirdled with a cloak of varied tinted foliage, now fading into the softest pearl greys, is a picture one loves to linger before. Around us, beside this old patriarch among the hills, we have in the south-east the heights of Gadesing, crowned by its ruined fort, on the south-west Datar-no-dongar, with the hills of Makhan Kuudi, Taktakgiyo, Sazadiari, and Pavandhoda between, and the low pass on the eastern slopes of Girnar known as Surya-kund-ki-godi. In the middle of this beautiful valley, then, thus cut off from the outside world, upon a rock knoll, stands the great mound known as the Boria *Stupa* or the Lakha Medi (the abode of Lakha). The ground on every side between it and the western edge of the valley is strewn with fragments of bricks, and here and there are small mounds which look much like the remains of little *stupas*. Directly eastward of the big *stupa*, and on the eastern edge of the valley, is the small temple of Bor Devi, so called from the Bor trees which surround it.[15]

The valley is visited by those who come to pay obeisance at the Bhor Devi temple. Hardly anyone – other than those who enjoy burying their noses in antiquarian remains – remembers a colossal stupa in the jungle adjacent to the temple excavated in 1889 by J.M. Campbell. A massive cut that he left in his wake at Lakha Medi – a consequence of his dig – looks like a large gash on a gasping brick body, confirming the plausibility of the hymnal image of a riven rock spouting blood. The stupa is made of solid brick in herringbone bond, which is why, despite Campbell's hack work, it has not collapsed. Inside it, in a stone coffer, was found a pot, also made of stone, containing relic boxes of copper, silver, and gold, precious stone, and a relic which "had the appearance of a dried twig". Neither an epigraph nor a coin

---

[15] Cousens (1891): 18.

were found that might have helped to more precisely date the stupa. The likelihood that it is of Ashokan origin is suggested by it being, like many Mauryan stupas, a solid brick structure. And there is, additionally, the Ashokan stamp of relics within it. The clincher is of course the existence almost within hailing distance of it of Ashoka's majestically inscribed edicts.

A Buddhist monastic set-up here in the time of Ashoka is virtually certain. It will have been the start of a Buddhist presence in the Junagadh–Girnar area, and over time there is evidence of its substantial expansion: there are Buddhist caves in Junagadh, and the caves of Uparkot (the upper citadel) were discovered by Bhagwanlal in 1868. In a part of the forest – within the Hasnapur Dam area and close to a local religious place called Jina Baba ki Samadhi – a stupa site is discernible.[16] Then there is Intawa, a Buddhist monastic site in the midst of thick jungle, on a hill above Bhavnath. Intawa was excavated in 1949 and yielded the foundations of monasteries, as also artefacts ranging from water pots and coins to a rounded clay seal identifying itself as belonging to the Bhikshu Samgha of the vihara of Maharaja Rudrasena.[17] This is likely to have been Rudrasena I (199–222 CE) – not the king who repaired the broken dam, but a later ruler. The seal inscription shows Intawa quite singularly and with absolute certainty as the datable early historic site of the area.

A pattern can be traced within the region's ancient monuments. The Girnar forested tract does not have a great deal of flat land; from what I could see, there are four small valleys between the Girnar range and the surrounding hills, three of which are at Bhavnath, Hasnapur, and Bhordevi, with the fourth at Surajkund showing an old well. The famous Girnar "parikrama", which starts annually in November, begins at Bhavnath, passes

---

[16] Some of these sites, including Jina Baba ki Madi, which she described as a "'samadhi", find mention in Shubhra Pramanaik's description of the fieldwork that she undertook there (2004–5): 181.

[17] Chhabra (1949–50): 174–5.

through the forest via Intawa, reaches Jina Baba ki Madi, and then crosses Madvela to reach Bhordevi – from where pilgrims move back to Bhavnath. At the traditional halting places in this pilgrimage circuit lie the ruins of Buddhist structures. It would seem that, much before its fame as a centre of Jain and Hindu worship – which continues to be its current form – Girnar was sacred to the Buddhists, and possibly the earliest circuit of worship in and around it was a Buddhist one; and therefore it seems possible to believe that the origins of the religious character of this location can be traced all the way back to Ashoka.

This ambit involving Buddhists is not certified by written tradition. But conjectural plausibility lies in seeing that the earliest Buddhist to have left his thoughts on a Junagadh rock, and who in all probability constructed a stupa in an adjoining forest, was none other than Ashoka, and that the pilgrimages here, unknown to the pilgrims, are implicit homage to him – as they probably more explicitly were in the hearts of ancient pilgrims. As his religion proliferated in the area, he may even have been invoked as the guardian of Buddhists here 2000+ years ago – a tradition the Japanese tourist I saw at the Girnar rock was unknowingly continuing.

Looking Back at Barabar

THE BARABAR HILLS are easily approached from Jehanabad, a town in south Bihar whose name appealed to me because of its connection with a distinguished seventeenth-century royal woman. I had heard it had been named for Jahanara Begum because she is said to have supervised and managed a "mandi" (marketplace) here in the seventeenth century, set up for the hungry and starving in a famine.[1] Precisely when Jahanarabad became Jehanabad remains unclear – the town and district are now both Jehanabad. Near the town is the dargah of a Sufi woman saint, perhaps the first such shrine of a woman saint to have popped up in India. She was called Bibi Kamal Sahiba and her resting place is still patronised by devotees in search of healing. My journey to Jehanabad was in search of similar holy characters and their patron, except mine were dead brown males

---

[1] The scholar of medieval history Farhat Hasan informs me that no contemporary Mughal sources mention any such association. So this may well be part of popular folklore which came to be recorded in the nineteenth century.

who lived in the area more than a millennium before the Mughal days of Bibi Kamal Sahiba.

An ancient sect known as the Ajivikas had once lived in the Barabar hills, in the vicinity of Jehanabad. The hills had been made famous by Ashoka: he had had tonnes of granite gouged out of its rock faces, creating caves for this sect as well as for other unnamed ascetics. The Ajivikas believed in an overwhelmingly fatalistic doctrine of predestination with no space for human will. They enjoyed much patronage in the court of Magadha – as this part of Bihar was then called – in the sixth century BCE.[2] So did other religious faiths from the same period, such as those of the Buddha and Mahavira. But we know much less about the Ajivikas than we do about the Buddhists and the Jains because no modern adherents of this sect have persisted into our time. The religion vanished completely – there is, at least no reference to its existence after the sixth century CE – which makes the creation of elaborate caves for them now seem strangely enigmatic. The hollows were fashioned on the orders of an emperor in whose court these ascetics are likely to have enjoyed much power and patronage, else he would hardly have spent the substantial sum involved in providing them a habitat. The Ajivikas lived naked and performed penances of the most rigorous nature, ranging from lying on beds of thorns to deliberately exposing themselves to the bitter chill of winds at night. It seems odd that a group so keen on self-flagellation came to be provided with stunning habitations – or stunning at least by the standards of their day. The walls of their caves show a mirror-polished glitter that makes them both quite lustrous and strangely at variance with the worldliness they were so interested in eschewing. No doubt it was possible to mortify the flesh even within an aesthetically pleasing home environment.

What made Ashoka bring architectural grandeur into the

[2] An excellent overview of the history and doctrines of the Ajivikas is Basham (1951).

lives of these ascetics? What was the landscape like where these caves stood? Who were some of the later kings and commoners that had made their presence known in this region via signs and inscriptions? These were some of the big questions that kept popping up in my head all day and leaching into my dreams of the ancient world at night. The best way to find some answers was to make haste to the Barabar hills and see things for myself.

The Barabar caves had also seemed a good location for the "ground reality" of a famous novel, with the dark interior of one of these caves featuring as the most critical point within the heart of the story: historians with an interest in fiction will know immediately that I am referring here to one of the most profound classics of the English canon, E.M. Forster's *A Passage to India* (1924). The novel dramatises the conflict in colonial India between the liberal and spiritual point of view on the one hand, and the colonial and racist on the other. The most crucial event in the novel takes place when the anti-heroine Adela Quested imagines she has been molested by the protagonist, Dr Aziz, during the picnic of their group to the Barabar caves (in the novel they are called the "Marabar caves").[3] Subsequently, over an ephiphanic moment in a courtroom where the conspicuously brown Dr Aziz is being tried for attempted rape of the vulnerably white Adela, the woman has the guts to confess she was mistaken: what she had experienced in the darkness of the cave was not a molestation but a hallucination. A frightening echo in the cave could, Forster suggests, be interpreted as either a divine "Om" or a catastrophic "Boum", depending upon the state of mind and historical circumstances of the person interpreting the echo: Adela's sexually fraught state in the caves had made her understand the echo negatively.[4]

---

[3] A fine study of historical material relevant to Forster's understanding of India is Das, *E.M. Forster's India*.
[4] See "Caves", the second section of the novel, in Forster (1924).

Ideally, no one visiting the Barabar caves should enter them without reading the Forster masterpiece because it enhances the experience, adding a new perspective on how to understand these caves. Having read the book, it struck me, for instance, that these grottoes of old times were perhaps in line, after all, with the needs of a self-flagellating bunch of ascetics. Adela's surname, "Quested", suggests the idea of life as a quest, and ascetics are always questing for the divine. And Adela Quested's traumatic experience – a mix of apprehension, fright, bewilderment, hallucination – suggests a Sartrean and Beavoirean existential way of first questioning life and then arriving at a deeply personal and distinctively individual meaning. This too is in line with what the ascetic seeks in the wilderness. Ascetics of a sceptical temperament keen on flogging their own flesh in order to experience life's extremes would perhaps have felt perfectly at home in these caves, for they would undoubtedly have stretched them psychologically, their echoes confirming a godless universe absent of meaning.

I followed the trail to the Ajivikas on an autumn morning in early October 2012. It took a while to reach the caves, some twenty-five km from Jahanabad. From the path that I took the caves were not visible since they are located low in the hills, and I was approaching them by first going to the summit from another direction and then descending. The path had been chosen by my host, Balamurugan Devaraj, the district magistrate of Jehanabad District in Bihar. In 2011 Bala had ended a decades-long practice of stone mining, much of it illegal, in these hills. That morning he gave me a sense of how he had managed the crackdown, as also a sense of how the cracks had developed in the caves because of explosives used by the criminal stone extracters.

I remember Bala as an amazingly committed officer, as one who cared for the history of the region in general and the conservation of these caves in particular. His energy ensured that, apart from the caves, I visited all kinds of places, including the local museum in the town. The museum had a library with an impressive collection of Hindi books, as also English titles such as *David Copperfield*, *Pygmalion*, and *India After Gandhi* – the last a personal modern history favourite which made me realise how connected this remote part of Bihar was with the world beyond it. The Ajivikas here in the third century BC had occupied caves carved out for them by a metropolitan emperor; centuries later a metropolitan novelist had made them the centre of his depiction of the beating heart of India; a nearby library associated with them seemed to have linked them to mainstream India via a readable history; and here I was, trying to see them through Ashoka's eyes so that I could transmit something of what I saw to readers of my book. It was heartening to see a small-town museum in the boondocks of Bihar stocking books that, presumably, at least a few people in Jehanabad had borrowed and read.

When you walk uphill on the dirt path in that backyard of the known universe, as I did with Bala that October morning, what you get to see is not the landscape evoked by books on the caves. Instead, there are an overwhelmingly large number of religious sight-markers which give a sense of pilgrims who had trodden these hills over the past 1500 years or more. The path was strewn with historic stone images of Hindu gods and goddesses – paunchy Ganeshas, an athletic-looking Varaha (an avatar of the god Vishnu), elaborately carved Vishnu images, and superb representations of Siva and Parvati looking utterly loverly as they sat side by side (Figs 4.1 and 4.2). Old niches carved into the rocks were marked by lines of shivalings carved into rocky niches. The carvings were crafted in a style that suggested an antiquity between the fifth and seventh centuries CE. However, the generous and fresh vermilion-painted foreheads of the stone deities, some of them having recently been adorned with red cloth, were reminders of modern pilgrim footfalls. Their

Fig. 4.1: An athletic-looking Varaha

tracks always led up, beyond the elevation of the caves, to the Siddeshwarnath temple.

This temple crowns one of the highest peaks in the range. The structure is modern, but built on the remnants of an older shrine (Fig. 4.3). Detached architectural elements have been cemented into, and awkwardly poke out of, the base of the modern superstructure. Inside the sanctum sanctorum is a stone linga which seemed to have been worshipped that very morning with rice and purple periwinkle. The smoothened and black character of the object of worship suggested many decades of prayer here.

As on the way up, there was a profusion of images in the temple precincts. Images of the Devi, presumably Durga, of the

Fig. 4.2: A loverly Siva and Parvati among old images

Fig. 4.3: Old images in a new structure of the Siddeshwarnath temple complex

celestial Siva-Parvati couple, and of their son Ganesha, along with Shiva lingas, were evident in and around the courtyard and subsidiary structures. Their craftsmanship suggested a date after the fifth century CE; some were possibly designed a couple of centuries later.

As I later learnt, Hindu worship at this spot was not new. The archaeologist J.D. Beglar, in a tour of the area in 1872–3, had been struck by the number of idols littered over the landscape. These he had described on the path leading up to the temple as including statues "both detached and sculptured on the rock". Then, as now, it was a modern living shrine with a crowd of ancient images:

> The temple now contains Brahmanical deities, and is frequented by Hindu pilgrims. Close to it was another, of which only traces of the foundation exist. This was also Brahmanical, judging from a lingam and fragments of statues on the site; and it does not appear to me that these temples were originally Buddhist, as they do not face the east, and because there is in the existing temple a lingam which I was informed by my Hindu servant (I was not allowed to enter) to have been deeply embedded, and apparently in its original position (it is known as Siddeshwara). But whether they were originally Buddhist or not, Buddhist temples must at one time have existed in the vicinity, for Buddhist statues are to be found within the precincts of the temple; they are now worshipped as Brahmanical deities.[5]

Presently, there is nothing Buddhist around the temple. It may well be that since Beglar was following the footsteps of Xuanzang, the seventh-century Chinese pilgrim-traveller, he imagined such images in the crowd of sculpture there. He was much disappointed that his search had not led to the sighting of any Buddhist structure at all and consoled himself by recounting that Xuanzang had, in fact, not described any "Buddhist institutions of the hill".[6]

---

[5] Beglar and Cunningham (1878): 36.
[6] Ibid.: 37. In spite of the Chinese pilgrim not mentioning anything Buddhist

But more than the Siddeshwarnath temple, it was the view from where it perched that was stunning. The hills that stretched out below were clothed in the gorgeous green foliage that follows months of monsoon rain. The trees and undergrowth gave way, here and there, to granitic rocks, and there was the occasional large reservoir glinting in the morning sun with the slow meandering Phalgu river in the background. Looking out, you saw in the distance the outcrop which had seen such strenuous activity on behalf of Ashoka in his day. At first sight it seemed to resemble the gigantic creature that had in the past been described as whale-shaped. It was a rocky curvilinear mass that did indeed seem like a massive Humpback whale on a bed of sea green.

Three caves lie inside the whale, all built at Ashoka's instance; they are entirely within the hump area and one lies inside an outcrop some distance from it. Two of the caves are double-chambered. The Sudama cave's smaller chamber was fashioned into a hut of stone (Fig. 4.4). Carved out of the rock, it imitated a form more often seen in wood and bamboo: it seemed to me most suitable for ascetics. The modern name for one of the caves is, in fact, Vishwa Jhompri, meaning "universal hut" or a "hut of the world". It is quite another matter, and rather ironic, that the money that will have been required to make these caves was enormous, and a very far cry from anything that those who lived in huts could ever have afforded. Much was also spent in terms of energy and expertise on the Lomasha Rishi cave – which is adjacent to the Sudama cave – specially on its finely carved architrave above the exterior entrance (Fig. 4.5). Unlike other caves, it does not carry an Ashokan epigraph but its polish and architecture is manifestly Ashokan. The design is of elephants

---

there, Beglar was convinced it was identifiable as the hill of Buddha described by Xuanzang.

Fig. 4.4: Interior of the Sudama cave

Fig. 4.5: Ashokan carved architrave on the exterior of the Lomasha Rishi cave with the epigraph of Anantavarman just above the entrance

moving from both directions towards a central stupa, with a lattice screen made of intersecting circles. Did the inhabitants realise this screen was of the same design that was carved on a throne ("vajrasana") made by Ashoka's craftsmen in honour of the Buddha at Mahabodhi? The throne makers may well have been those employed to decorate the Bihar caves.

The last of the emperor's dedications in this outcrop is now known as Karna Chaupar. Polished to a high lustre, its inscription does not mention the Ajivikas but records that the emperor dedicated it for shelter during the rainy season.

Ashoka's epigraphs are short and their brevity is starkly at variance with the caves, which are magnificently elaborate in their conception. The vaulted roofs, inclining walls, and proportions of the rooms have a highly developed aesthetic underlying them which is enhanced by the remarkable polish. The caves were certainly solid enough to keep the rain out for the ascetics who inhabited them. But the workmen who created these rock solid shelters, chipping and chiselling for months on end, must have cursed roundly under their breath. If they were the same as the artisans who had carved Ashoka's words into rock, their execrations would have been worth hearing, for carving up a cave is a project of an entirely different order from inscribing words on a slab, and the work on these caves would have been back-breaking. One set of craftspeople may have lost patience, resulting in the Lomasha Rishi cave – the one with the elaborately carved gateway arch – being only partially finished, the chisel marks being still visible on its walls and ceiling. The argument has been made that this was because the cave developed cracks as it was being hacked into shape and so had to be abandoned.[7] But I prefer to conjecture that a cursing, swearing, and fed-up workforce left it incomplete. It is certain that the cave wasn't finished to the

---

[7] For the caves and their architecture, Gupta (1980): 189–92 and 202–21. For the epigraphs, Hultzsch (1925): 181–2.

standard that Ashokan edifices mostly reveal. What I'm certain is that those ascetics of antiquity will have marvelled, as I did, at the enormous task that had been accomplished to make such a fine retreat for the rainy season. If a couple of these were used, as has been argued, for voluntary death by the Ajivikas, their munificence seems even more incongruous.[8]

There is also something unusually stark about the rough granite outside and the smooth glitter of the walls inside. All around I saw scenarios of contrast: the bright-green hills and the dark inky interiors, the chirping birds and the chattering humans, the perfect silence desired inside the caves and the resounding echo of every little sound. In *A Passage to India* Forster, who was quite explicit about the influence on him of the use of leitmotifs by Beethoven and Wagner and Proust, turns the echo of the caves into a leitmotif of his own. In his novel, part of the mystery of India, the universe, and microcosmically the world within every individual's head consists in the impossibility of ascribing any single or final meaning to the echo. One of the characters, Mrs Moore, dies with the echo of the caves in her head while she is journeying back to England on a ship. Adela Quested is, as we have seen, misled by the echo into believing she has been molested. Had I asked myself how the cave had echoed in *my* head, the straight answer would have been an echo which said "Ashoka". The transition that I in fact experienced in those caves, however, gave me the feeling of being at a crossing where, by setting foot inside the strange interiors of the caves, everything that I was comfortable and familiar with was being left behind. The feeling of entering a kind of Nothingness is one possible interpretation provided in relation to characters entering the Marabar caves in the Forster novel, and my entry into them, in retrospect, showed me once more the superior apprehension and expressive power of poets and novelists in conveying feeling – in this case something

---

[8] This is the argument of Majumdar (2017).

as difficult to convey as the feeling of Nothingness when entering an Ashokan cave. Religious abodes of varying types have been made for thousands of years, but to me these were the most staggering and the most singular and the most unfamiliar that I had experienced of a time so remote from ours.

Many centuries later, as Ashoka came to be remembered and his life written about, the Ajivika order appears in stories and legends around his birth. Characters from this sect, like the witches in *Macbeth*, predict that he will one day be king. These literary – perhaps consciously mythologising – accounts do not mention the Barabar cave endowments, they speak only of those to whom they were made: for instance, in the *Ashokavadana*, the legendary biography of the emperor, his "coming" as emperor of India is predicted when he is still a prince.[9] The commentary on the Sri Lankan chronicle *Mahavamsa* sees his ascension as coming to pass even before Ashoka is born, and here again the oracle is an Ajivika. In this latter account, Ashoka's mother, when pregnant with him, craves all kinds of unusual and odd things, which grows into a matter of concern for her husband, the king Bindusara.[10] It was very probably the memory of Ashoka's patronage of this sect, at places such as the Barabar caves, which made these later chroniclers so specifically endow an Ajivika with the power of prophecy.

The caves have probably changed much less over time than the endowments. On the rock surfaces there is evidence of copious messaging pointing to things that came to pass in the caves. The clearest change is a deliberate erasure: the letters specifying Ajivikas in the Ashokan message in the Sudama cave were more or less obliterated. Those who occupied the cave subsequent to

---

[9] For the Ajivika story in *Ashokavadana*, Strong (1989): 198–204.
[10] *Vamsatthappakasini* is cited on this point by Guruge (1993): 26.

the Ajivikas were almost certainly of another faith and possibly hostile to the Ajivikas; they may have feared that Ajivikas might at some point turn up and claim it as theirs, the rock carving being a kind of nameplate of earlier inhabitants that the new owners naturally did not want displayed. There are no Ajivikas after the early sixth century CE, certainly none that appear in epigraphs or texts in India, and therefore this name erasure is likely to have been before then. Interestingly, there was no such apprehension *vis-à-vis* Ashoka once he was dead and gone: the allusion to Piyadasina, which was what Ashoka called himself here, remained unharmed. Th nameplate erasure, though, is not in evidence at another cave, the Vishwa Jhompri cave. Was this a consequence of its secluded location, at some distance from the primary cave-inhabited outcrop?

Sundry travellers and mendicants had wandered this region, one or some of whom may well have been responsible for the effort to scrub out the Ajivikas. Some of these later folk carved new words in the caves. Predominantly, these elaborate ascetic dwellings appear to have evoked austerity and deprivation: "Klesha kantara", which means a forest of pain, is inscribed in the fourth–fifth century CE in the Lomasha Rishi and Sudama caves; it is possible that the phrase alludes to ascetics, including the Ajivikas.[11] "Daridra kantara" in the Karna Chaupad cave, meaning a forest tract for the poor, is another such message of the fifth–sixth century CE.[12] The allusion is either to the poor or to those undergoing hardship.

There were others more interested in imprinting their own names on the cave walls. Around the time that the Karna Chaupad cave brought to mind poverty to one scrawler, another wrote "Vikatatungashiva", which could be his own name or that of the deity he worshipped.[13] A little later yet another character

[11] Majumdar (2017): 40.
[12] Ibid.: 47.
[13] Ibid.: 46.

tarried long enough to engrave his name, "Bodhimula", on the doorframes of the Lomasha Rishi and Sudama caves, this name suggesting he was a Buddhist.[14] Such graffiti is all too common nowadays, but visitors appear to have been far fewer and more restrained in ancient India.

Beyond the deletions and stray graffiti, a ruler decided to get messages inscribed here more than 800 years after Ashoka. He was a Maukhari ruler called Anantavarman who came along here from his base in south Bihar. Whether he was related to the better-known Maukhari rulers of Kannauj in Uttar Pradesh is unclear, but he was, like them, taking advantage of the increasingly weak successors of the imperial Guptas – known to historians as the later Guptas of Magadha. Anantavarman is familiar now mainly from his epigraphic markers in these hills, and many of them suggest a conquering ruler.[15]

He was born, he tells us, in the family of Maukhari scions, and the words that he caused to be inscribed were meant to highlight the military prowess of his family. His father Shardulavarman could cast "in anger his scowling eye" on any enemy and was known to be "Death to hostile kings". This was only to be expected, belonging as they all did, he tells us, to the Kshatriya "kula" or warrior family that had earned glory by "waging many battles". From these words and lines he appears to be recording acts of aggrandisement. The aggrandisement includes the promotion of his preferred form of religious worship. His programme aimed to Hinduise this area – Fig. 4.5 shows his epigraph just above the entrance. He says he has granted away the Lomasha Rishi cave to image worshippers. His message etched outside the cave, above the beautiful elephant panel, says he has had a Krishna image installed here. No such Krishna image has been found, but its consecration by a royal in Anantavarman's time would

---

[14] Ibid.: 43, 47.
[15] Thaplyal (1985): 133–6.

have ensured that the cave became a Vaishnava shrine. Almost certainly, this starts the Vaishnava faith in this part of the landscape of Bihar.[16] There are more lines by Anantavarman – and more in praise of himself as a virtuous man and as one successful in fighting off the enemies of his father, than in praise of the lord to whom the cave was dedicated.

Anantavarman changed the character of the Lomasha Rishi cave, and his conversion of caves for ascetics into shrines of worship here extended into the neighbouring Nagarjuni hills. There, Ashoka's grandson Dasharatha had gouged out caves similar to those made by his grandfather – they too were for the Ajivikas. Anantavarman's transformation of them into Hindu enclaves is engraved near their entrance. One cave is now dedicated to an image of Siva in the form of Bhutapati, and his wife Parvati, described as Devi. In another cave, Anantavarman announces that that he has granted a village to the goddess Bhavani; resumably the cave too was now her abode.[17]

In the years since my visit to these caves I have thought many times about Barabar and the surrounding hills as they are now, as against what they were like in Ashoka's day and later. Two sorts of people now take the route to the Barabar hills. There are those like me who, fixated on Ashoka, arrive because of what they have read about the caves' connection with him. Among foreigners, on the other hand, the fixation is Forster's *Passage to India*: the comments of Europeans and Australians that I saw in the visitor's book there bear this out. "It was exciting and moving to be in the caves which E.M. Forster wrote about" is how a British couple reacted, and an Australian couple similarly "came to the caves because it is mentioned in E.M. Forster's *A Passage to India*." One Indian visitor's comments revealed to me an uncommonly deep interest and knowledge of both Ashoka and Forster. Anup Mukherji, a civil servant who had retired as Chief Secretary of

[16] Amar (2012): 165.
[17] Thaplyal (1985): 135–6.

Bihar – in horrifyingly hierarchical India chief secretaries are practically deities in their own right – drove himself to Barabar in the spring of 2012. He noted how impressive the caves were, "... and to think that these rock cut caves were carved into solid granite rock around 253 BC without any modern implements! It fills me with wonder and pride ... no wonder E.M. Forster was inspired and saw in the caves the crux of the dilemma of the Empire & her subjects!" (Fig. 4.6). This Mukherji was obviously a chip off the old block – in fact off a very old block – for an Indian civil servant neither corrupt nor semi-literate is now as seldom seen as the Siberian crane.

The run-of-the-mill visitors, though, the sort that put their names down in the visitor's book, are a minority in relation to the religious traffic. For pilgrims, the point of preference is not the caves but the pinnacle where the Siddeshwarnath temple stands. Before the caves came to be protected by the Archaeological Survey of India, large numbers of such pilgrims would cook and live at the level ground around the whale-shaped cave-bearing

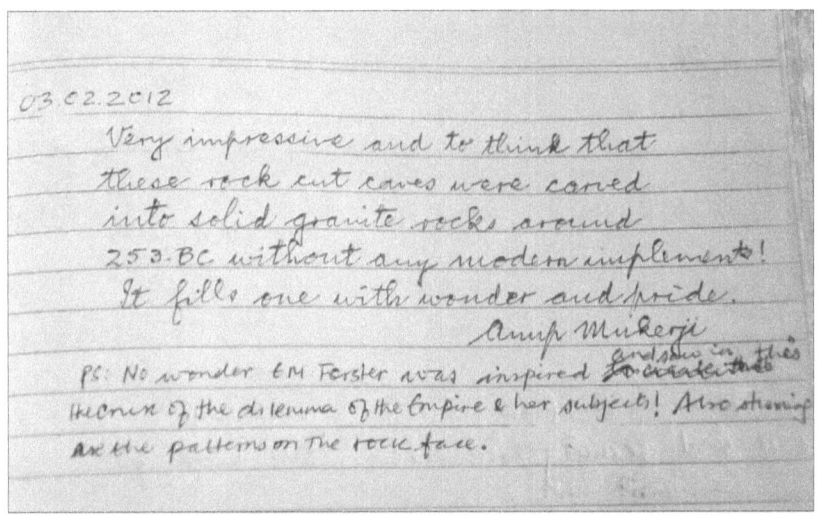

Fig. 4.6: Anup Mukherji's comments in the visitor's book at Barabar

rock during the annual fair. Alexander Cunningham, surveying the area in 1861–2, noted that the ground was "strewn with broken bricks and fragments of pottery" and the rubbish had "accumulated to a height of three feet above the floor of the caves."[18] Garbage, as often in Indian pilgrimage sites, had overtaken worship. Fortunately, the ground around the caves now is no longer a rubbish dump.

Looking back at the long history of these hills, what is also evident to me is that whereas Ashoka's legacy has not lived on, Anantavarman's has. The Ajivika sect faded, Buddhism declined, and both gave way to Hindu worship, which expanded and flourished. Some of this expansion is probably contrary to what Anantavarman would have wanted: the worshippers of his day abandoned the caves, preferring to perch above and beyond them. The pilgrim throngs now are all headed there, to the temple. To almost all of them, Ashoka does not reverberate even faintly as an echo.

---

[18] Cunningham (1871): 43.

Searching Siblings in Sri Lanka

SOME YEARS AGO there was something of a furore in India when the name Bombay was changed to Mumbai in deference to the local Marathi preference. Kolkata and Bengaluru for Calcutta and Bangalore have been other prominent changes in Indian place names. As an aspect of slow decolonisation and Eastern distancing from the West, Burma is now Myanmar and Ceylon Sri Lanka.

It is Sri Lanka – or Tambapanni, or Tamraparni, or Tamrapanni, as it was known in antiquity – to which I now move. The island's old name was what I had encountered in Ashoka's edicts. Taprobane, presumably deriving from Tamrapanni, continued to be current in the second century CE because the Egyptian geographer Ptolemy used it when describing the island.[1] Ptolemy

---

[1] Taprobane is also the name of a very tiny island, not far from Galle in southern Sri Lanka, on which the writer-scientist Arthur C. Clarke found just about enough space to build his house.

is known to have put together many details about geographical places, especially on the Indian Ocean coasts of Africa and Asia.[2] Nearly two hundred years after Ptolemy and some six hundred years after Ashoka, Tambapanni appeared in the *Dipavamsa*, a fourth-century CE Pali chronicle of Sri Lanka. Only the name appears in the king's epigraphs, whereas in the text we find an account of the naming. Tambapanni, says the *Dipavamsa*, derives from the red dust that smeared the hands and feet of a few hundred followers of Vijaya, who arrived on the island from India and grew into a ruler. He and his followers are said to have arrived many centuries ago, exhausted by the journey and able only to crawl on the ground. When they finally managed to stand upright, their hands were copper-coloured and, "tamba" being the word for copper, the location came to be known as Tambapanni.[3] Some time later, Tambapanni was described in unflattering terms within the same text, by a monk from India who declared that "Tambapanni has entirely been subdued by obstacles and passion in consequence of the obscurity of error and of the darkness of ignorance and of (worldly) existence." At this point the name seems to have expanded into that of the entire island.

The Buddhist monk claimed, as missionaries often do, that before his intervention on behalf of a superior truth, the territory he was venturing into was beset by envy, ignorance, and selfishness. He had been exhorted to go to Tamraparni because by preaching the religion of the Buddha there he would destroy "the darkness of error and throw light". There is, in fact, a web of allusions around this famous monk, as also around his younger sibling, a nun. Mahinda and Sanghamitta were their names and, since they were ordained Buddhists, the honorifics "Maha-thera"

[2] Gokhale (2004). An excellent study of Greek and Roman references to Sri Lanka is Weerakkody (1997), which cites a range of sources to argue that the best-known Greek and Roman name for it was Taprobane.

[3] *Dipavamsa* 9.29. Oldenberg 1879 (reprint 1982): 162.

and "theri" were added on, making them Mahathera Mahinda or Mahamahinda-thera, and Theri Sanghamitta or Sanghamitta-theri. They are said to have arrived in Sri Lanka in the third century BCE; the brother came first and was followed by the sister. Both were the children of Ashoka and Devi. If Ashoka is writ large over the landscape of the Indian subcontinent, the siblings overshadow their father in Sri Lanka.

I went off in search of them to the island in 2019. While Ashoka, given the number of his queens, is likely to have "on many multiplied his kind" – to borrow Dryden's phrase – only two of his progeny are recalled as having travelled to Sri Lanka and making it their home. Mahinda and Sanghamitta are the most celebrated ancient Indians there, apart of course from the Buddha himself.

I decided to begin by following the trail of the sister. Sanghamitta's spoor led me to a part of Sri Lanka that I had never visited, the Jaffna peninsula, now generally remembered as the heartland of the movement of the Liberation Tigers of Tamil Eelam. The war between the army and Tamil militants resulted, from the 1970s on, in much loss of life and property, including the destruction of the precious Jaffna Public Library, the insurrection being brutally and comprehensively snuffed out in 2009. But this is merely contemporary history that, in my head, can't hold a candle to the region's fascinating ancient and longer-term history. For me the Jaffna coast's pre-eminent claim to fame is Buddhist, for it was here that the ship carrying Sanghamitta was supposed to have docked.

Ratna, our driver Lakshana, and I travelled north on the advice of our guide in Sri Lanka, the archaeologist-diplomat Sudharshan Seneviratne: he had insisted we leave early, so we were out by five in the morning and anticipated reaching Jaffna a little after noon.

March in Sri Lanka can be warm, but at that time of morning it was cool on a highway lined with mango and palm trees and many whose names we did not know. Sometimes we whizzed by houses and shops, swamps and other waterbodies, with many more stretches of water in a fairly low-lying flat terrain as we approached our destination. The peninsula, with the sea on three sides, has the Jaffna lagoon towards its south. A small strip of land is all that connects the rest of the island with Jaffna. It struck me that if Sanghamitta had indeed landed on the coast and then travelled south inland, she too would have been struck by the contrast between this water-beset peninsula and the interior political capital of Anuradhapura, where she is said to have reached.

I had read the two key Sri Lankan Pali chronicles (in English translation) before starting my Sri Lanka travels, mainly to soak in the many compelling details in them about Sanghamitta's journey. These two chronicles are the *Dipavamsa* and the *Mahavamsa*; both are said to be based on older materials and therefore have frequently been used – even while being contested – as sources of history.[4] The "histories" in them include so many miracles and myths – alongside the events that are said to have transpired in the third century BCE and later – that it is necessary to take what they assert with a large pinch of salt. The *Mahavamsa* is the more expansive and coherently organised of the two. It claims to be the result of a considerable attempt at removing repetitions while retaining an account of all that its author considered essential. Its author, or rather compiler, was the monk Mahanama, who lived in the middle of the first millennium CE at Anuradhapura, the heart of "Theravada" Buddhism. The religion was undergoing a renewal here after the end of some

---

[4] For a sense of the debate at the beginning of the twentieth century in relation to their historical value, see Geiger's introduction to the *Mahavamsa*, Geiger (1912). For an overview of the Buddhist chronicles of Sri Lanka, Hazra (1986).

decades of what has been described as Tamil rule in the region, Theravada being the name prefixed to the oldest surviving strand of Buddhism – as preserved in the Pali canon.

The political changes at the time of the composition of the *Mahavamsa*, and the nature of Buddhism within that antique context, was explained to me some years later by a renowned Sri Lankan scholar, Osmund Bopearachchi. In the fifth century, he said, King Dhatusena most likely ruled the country, having reunited it after defeating the South Indian invaders. To paraphrase this scholar, the primary purpose of the *Mahavamsa* is to show Tamils as the invading demons – the Yakshas – of Sri Lanka: the Buddha and his messengers had come to the island to purify it of these demons. An early king of the Anuradhapura kingdom, Dutugamunu, had in the second century BCE fought a great war against a Tamil king to save Buddhism. Dutugamunu's Tamil enemy was an old king who had in fact ruled his country justly: yet it had to be shown that the cause of the Sinhala king was nobler. The chronicle was written – deploying much literary animus – to show the superiority of the Sinhalese race over the Dravidians. The *Mahavamsa* also describes the Anuradhapura Mahavihara as the seat of Theravada Buddhism, ignoring all the other monasteries in Anuradhapura practising the Mahayana form of Buddhism. In short, the story of Mahinda, which is full of miraculous events, is a way of exaggerating the supernatural superiority of the Buddha to the Yakshas.

It became evident to me via Bopearachchi's wisdom that the *Mahavamsa* provides much more material than does your typical canonical text. It certainly seems to give historians of ancient South Asia most of what they need: the Buddha, as well as myriad other sacred personnel, including Yakshas and Nagas; kings of India and Lanka who sent gifts to each other and maintained links through marriage even while they fought amongst themselves; wars and killing; the founding of settlements and religious institutions; journeys and jamborees; and threading all this the overarching conception that the island was divinely ordained by the Buddha for the maintenance of the dhamma through Buddhist kingship.[5] Naturally, for Mahanama the compiler, the arrival of a female Buddhist emissary carrying precious religious cargo from India, and being received by a newly converted Buddhist king, were subjects that required a suitably resplendent description.

It would appear that Sanghamitta set off from the port of Tamralipti on the eastern coast of Bengal, boarding a big ship that took her to Lanka. She landed on the Jaffna coast, at a place known as Jambukola (now Jambukola Patuna). The reason for her journey is made clear – at the request of the Lanka king Devanampiya Tissa (hereafter "DT"), "Dhammasoka" had dispatched his daughter Sanghamitta to his island. This monarch's queen, Anula, lived along with other lay disciples in a vihara (monastery), but she could only make the desired transition into becoming a Buddhist renunciant if she were ordained by a bhikkuni (Buddhist nun). Ashoka's son, Mahinda, who was already on his mission to the island, therefore sent a message to his father asking that Sanghamitta be sent to do the needful. He added that she also be asked to bring with her the "south branch" of the great Bodhi tree.[6] This was the tree of utmost sacredness under which Siddhartha Gautama had become the Buddha.

In ancient times, unless they were conquering each others' lands, it was rare for monarchs to come face to face. Kings were in touch through envoys and friendships between them came about through exchanges of various kinds. It was in this sense that, as the *Mahavamsa* puts it, "Devanampiyatissa and Dhammasoka had been friends a long time, though they had never seen each other."[7] Ashoka mentions Tamraparni in his Thirteenth Rock Edict – along with a slew of states ranging from those on

---

[5] Wijeyeratne (2007): 164.
[6] *Mahavamsa* XVIII.14–15; Geiger (1912): 123.
[7] *Mahavamsa* XI.19; ibid.: 78.

Mediterranean shores to the Cholas and Pandyas in the peninsular south of India – as part of his sphere of dhammic influence.[8] Gifts too had been exchanged: "DT" had sent precious gems, pearls, and three priceless bamboo stems with his envoys to the Indian king.[9] Ashoka had sent return gifts. These included a sword and parasol, the water of the Ganga river, herbs, mountain rice, and even "a maiden in the flower of youth".[10] These were said to have been used, on Ashoka's request, for a second consecration of the Sri Lanka ruler. How the young girl was used was not specified.

The most powerful monk in Ashoka's empire, Mogaliputta, decided to send monks on missions to convert a variety of lands to the faith of the Buddha, from Kashmir and Gandhara to the Yavana country.[11] And for the "theras" (senior and respected monks) venturing into the "lovely island of Lanka" he chose the son of Ashoka himself. Mahinda was accompanied by two of his relatives, Sumana Samanera (Sanghamitta's son) and Bhaduka (a cousin's son), as well as four other monks named Itthiya, Uttiya, Sambala, and Bhaddasala. This mission pushed the relationship of the two kings in an entirely new direction. This was followed by Sanghamitta's journey to ordain the queen, and no doubt the women of Lanka, which struck me as impressive, given the generally subordinate position of women at the time. The narrative focuses largely on her instrumental function in carrying the Bodhi tree – symbolically, she seeds Tamraparni's soil with Buddhism.

A sapling had been sprouted from the Bodhi tree to properly equip Sanghamitta as the emissary of Buddhism. Apparently, when Ashoka approached the tree with folded hands, "from its

---

[8] See, for instance, lines XVII–XIX, Erragudi Edict XIII; Sircar (1979): 85.

[9] *Mahavamsa* XI.11–14; Geiger (1912): 78.

[10] *Mahavamsa* XI.; ibid.: 28–33.

[11] *Mahavamsa* XII; ibid.: 1–8.

south bough the branches vanished, leaving a stump four cubits long."[12] A golden vase fashioned by Vishwakamma (Vishvakarma), in his avatar as a goldsmith, was ready at hand. Along the very point where Ashoka had drawn a line in the bough, a section miraculously severed itself and floated above the vase; roots then sprouted downwards and, as the plant settled itself in the vase, "the earth quaked and wonders of many kinds came to pass."[13] As Calpurnia put it to Julius Caesar, "When beggars die, there are no comets seen/ The heavens themselves blaze forth the death of princes." The equivalents in the Sri Lankan Buddhist tradition seem to have been fresh starts inaugurated by earthquakes, which always portend great occurrences and are frequent in the *Mahavamsa*.

So, bearing the Bodhi branch in this golden vessel Sanghamitta, accompanied by bhikkunis, embarked on the ship, her father apprehensive and filled with sorrow – at being parted not from his daughter but from the Bodhi tree: "Dhammasoka returned weeping and lamenting to his capital", it says, and the text is explicit that his tears were falling not for Sanghamitta. Clearly, the devout Buddhist compiler wishes to emphasise Ashoka's greater devotion to the Buddha than to his own daughter, a theme reminiscent of the demand made by Jehovah of Abraham when asking him to sacrifice Isaac. An emperor having to sacrifice a sapling, however, makes the sorrow seem somewhat ridiculous since the parent tree, even if short of a branch, was still very much around in Bodh Gaya. Unlike the *Mahavamsa*'s account of the arrival of Mahinda under the chapter title "The Coming of Mahinda", its chapter on Sanghamitta's arrival is "The Coming of the Bodhi-tree". The entire narrative is focused on the "king of men", i.e. DT, receiving from her "the king of trees", with Sanghamitta as the necessary appendage clutching it.

[12] *Mahavamsa* XVIII; ibid.: 34.
[13] *Mahavamsa* XVIII; ibid.: 44 and 50.

The holy tree's arrival and ensuing ceremonies are described: "he, the splendid (king), descended even neck-deep into water; and when together with sixteen persons (of noble families) he had taken the great Bodhi-tree upon his head, had lifted it down upon the shore and caused it to be set in a beautiful pavilion, the king of Lanka worshipped it by (bestowing on it) the kingship of Lanka."[14] The entire length of the road from Jambukola to Anuradhapura – a distance of over 200 km – was prepared to ensure unimpeded travel for the precious cargo and its bearer.

In following this *Mahavamsa* narrative the question in my head was whether the Jaffna region had yielded traces of ancient habitations and early Buddhism contemporary with the tale. If there were any at all, it would suggest some broad historical trends, even if specific identifications proved impossible. Archaeology is frequently invoked to test the historical reliability of chronicles in Asia and Europe, and the idea of juxtaposing material remains with the story of Sanghamitta's arrival was exciting.

The ship bearing Sanghamitta and the Bodhi tree had docked at what has been identified as Jambukola Patuna, several kilometres north of Jaffna town. The coastline here appears conducive to natural harbours for ships, suggesting its suitability for habitations as well, but nothing ancient is evident in the environs. The only visible heritage of Buddhism here are modern fabrications – a stupa, statues of Sanghamitta, paintings of her landing, and boats allowing visitors to imagine how the daughter of India's most famous Buddhist ruler arrived among Sri Lanka's first Buddhist king (Figs 5.1 and 5.2). The most prominent of the Sanghamitta statues was unveiled by Shiranthi Wickramasinghe Rajapaksa shortly after the Jaffna peninsula was pacified by the Sri Lankan army, the unveiler being the wife of the Sri Lankan

[14] *Mahavamsa* XIX; ibid.: 29–34.

Fig. 5.1: Sanghamitta carrying the Bodhi tree, being received by the king

president, Mahinda Rajapaksa. A plaque says the memorial is an acknowledgement of Buddhist devotees as well as the arrival here of a branch of the Bodhi tree. Since the end of the civil war many Sinhala pilgrims and visitors have added this location to their travel itineraries and no one seems much bothered by the fact that no ancient remains are visible here. Jambukola Patuna remains under a fairly formidable security cover.

Other parts of the Jaffna region have, however, yielded ancient remains which possibly provide a historical frame for the nar-

Fig. 5.2: Model of the ship that carried Sanghamitta at Jambukola Patuna

rative about Sanghamitta's arrival in Jaffna. One of these is the Vallipuram Vishnu temple area. Named after the village in its vicinity, this temple complex looks like a small oasis among sand dunes dotted with clumps of grass and tall coconut trees. The dunes continue till the coast that fringes the northernmost part of the Jaffna peninsula: the temple is not far from where the Palk Straits and the Bay of Bengal meet, a place of stunning natural beauty and ambience. It is quite the opposite of what lies across the waters at Kanyakumari in India, where the crush of crowds makes the experience of being at the southern geographical edge of the subcontinent much like being in the crush of the rest of urban India.

Vallipuram has revealed relics with unmistakable Buddhist affiliations. One of these is a second–third century CE gold plaque in the Colombo National Museum. Its four lines in Prakrit attest to the setting up of a Buddhist temple called Piyanguka by the minister of a king. This shrine came to have images later – evident from a Buddha stone statue unearthed very close to the Vallipuram temple. Unluckily, the fate of all imperial loot befell this statue as well: it can no longer be seen in Sri Lanka because in 1906 it was presented by the British governor, Sir Henry Blake, to the king of Siam (Thailand).[15] Buddhist images are usually found in viharas and chaityas, so this statue is likely to have been in the temple mentioned in the epigraph.

There are also literary allusions to viharas in this area, which was known as Nagadipa; in the *Mahavamsa*, Jamukolavihara is mentioned as being in Nagadipa.[16] There are also viharas in Nagadipa which cluster around the second and beginning of the third century CE, which kings are said to have built and restored.[17] So the epigraph and the Buddha from Vallipuram form part of a larger Buddhist landscape in this part of the Jaffna peninsula – which the compiler of the *Mahavamsa* may well have been aware of.

Buddhists were not the first to inhabit the strip of land where the Vishnu temple stands. Before them were those who buried their dead in megaliths. An early grave here yielded a pot in a cist, and pottery including black and red ware which was found strewn beyond the burials. Potsherd distribution, sporadic in the surrounding areas of the temple, was intense in a mound north of the temple.[18] Sacred places everywhere frequently have religious structures of different faiths appearing as successive overlays, or sometimes standing adjacent to each other. So, the fact that an ancient burial site became the site for a Buddhist

---

[15] Schalk (1996): 295–312.

[16] *Mahavamsa* XX. Geiger (1912): 25.

[17] Pieris (1917): 12; Schalk (1996): 297. King Mahallanaga (136–43 CE) built a vihara called Salipabbatam, King Kanithatissaka (167–86) restored the Nagadipa ghara and King Voharika Tissa (209–31) built a wall in a vihara called Tissa.

[18] Raghupathy 1987: 83.

vihara to be set up, and where in the thirteenth century a Vishnu temple was constructed, is unsurprising. My Jaffna mentor and guide, Professor Krishnarajah Selliah of the University of Jaffna, pointed out that the contemporary history of India too has found a place at Vallipuram – on its towering gopuram (entrance tower), within a crowd of colourful divine and living beings, is an image of Mahatma Gandhi. He has been integrated into the temple architecture. To me he seemed to stand out more than the Vishnu avataras, because no Gandhi statue elsewhere graces a gopuram.[19]

Archaeological remains of various kinds are also part of a famous stupa complex in Kantarodai, in the suburbs of Jaffna. The area has an entirely rural feel to it, with many ponds and tanks around, the Kantarodai Kulam alone covering some forty acres. The most visible ancient feature of Kantarodai is a series of small stupas, all reconstructed by the Department of Archaeology of Sri Lanka over the original bases that were found (Fig. 5.3). The stupas are built over burials. A two-metre or so high archaeological mound is also visible in Kantarodai. It was described in the 1980s as being some two square km in its spatial dimensions, the entire modern village being situated on parts of it.[20] Punch-marked silver coins of the sort common in the late centuries BCE, and later Pandyan coins of South India as well as Roman specimens, have been found here. Roman-type pottery called "rouletted ware", of which the designs were initially thought to be made by a roulette but could well have been made with sharp pointed metal strips, strengthens the possibility of an ancient Roman connection.[21] Strong maritime links are likely to have been through an entrepôt on the Palk Strait, barely ten km distant.

[19] Lahiri (2019).
[20] Raghupathy (1987): 57; also Godakumbura (1968).
[21] Rouletted wares are present at Kantarodai, Mantai, Tissamaharama, and Ambalantota in Sri Lanka. See Rajan (2011): 191. For a study of the technique, Begley (1988).

Fig. 5.3: Small stupas at Kantarodai

A pre-Buddhist megalithic culture was revealed to have existed here in excavations conducted in 1970.[22] Estimates of its dates have ranged from the second millennium BCE to 300 BCE.[23] Much like the Vallipuram Vishnu temple area, this forms the cultural base beneath a Buddhist overlay. What all this makes obvious is that, before Buddhism was established here, Kantarodai had long had community trade contacts and a megalithic burial tradition. Potsherds and beads here and at a nearby site, Annaikoddai, show Brahmi alphabets, suggesting maritime trade. When the *Mahavamsa* was written in the fifth century CE, it would have been common knowledge that there had been early Buddhist communities in Jaffna.

In her study of the period after the Sri Lankan civil war the architectural historian Anoma Pieris has analysed heritage tourism around Buddhist sites in northern Sri Lanka. She says their

[22] For a summary of the excavations of the 1970s, Raghupathy (1987).
[23] Murphy, *et al.* (2018).

histories have been told in ways that minimise their many ancient links.[24] Meanwhile the tourism to these sites has increased because the civil war had made them inaccessible for decades and people are keen to make up for lost time. The result is that more and more tourists are now being made to believe that this region was dominantly Sinhala-Buddhist – a notion which of course is contested by Jaffna Tamils and the Tamil diaspora. Kantarodai is now, perhaps like Tibet, an example of a place where a new regime is busy resignifying the territory's past in line with its own nationalist aims. An archaeological history antedating Buddhism is being slipped into a narrative described as an "imagined cosmos of Sinhala-Buddhist territory – encompassing national and transnational Buddhist sites."[25] Naturally, Kantarodai's reconstitution in a Sinhala form through these modern tourism practices "incites and frustrates Tamil nationalism claims". Tamil counterclaims have appeared in *Global-Tamil News*, identifying Kantarodai "as evidence of the Great Stone Age (pre-Buddhist, megalithic-period inhabitants)" who were, in this argument, the original settlers, making the "Tamil cause . . . justified on the basis of regional presence, and the Sinhala cause on histories of colonisation and conversion." The security presence that I saw at Buddhist sites in Jaffna in 2019 was much the same as described by Pieris for the period between 2010 and 2014, when the "act of repossession . . . was initially achieved through visitor numbers, and later formalised by the military presence that managed and asserted the claim."[26]

Was there a similar repossession in ancient times? Certainly, if archaeology is juxtaposed with the *Mahavamsa*, it would seem so. The text mentions the arrival from India in the sixth–fifth centuries BCE of Vijaya – possibly an Indian man who would be

[24] Pieris (2019): ch. 6.
[25] Ibid.: 149.
[26] I have described the claims around Kantarodai but a similar controversy exists in relation to the Vallipuram gold plate. See Veluppillai (1981).

king of Sri Lanka – with his followers, but it does not say what existed by way of earlier culture or belief systems in the Jaffna area. Being primarily a chronicle for Buddhists put together by Buddhist monks, there was no thought of pleasing me when it was written. What the archaeologist's spade has revealed, on the other hand, is flourishing commerce among people who buried their dead in megaliths and with a paraphernalia of seals and writing that have much in common with contemporary Tamil Nadu. Some visual residue and general impress of all this must surely have been known to the composer of the *Mahavamsa*.

From Jaffna the Bodhi tree journeyed to Anuradhapura. On the fourteenth day after its arrival in Lanka the sapling is said to have been brought to the neighbourhood of the city by DT. Floating incandescent in the air and sparkling with abandon, it filled people with faith before coming down to earth and making the firmament quake. Eight shoots sprang from it, which were then planted at various sacred places. One of these was at Jambukola, where the sapling had stood after leaving the ship; other places where shoots were planted included monasteries like the Thuparama and the Issarasamanarama.[27] A sacred topography stretching from the shores of Jaffna to interior Anuradhapura and its suburbs was thereby grafted around the Bodhi tree.

As for the nun herself, she continues to get short shrift: Queen Anula and her following received "the pabbaja from the theri Sanghamitta" and attained enlightenment.[28] Sanghamitta, perhaps seeing how inconsequential she was, soon decided to do other things. She set up twelve buildings in the Upasikavihara where she dwelt with fellow nuns. She converted three of these edifices into memorials around the ship on which she and

---

[27] *Mahavamsa* XIX; Geiger (1912): 60–3.
[28] *Mahavamsa* XIX; ibid.: 65.

the Bodhi tree had arrived. In one of these buildings, says the chronicle, she had the mast of the ship set up, in one the rudder, and in one the helm.[29] Memorialising branches out from the tree into a sacralisation of the transmitting apparatus, this being a Sanghamittan brainwave. Or perhaps she found it wasn't such a brainwave after all: with three buildings converted into memorials, Sanghamitta found even her lodgings in the vihara much too crowded for comfort. So she set up another, more remote and peaceful, abode for the nuns; the king, on hearing this, ordered a nunnery to be built for the bhikkunis. This was made near a cool and flowery place on the edge of the city, with the king's state elephant living next door, tethered to a post. The proximity of the pachyderm caused the nunnery to be named Hatthalhaka-vihara.[30]

Beyond the tale of Sanghamitta coming across from India and settling in Anuradhapura, it is Mahinda, the brother, who dominates the Buddhist stories. As noted, he had arrived with his fellow monks well before her. They all came, according to the text, by the aerial route, following the example of the Buddha, who had himself alighted in Sri Lanka by flying there like Hanuman of the Ramayana. In those days, if you were a god, you flew, sailing being for mere mortals. And so Mahinda, "the (thera) of wondrous powers, coming hither with his following alighted on the pleasant Missaka-mountain, on the Sila peak on the open and fair Ambatthala" (Fig. 5.4).[31] Silakuta is the northern peak of the Mihintale mountain and the tableland below it is Ambatthala. Mihintale is a mere fifteen km from Anuradhapura, where Mahinda would later go. At this point in time matters appear to have been divinely arranged for DT to be on a hunting expedition with his men around the area. Seeing an elk stag, he pursued it towards the Mihintale mountain. The

[29] *Mahavamsa* XIX; ibid.: 70.
[30] *Mahavamsa* XIX; ibid.: 83.
[31] *Mahavamsa* XIII; ibid.: 20.

Fig. 5.4: The Missaka mountain in Mihintale, with a line of visitors

stag so pursued was none other than a "deva of the mountain" who wanted to lead the king to where the monks were. Their first one-to-one encounter had been prearranged by the deva-elk to preclude all difficulty:

> Thinking: "if he sees too many (people) he will be too much afraid," the thera let (the king) see him alone. When the king beheld him

he stood still terrified. The thera said to him: "Come hither, Tissa." Then, from the calling of him by his name, Tissa, thought forthwith: "(That is) a yakkha." "Samanas are we, O great king, disciples of the King of Truth. From compassion toward thee are we come hither from Jambudipa," thus said the thera. When the king heard this fear left him. And remembering the message of his friend, and persuaded that these were samanas, he laid down bow and arrow aside and approaching the sage he exchanged greetings with the thera and sat down near him.[32]

On the same day, after preaching to him, Mahinda converted the king and the forty thousand men who had accompanied DT on the hunt. Later, he miraculously preached the dhamma over the whole of Lanka even though he was in Mihintale. On the next day he, along with the other samaneras, "rose in the air and by their miraculous power they descended to the east of the city" of Anuradhapura.[33]

The narrative then consciously fashions an account of the creation and consolidation of a religious landscape revolving around the arrival of Mahinda in Sri Lanka, the template here being the Buddha and his travels in ancient India. Where the theras alight for the first time, a chaitya is built on the spot and comes to be called Pathamcetiya. Later, when at the behest of DT the theras turn back from the path to Mihintale, a chetiya (chaitya) happens to be built right there called Nivattacetiya – literally, "the turning-back chetiya". They are then taken to the verdant Mahamegha-vana, and the next day they accept this park as a gift from the king.

What follows all this gift-giving is a kind of mapping of various areas that meshes seamlessly with the quaking of the earth. Mahinda, we are told, knew what was the right or wrong place for a sacred building. Many of these sites, Mahinda informed the king, were places that had been visited by former Buddhas – it

---

[32] *Mahavamsa* XIV; ibid.: 6–10.
[33] *Mahavamsa* XIV; ibid.: 44.

does not seem to matter to the chronicler that Lanka, having only been converted to Buddhism by Mahinda, is therefore implicitly being shown as resistant to earlier incarnations of the Buddha.

Illogicalities and inconsistencies in fact never get in the way of this chronicler, who soldiers on heedless. He tells us that by the side of the Kakudha pond a place was deemed fitting for a stupa. Sure enough the iconic great stupa in Anuradhapura – known as the Ruwanweli stupa – came up right there after a monk worshipped the spot "with campaka-flowers brought by the king."[34] The culmination of all this is the construction of the Anuradhapura Mahavihara, the Great Monastery of the area. Its boundaries had been marked with a plough by the king himself, as also the locations of various buildings which he then ordered built: "Then did he set up a building for the great Bodhi-tree, the Lohapasada, a salaka house, and a seemly refectory. He built many parivenas in an excellent manner, and bathing tanks and buildings for repose, by night and by day, and so forth."[35] Dighasandana, the commander of the king's troops, also built "a little pasada for the thera with eight great pillars. This famed parivena, the home of renowned men, is called Dighasandase-napati-parivena." The buildings of the Mahavihara are named after monuments that existed in the fifth century CE, when the *Mahavamsa* was written.[36]

Next, Mahinda and the theras go off to spend the rainy season at Mihintale, where the king establishes a chetiya made of sixty-eight rock cells. Soon, at the request of DT, relics of the Buddha arrive from Ashoka, as also from Sakka, the king of the gods. This is followed by the arrival of Sanghamitta and the Bodhi tree.

The landscape in and around Mihintale, and Anuradhapura with its historic structures – the more recent ones are all helpfully

---

[34] *Mahavamsa* XV; ibid.: 56.

[35] *Mahavamsa* XV; ibid.: 205–6.

[36] Osmund Bopearachchi underlined this point in his reading of this chapter.

labelled – are fascinatingly in sync to this day with the *Mahavamsa*'s descriptions. What exists on the ground confirms the text. And this is how the pious see Anuradhapura and Mihintale; the fact that the chronological antecedents of the structures don't always fit with the textual narrative is something they are either oblivious of or is, from their perspective, beside the point. Perhaps the largest number of visitors here are believers wanting to worship, which is a very far cry from a historian in search of archaeological certitude.

The strongest connection between text and archaeology, it seemed to me, lay near the Missaka mountain in Mihintale – the peak on which Mahinda is said to have descended. Here, in the Mihindu Seya, lie a portion of his relics. There is also a first-century CE inscription on the Mihintale rock recording donations made towards the maintenance of images of Mahinda, along with those of the three theras Itthiya, Uttiya, and Bhadrasala (Fig. 5.5). The *Mahavamsa* flavours Anuradhapura even more expansively: the Jaya Sri Maha Bodhi in the royal park

Fig. 5.5: Mihindu Seya

of Mahamegha-vana, the Mahavihara alms hall, and the vast panoply of stupas and monastic establishments are all concrete evidence of the Buddhist record preserved within this text.[37]

It struck me that this tale of the establishment of Buddhism in Lanka has been told as a right royal saga in which two kings, one Lankan and the other Indian, and the children of the Indian king, share the honours. The tale is skilfully fashioned to focus mainly on royals, shown playing a decisive role in the island's conversion. The question worth asking remains: does the *Mahavamsa* also provide us an accurate record of the large range of physical locales in which the early archaeological evidence of Buddhism has been discovered?

Both at Mihintale, near the Kanthaka Cetiya, and in the vicinity of Anuradhapura at Vessagiriya, are several rocky areas with shelters and caves showing early Brahmi epigraphs inscribed on their drip ledges (Figs 5.6 and 5.7). Who were the patrons of these caves? Who were the inscribers? How different is their story from what is recounted in the *Mahavamsa*? Thinking back to the Buddhist sites in India where epigraphs of this length exist, my intuition was that there will have been a multiplicity of chronologically discrete people who carved these letters on rocks. I later discovered that there are in fact a very large number of historic spots in Sri Lanka where such inscriptions are to be found.

A correlating of text and archaeology by the archaeologist Robin Coningham has pointed to many entangled issues that prevent any straightforward equations between the two. Coningham points out that, from the perspective of archaeology, the early Buddhist establishments mentioned within the chronicle

---

[37] For a description of the monasteries and monastic planning, Silva (2006); as also Pichard and Lagirarde (2013).

Fig. 5.6: Brahmi epigraph at Mihintale

Fig. 5.7: Brahmi epigraph at Vessagiriya

are not really recognisably early at all because of their overlayering by later constructions: "they have been so developed and expanded by later kings that no traces of the original structures have been identified."[38] On the cave dwellings, his view is that they are identifiable as early Buddhist establishments of the type that don't dominate the text but do have a visible presence in many parts of Sri Lanka.

The sheer number of such caves and epigraphs is best appreciated in a superb compendium of the Brahmi inscriptions of Sri Lanka by the celebrated archaeologist-epigrapher S. Paranavitana.[39] About a thousand of these are arrayed in his book, even as he points to the possible existence of many more. The first explorer, he thinks,

> might have approached a particular cave from a direction in which a precipitous drop of the rock side makes progress to a cave with inscriptions impossible, and it would take half a day to approach it from another direction . . . Even in those caves visited by him, certain inscriptions may have escaped his notice, due to the diminutive size and lack of depth of the letters, or for the reason that the light falls to a cave from the wrong direction, or that the letters are made invisible from the ground due to vegetation or moss. A subsequent explorer might find such impediments removed by natural causes.[40]

What do these caves and inscriptions reveal? Many of them, says Paranavitana, go back to the third century BCE, the script of the epigraphs being the same as that in "the edicts of Asoka"; and the writing seems to evolve in a way that can be found on "the railings and toranas at Bharhut and Sanci", i.e. up to the first century CE.[41] These are short donative epigraphs which provide the affiliations – royal, religious, and sometimes socio-economic –

---

[38] Coningham (1995): 228.
[39] Paranavitana (1970).
[40] Ibid.: vi.
[41] Ibid.: xvii.

of the donors. Coningham, who did a quantitative analysis of these, makes the argument that there is a disjunction between what they reveal about royal patrons and what the Buddhist chronicles foreground: there are nearly eighty royal donors, whereas only a few of these donors are identifiable in the chronicles. He pinpoints the quite significant fact of the absence of even the very king of Lanka, DT, named as Ashoka's ally. Paranavitana's compendium, in Coningham's view, "failed to identify . . . a single donation from the first royal patron of Buddhism, Devanampiya Tissa."[42]

This silence around DT in the epigraphs is interesting. Could the reason for it be that DT's munificence was self-evident and not in need of epigraphic restatement? This is sometimes the case with royal patrons in ancient India. Near Vidisha, the grand Varaha panel at Udayagiri was designed to broadcast the political ambition of the Gupta monarch Chandragupta II (*c.* fifth century CE). But no epigraph at the site seems to have been instituted by the ruler himself. This is also so with the Vishnu-Narayana panel, which depicts the god in cosmic sleep higher up on the same hill: nothing by way of inscription shows the king's name. The patrons in such cases may have seemed too well known to have been made even more well known. One scholar, Hans Bakker, puts this very well when saying that Chandragupta's "own monumental plans, such as the Varaha and Narayana panels, were apparently so obvious that they needed no special commemoration in the form of dedicatory inscriptions."[43] The absence of DT in Sri Lanka is conceivably for the same reason; the lack of specific mention of the monarch is not, in any case, exceptional.

The king as *donor* is not apparent, but his name is part of the rolls of honour in the terrain all the same. At Mihintale an

[42] Coningham (1995): 231.
[43] Bakker (2010): 464.

epigraph may have been dedicated by a member of the extended household of DT for it says this was the cave of "the female lay-devotee Varunadatta, sister of the wife of the great king Devanampiya."[44] Also worth noticing are characters who figure in both chronicle and epigraph: three epigraphs connected with the king's brother and his family are connectable with mentions of this sibling in the *Mahavamsa*.[45] All three epigraphs are at Mihintale and relate to Uttiya – called "Uti" in the epigraphs – DT's younger brother, who reigned for ten years after him. Mihintale, as noted, is connected with Mahinda-thera, and the Kanthakacetiya there was established by DT. So, caves dedicated by DT's brother's household seem logical. Interestingly Uti was also titled "Devanampiya", meaning "beloved of the gods", this being the title first used by Ashoka himself. Several rulers in ancient Lanka use this title, which speaks of the invisible influence on the island of Ashoka.

Ashoka's son as an actual historical figure who converted DT to Buddhism is supported by an epigraph. Mahinda-thera figures in an inscription from Rajagala in eastern Sri Lanka at the site of a stupa. This stupa enshrined the relics of Mahinda and another monk called Idika. The epigraph says it "is the stupa of the elder Idika and the elder Mahinda, who came to this Island by its foremost good fortune."[46] Idika, or Itthiya, is one of the theras in the *Mahavamsa* mentioned as having come to Lanka with Mahinda. The historical ramifications of the epigraphic allusions to Mahinda and Idika are offered thus by Paranavitana: "The association of Mahida-tera with Idika-tera, and the mention in particular of their having come to Ceylon, presumably from

---

[44] No. 2, ibid.

[45] Nos 34, 46, and 47 in Paranavitana (1970): 3 and 4. No. 34 mentions the donation of a cave by a princess who was the daughter of Uttiya, who gave it to the Samgha for the benefit of her mother and father. No. 46 is the cave of Sumanadevi, wife of Uttiya, while No. 47 is fragmentary but mentions the creation of an unspecified structure by Uttiya himself.

[46] No. 468, ibid.

outside, leave no room for doubt that the reference in the inscription is to Saint Mahinda, the apostle of Buddhism in Ceylon" (Figs 5.8 and 5.9).[47]

Many other patrons of Buddhism emerge in these epigraphs. Paranavitana's study reveals treasurers, chiefs, royal physicians, teachers, gamikas (prominent village people), gapatis (lit. householders; usually, well-to-do people), craftsmen, Brahmans, and relatives of Brahmans.[48] This eclectic base of early Buddhism is not reflected in the Pali chronicles. Instead, the centre of their world is the devotion and patronage of rulers.

All the rulers who figure on the cave dwellings do not recur in the chronicles. Three generations of a previously unknown royal family appear in four inscriptions of the Kandy-Matale region – Pacina Rajha Naga, his sons Rajha Abaya and Tiss-aya (prince), and his grandson Tisa-aya. Another such is Rajha Shiva of Olamgala; and in Occappukallu there is a "rajha-puta"

Fig. 5.8: Epigraph at Rajagala. *Courtesy* Osmund Bopearachchi

[47] Ibid.: ci.
[48] Ibid.: lxviii–ci.

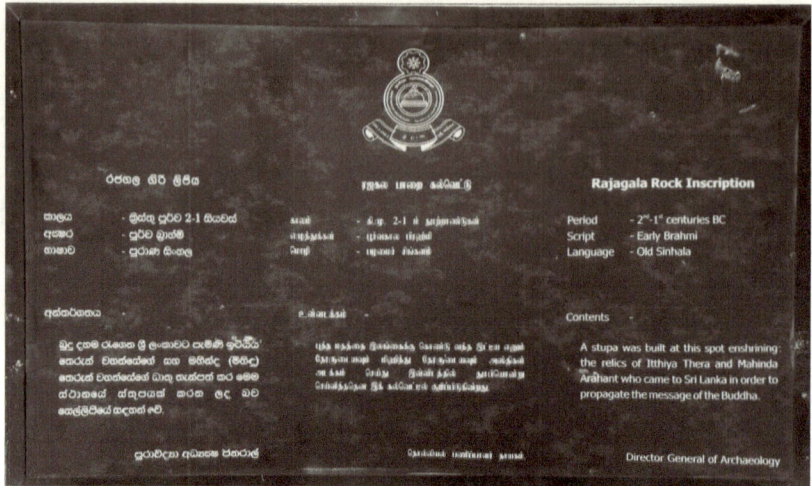

Fig. 5.9: Description of contents of the Rajagala rock inscription. *Courtesy* Osmund Bopearachchi

(prince) whose name cannot be recognised in the chronicles: Paranavitana draws attention to such figures as local rulers and princes who do not feature in the ancient literature.[49]

Since these were, all the same, royal donors and supporters of Buddhism, how may one explain their absence in the chronicles? Coningham suggests

> that they are not mentioned in the *Dipavamsa* and *Mahavamsa* because, when the records of the earlier periods were composed in the fifth century AD by the monks of the Mahavihara, the Anuradhapura kingdom had successfully absorbed the island's other kingdoms. The chronicles thus . . . may represent a contrived ecclesiastical tradition legitimising the contemporaneous status quo by awarding a central position to the successful kings of Anuradhapura and ignoring the contributions of the failed kings.[50]

In short, the many-layered patronage history of early Buddhism on the ground in Sri Lanka is far from identical with its textual tradition.

[49] Ibid.: lxiv.
[50] Coningham (1995): 232.

As regards illustrative evidence, it is interesting that it derives from the texts rather than from the epigraphs: what is graphically imaged later in various artistic forms is linkable largely to the chronicles. During the reign of an eighteenth-century king of Kandy, Kirti Sri Rajasinha (1747–1782), the Dambulla caves – copiously painting the early history of Buddhist practices – drew their subjects from the ancient texts. Paintings in this tradition show the ploughing of the monastic boundaries of the temple complex at Anuradhapura, the arrival of the Bodhi tree there, and the placing of the Buddha's relics in the Thuparama – the first stupa to be built in Lanka.[51]

Elements of these historic themes permeate Sri Lanka's villages in all kinds of forms. A group of people in the late-nineteenth century claimed special privileges because of their association with the Bodhi tree. Alluding to the nineteenth-century British official R.W. Ievers, who worked on the North-Central Province, one scholar says this official had "asserted that there was a special caste in the region, constituted by a group who claimed that their ancestors had come to Sri Lanka with the Bo tree. He reported the attendant oral tradition: this caste claimed that their ancestors had been given the task of protecting the Bo tree from monkeys by using arrows."[52] The truth or otherwise of such claims to exalted ancestry is moot: such claims in India are often cases of what is called "sanskritisation" – the assertion of superior status by a caste or social group, often by cooking up a genealogy which shows descent from the gods.

So where, over this long march in the trail of my favourite monarch of ancient India, was I now in relation to the big man himself? I had sniffed the spoor of his children, but was there any whiff of the father? Sri Lanka seemed to resemble the land

---

[51] Sivasundaram (2007): 122–3.
[52] Ibid.: 126.

of a holy trinity with the main prong of the trinity missing: the holy son and the spiritual daughter were everywhere, whereas Ashoka the Father did not seem to make it here even as the Holy Ghost.

However, when I moved away from the domain of religious colonisation and the demarcation of sacred spaces in the island, I discovered that there was in fact an arena where Ashoka had squeezed through – the realm of state affairs. What is thought of as an important Ashokan element of governance persists to this day in Sri Lanka. This is the idea of an Ashokan purification of the polity to ensure governance by consensus. One of the abiding political leitmotifs here, as in India, relates to the purification of the Samgha that Ashoka is supposed to have undertaken within his lifetime. His opposition to divisions and faction fights and schisms ("samghabheda") is inscribed on pillars in Sarnath, Sanchi and Kaushambi/Allahabad.[53] In the Lankan chronicles, a different form of purification seems in evidence as an Ashokan inheritance – in which the Samgha rather than the king reigns supreme. One scholar has drawn attention to the *Mahavamsa*'s telling of the story of how the Third Council of Buddhism – not mentioned in Ashokan edicts – came to be convened by the emperor. The backdrop to this Council was the venality of the bhikkus in the Ashokarama – Ashoka's monastery – a body that had expanded because of Ashoka's generosity, and which had thus come to harbour many heretics. The organisation having bloated to take in these non-believers, the pious bhikkus of the order refused to hold the Uposatha – the periodic day of observance and meditation among Buddhists. Thereupon Ashoka decided to purify the order. At first, in his house-cleaning effort, he made a bad move: he struck off the heads of several unacceptable theras.[54] Later, a happier form of cleansing was followed,

---

[53] For details, Lahiri (2015): 255–6.
[54] Tambiah (1976): 167.

and in this the monk Mogaliputta held the reins. While Ashoka and the thera sat side by side and spoke of many matters, it was Mogaliputta rather than Ashoka who put things in order during the Third Council: "the monarch asked the thera: 'Sir, does the Sambuddha (really) teach the Vibhajja-doctrine?' The thera answered: 'Yes.' And when the king knew this, he was glad at heart and said: 'Since the community is (henceforth) purified, sir, therefore should the brotherhood hold the uposatha-festival."[55] We are told that this "story is unambiguous that the king and the great *thera* sat together, that it was the king who asked the questions but accepted the *thera's* version about the adequacy of the answers."[56] Modern management gurus preach "delegation of duties" to presidents of corporations. The Ashoka story here seems to show management wisdom has been going strong for close to 2500 years.

This example of the Samgha's purification in Ashoka's time apparently became a moral template model for later Buddhist kings in Sri Lanka. Parakramabahu I in the twelfth century received help from various theras to expel presumably rogue and apostate bhikkus from the Samgha: the king, "in the manner of Asoka, first acquainted himself with a knowledge of the laws of the Buddha," which enabled him to "discriminate between failure and non-failure."[57] Parakramabahu himself was supposedly present as the protector of the court on the occasion; he is said to have stood on his feet through the entire night, taking part in the proceedings. At the end of it all the unworthy bhikkus were cast out and made to wear the garb of laymen, which was widely recognised as a status insult. But in order that these demoted bhikkus not harm the order, they were assigned lucrative positions by the king. This last act of the Sri Lankan king, incidentally, is unlike anything that Ashoka is historically reported

[55] Ibid.: 168.
[56] Ibid.
[57] Cited in ibid.: 168.

to have done. What it suggests is the power and influence of "unworthy bhikkus" in the twelfth century.

If Parakramabahu I followed the example of Ashoka, as is asserted in the Sri Lankan chronicles, Sinhalese kings in general are supposed to have seen themselves following the Ashokan persona in a number of other ways. DT and his brother both took on Ashoka's nom de plume for themselves, this being an example of a "conscious desire to establish a genealogy to the Ashokan state."[58] The worship of relics is another Ashokan hangover: Ashoka is supposed to have not merely worshipped them but redistributed them across a vast territory, and various Sinhalese kings subordinated themselves "to relics, which refracted the immanence of the Buddha."[59] Stupas that included ossuaries and housed all manner of Buddhist relics were also something that the Lankan kings seemed to have grown rather fond of building. The manner in which the *Mahavamsa* invests the figure of Ashoka with responsibility for protection and proliferation of the dhamma – which Sinhalese rulers were expected to follow – means that "Asoka emerges as a sectarian Theravada Buddhist, an image that is, of course, totally inconsistent with that provided for" in his own edicts.[60] This contradiction between on the one hand the king's image of himself – or rather what is historically clear about the image he wished to project – and what the Pali chronicles assert on the other also suggests that in their narratives the priestly elite of Lanka purposively reshaped not merely the political history of their own island but also that of India.

The entire history of Sri Lanka, as told by the *Mahavamsa*, makes the island out to be the Chosen Land, chosen by the Buddha himself and, as predicted by him, converted to the Buddhist faith by the son of Ashoka. Origin myths of this variety exist in

[58] Wijeyeratne (2007): 165.
[59] Ibid.: 162.
[60] Ibid.: 165.

the sacred texts and sagas of most societies and over time become a part of national belief systems. The Ramayana and the Mahabharata in India, the Old Testament in Israel, and the Norse sagas in Scandinavia weave together politics, governance ideals, and religion into larger potboilers where superhuman heroes overcome monumental challenges before an ideal is realised. Similar challenges face the monarchs of the Pali chronicles and are elaborately described. They do however differ in their accounts from the Ashokan edicts, where the enemies of the state, such as the unconquered Atavikas (forest dwellers), are a very shadowy presence. In the *Mahavamsa* the enemies are often Tamils (Damilas). There is an entire chapter on "the victory of Dutthagamani" in which the king overpowers Damila rulers and slays Damilas. By the end of it, when "he had thus overpowered thirty-two Damila kings, Dutthagamani ruled over Lanka in single sovereignty."[61]

This is virtually a wholesale subversion of Ashoka and all that he represents in India. The historical Ashoka, as I and most Indians see him, was the epitome of the monarch seeking victory through peaceful means. In Sri Lanka, an all-encompassing territorial sovereignty is brutally established by a Buddhist king who is, at least putatively, of the same line of thought as Ashoka. For all the distortion, the indisputable fact remains that it is this chronicled image of Ashoka – the one developed in the Sri Lankan chronicles – that comes to be immensely influential in the ensuing centuries.

It was in his *Mahavamsa* incarnation that Ashoka journeyed across to South East Asia – where I continued in chase of him.

---

[61] *Mahavamsa*, see ch. XXV; Geiger (1912): 170–8.

6

Among Relics and Shrines in Myanmar

ON A LATE EVENING in December 2016, I went to see a few bone fragments of the Buddha in Mandalay. The city is located in central Myanmar and shows silhouettes of sundry political and religious structures. It takes its name after a hill, the only one in this part of the country, which dominates a large part of the cityscape – the part of it where a brick fort stands. This fort used to be the royal precinct of the last Burmese royal dynasty and began to be built when the capital was shifted by King Mindon (r. 1853–1878) from Amarapura to Mandalay. Amarapura is just outside Mandalay and has lakes with luminous water and bridges, as also relics and ruined walls fading into the horizon. The walls of the Mandalay fort are by contrast still impressively formidable, with battlements and multiple roofs, their size emphasised by a massive encircling moat. The Mandalay hill stands just beyond the fort. Devotees climb to its summit by foot – it is the only way to earn Buddhist merit when journeying to shrines. There are naturally many, including my family and myself, who on account of a mix of indolence and a lifelong failure to acquire heavenly merit of any kind, are resigned to taking the motor road and allowing the car to acquire merit via the blessings we shower upon it for so effortlessly getting us there. On reaching, one is greeted by the Buddhas and leogryphs that dot the hill slopes, along with a panoramic view of the city. The idea for us was, next, to quickly descend to the U-Khanti monastery, closer to the base of the hill, where the Buddha's relics lie.

U-Khanti (1867–1949), after whom the monastery is named, was a charismatic and influential ascetic who flourished in colonial Burma. The British were inordinately well disposed towards him and showered many favours on his head because, unlike Buddhist monks opposed to British rule, a steadfast feature of his exemplary piety was the distance he kept from political activism. He built and repaired shrines in and around Mandalay hill, and consequently in 1907 control of these shrines was granted to him by the rulers. U-Khanti made a clear distinction between the repair of old shrines and the construction of new ones, restoring those that were archaeologically significant with the consent of the Archaeological Survey. In fact he spent much more on the shrines than did the government. On those over which he had assumed primary responsibility, he spent over a million rupees – and this at a time when the total budget of the Archaeological Survey was only Rs 350,000.[1] So it was entirely appropriate for a monastery housing the Buddha's relics that were excavated by the Archaeological Survey to be named after him.

The hall in the U-Khanti monastery with the relics is announced by a board outside as the "Buddha's Collar-Bone Peshawar Relics worshipping place". An audience having been

---

[1] Woodward (1988). The quotations and ideas in this paragraph can be found on pp. 80 and 85.

prearranged for us with the guardian-monks, the casket containing the ancient relics was brought out, followed by an impressive exposition on their character and how they were found. The fragments inside the casket could not be seen, but even so this was the closest I was ever going to get to what was left of the Buddha. The irony of this as an experience in Myanmar, and not in India where the Buddha had lived and died, was not lost on me. Relics of the Buddha are of course around in Indian Buddhist stupas – Ashoka having been an avid collector and preserver of such relics – but easy accessibility is the mother of taking-for-granted and I had ignored them during stupa visits at home. It was the opposite feeling for me as a traveller unlikely to return to Mandalay, and therefore eager to savour and hoard as memory its most precious attractions.

The U-Khanti Hall is a kind of museum with a hotchpotch of things on display: an album of photographs showed the original casket and another a gold coin of King Kanishka – the beheaded king of the Mathura Museum – which had been found in the vicinity. The paintings decorating the hall included one depicting the carrying of the casket at a railway station, with monks and others in attendance. A family photograph of General Aung San showed his wife and the general gazing at each other while three of their children – a fourth died in infancy – look straight into the camera. Seven unarmed monks, mowed down by British troops on 10 February 1939, are on display close by. Ancient relics and modern reliquaries, worshipping clergy and monks in pools of blood, much-loved politicians and hated rulers, all mingle. This is often how museums attached to religious establishments are in South Asia and South East Asia.

Looking at this miscellany, I was reminded of why I had come with my family to see the Buddha's relics at Mandalay. Usually, in sagas of Ashoka, Buddhist relics which circulate way beyond their original burial places connect with Ashokan reconsecrations of them after old stupas have been dug up. This was the popular avatar of the ancient ruler that had circulated across Asia, at places where relics that Ashoka purportedly sent were believed to be enshrined. But knowledge of what in fact happened to the Buddha's bones in modern times illuminates far more. For the drama around the movement of the sage's bones was played out not by a ruler of the Buddhist faith but by a Christian state, and against the vast panorama of modern colonialism. This I had discovered many years before I went to Myanmar.

I had noticed descriptions of these small holy bones, the sort that came to Burma, in files of the Archaeological Survey. The British Raj, notings and correspondence showed, was actively involved in transfers of the ancient corporeal relics of the Buddha and his followers from the sites of their original interment. Several stupas that sundry European archaeologists and antiquarians had dug up contained such precious remains. Near Sanchi, as we have seen, relics were buried not far from where Ashoka built a stupa and set up a pillar: these had been removed by the officers of the East India Company who had excavated the stupas there. In the nineteenth century these Sanchi relics eventually reached museums in London.

A few decades later, after India came under direct British rule, the colonial government decided against this practice of institutionalised loot enriching its metropolitan museums. Instead of transporting relics discovered in excavations in British India back to England, they began to be moved to Buddhist countries in the hope that Britain would be perceived and lauded as a guardian of Buddhism. This is best described as relic diplomacy, with one such move – ensuing from an excavation of a Kanishka stupa at Shah-ji-ki Dheri in the North West Frontier Province – resulting in the Buddha's bones coming to rest in Mandalay. Burma was then under British rule, a bloody military pacification having concluded in abolishing the monarchy and exiling its last ruler,

King Thibaw, to India in 1885–6. Some decades later, the Buddha's bones were diplomatically repositioned in Burma, silently proclaiming Britain's munificence.

The journey of the relic bones, from where they were unearthed in distant Peshawar in India's north-west to Burma via Calcutta is a story in itself and could join the narrative tradition woven around journeys by precious jewels and precious bones – from Wilkie Collins' *The Moonstone* (1868) to Russell Martin's *Beethoven's Hair* (2000). D.B. Spooner, the officer of the Archaeological Survey of India who had conducted excavations at Shah-ji-ki Dheri in 1908–9 and discovered the bones, wrote an Archaeological Survey report about the dig.[2] Following government orders, Spooner travelled with his treasure to Calcutta and wrote an informal account of his journey in a letter to his uncle.[3] "The Bones of the Buddha were fastened around me," he says, as he sets off with his attendant posing as an armed guard, this guard being suitably decked up for the occasion in red and gold and told to keep his eye open for "three nights to guard the Relics". Three nights suggests an interminable train ride, and since Spooner is unlikely to have unfastened the Buddha's remains from his bosom while using the toilet, the spirit of the Buddha will have had to hold its nose each time its latest guardian had to answer the call of nature.

In Calcutta Spooner was treated to some esoteric ceremonies around the relics. He first met "the Dalai Lama of Tibet" in private so that the "living Buddha" could worship the relics, and this was where he "officially acknowledged them to be the Bones of himself 2500 years ago!" This was followed by a public ceremony at the throne room of Government House, fit setting for "the whole Government of India [to be] present in full uniform and about 200 of the great personages of the land including the Prince of Orleans." On this occasion Lord Minto, the viceroy,

---

[2] Spooner (1908–9): 48–50.
[3] Spooner (1910). Letter dated 6 April.

ceremonially presented the relics to the Burmese delegation. Spooner describes a long marble hallway leading to the throne room with tall Sikh lancers in uniform presenting arms as the dignitaries trooped in. The Buddha's bones, well blanched by the years and rattled by their journey after 2500 years of rest, are likely to have blanched a couple of shades more at the armed soldiers brandishing their weaponry as tribute to the remains of the most peace-loving South Asian ever. The casket in which the relics had originally been interred stayed back in India and is now in the Peshawar Museum in Pakistan. The bones were subsequently enshrined in the vicinity of Mandalay hill.

Buddhist relics from India have since made it a habit to travel to Myanmar off and on. In the early part of the twenty-first century, continuing their function as instruments of diplomatic goodwill, they signified a message of peace: in January 2016 a "Buddha relic bone" from the Hemis monastery in Ladakh was brought to Mandalay and then carried to prominent Myanmarese towns and villages by Ladakhi monks. This was apparently done to foster harmony, although it was rumoured in diplomatic circles that there was intelligence funding behind it, meaning that the monks who were the bearers and guardians of the bone may also have been doing some monkey business on the side. These monks returned to India after a few weeks.

My own journey to Myanmar, a more innocuous spying enterprise on Ashoka, was in pursuit of allusions and parallels in relation to him in the literature on Myanmar. There was something tantalisingly familiar in the stories of this oeuvre about relic-bearing stupas: the old Ashokan legends linked up in my mind with the modern movement of relics and Mandalay grew into a junction where the ancient Indian monarch intersected with modern relic journeys. What I wanted, most of all, was to satisfy my curiosity about these relics and the invocation of Ashoka in their vicinity.

The interconnection between Peshawar and Mandalay has analogues in the strong associations that exist between an image of the Buddha and epigraphs evoking Ashoka at another Mandalay shrine – the Mahamuni (Great Sage) temple. This is reckoned the holiest of Buddhist shrines and, much like the Peshawar relics, the image of Mahamuni within it, along with the inscriptions invoking Ashoka, were transplanted to the shrine from elsewhere.

The main shrine is dominated by a massively corpulent Buddha covered in gold leaf: he is so large here that the sanctum sanctorum looks like it was constructed around a very immobile *in situ* deity. Ashoka is to be found in a far less impressive place within the same complex, in a hall-like shed which houses an impressive collection of carved epigraphs. The shed is normally locked and not accessible to pilgrims, but the epigraphs, on stones arranged in rows, can be glimpsed through the grilled enclosure that houses them (Fig. 6.1). Many are copies of inscriptions, while a few are stones inscribed originally, many centuries ago. The temple's collection also includes palm leaf copies of epigraphs and these contain several that allude to Ashoka.

The epigraphs record dedications of all kinds and include allusions to stupas and temples that are said to have been built in Myanmar by Ashoka. Such stones begin to appear in the eleventh century, and their present existence in Mandalay is wholly fortuitous since they were brought in from all over Myanmar. Their origins are known from a list, published about a century ago, providing summary information about them, but enough to reveal their original location alongside basic details of donors and donative intent.

Several of these epigraphs, or their copies, were brought in from Bagan, which became the ancient capital under Anawrahta (r. 1044–1077), this king being widely regarded as creating an energetic eleventh-century Buddhist polity in the Irrawaddy river basin. His repute rests partly on all the shrines he created and repaired. An example of such work is mentioned in an

Fig. 6.1: A view of epigraphs collected by King Bodawpaya

inscription about the Tangyi pagoda in Bagan, which says it was repaired by Anawrahta in 1035 CE and originally built by "Siri Dhammasoka". The repairs apart, Anawrahta dedicated land, villages, and slaves to the stupa.[4]

Another dedication of the Shwe-in-dein pagoda in Indein village at Inle is also described as having been built by Ashoka, this time in an epigraph of a descendant of Anawrahta, King Alaungsithu (also known as Sithu I) in the twelfth century.[5] Indein is a village in the south-western corner of the Inle lake,

[4] Durosielle (1921): no. 142.
[5] Ibid.: no. 11.

with the pagoda complex perched on a hill. The legend of Ashoka having built it is apparently still remembered there. When it was refurbished with paintings in the 1960s, one of them showed the shrine under construction – and supervised by none other than Ashoka himself.[6] Alaungsithu made provisions for the continuous offering of rice and lights at this refurbished shrine. He is also said to have repaired a pagoda in Ngalengouk village in the Bankyi Lower Chindwin area: it too is described as built by Ashoka.[7] The Shwegu Dhamatha pagoda in Phyathi village in Pakangayi is yet another said to have owed its creation to "Siridhammasoka" and which, according to an inscription of 1196 CE, continued being given land and slaves.[8] These are all in different parts of Myanmar, Bagan being near the Irrawaddy river in the vast expanse of plains and Pakangayi not far from there. Inle, on the other hand, is in a mountainous area with a lake of more than a hundred sq. km, with floating villages and communities, while dormant volcanoes distinguish the Lower Chindwin area. These Bagan-based kings seem to have paid obeisance to Ashoka across a large swathe of the country.

How did this immense collection of epigraphs reach the compound of Mandalay's most holy shrine? They were apparently placed there in the eighteenth century by King Bodawpaya ("Lord Grandfather", 1782–1819), under whom the line of kings that formed the Konbaung dynasty reached the height of its power. The order to collect them came from the king himself, the reason being financial stress: the state revenues were dwindling and the monarch reckoned that by examining the inscriptions he might be able to distinguish non-taxable land given to the Buddhist Samgha from areas that were taxable. His idea – a bit like that of Henry VIII of England who destroyed monasteries partly to loot them – was to increase the resources of the state by reducing

---

[6] Stadtner (2015): 311.
[7] Durosielle (1921): no. 83.
[8] Ibid.: no. 143.

the resources of the Samgha which, he felt, had acquired too much wealth.⁹ Later, Bodawpaya decided to get a "New Chronicle" (or "Yazawinthit") written and ordered its author, Twinthin Taikwun Mahasitthu, to use the epigraphs in his work.¹⁰ Mahasitthu, being also the very man who had been centrally involved in making the epigraphic collection, was perhaps only too happy to have his interest in creating a historical record chime with the king's.

The epigraphs beg an obvious question: why is Ashoka's name invoked here, many hundred miles from Pataliputra, and from the eleventh century on, more than 1200 years after his reign? Ashoka in this context is almost certainly explicable as *the* renowned builder and restorer of stupas, and therefore as the inaugurating spirit behind every such subsequent enterprise far and wide. The epigraphs of Anawrahta and Alaungsithu show both kings fashioning themselves as saviours, repairers, patrons, and providers of ancient pagodas from Inle to Bagan and beyond. Ashoka, situated at the apex of the illustrious genealogy of rulership that they construct, adds lustre, sanctity, and Buddhist legitimacy to their kingship.

Could this trope – of Ashoka as builder of stupas in this region – have reached Myanmar via Sri Lanka? Relations between this region's rulers, starting from Anawrahta's time, and those of Sri Lanka such as Vijayabahu, who was Anawrahta's contemporary, varied from close to cordial. The ancient Ceylon of Bizet's setting in his *Pearl Fishers* (1863) is apparent here from the evidence of a trade in pearls and other gems, while Buddhist monks were sent from Bagan for the purification of the Samgha in Vijayabahu's kingdom. The texts of the Theravada tradition, such as the *Dipavamsa* and the *Mahavamsa*, reaching Bagan as a consequence of trade would seem logical and may have

⁹ Thwin (1979): 674.
¹⁰ Yi (1965): 56.

familiarised the region with Ashoka's name. However, in those texts Ashoka is not a relic-preserving stupa builder in Sri Lanka or anywhere in South East Asia. So, this avatar of his may have arrived via Ashoka-related stories which reached Myanmar via the chronicles. By the early-second millennium CE it seems to have been a widely established and popular mode of showing off the antiquity of places across Asia where stupas were built to associate them with the progenitor of such activity.

In place names and chronicles in the Rakhine state on the western coast of Myanmar I ran into Ashoka in another incarnation. Mrauk-U (Arakan), which is the old capital of Rakhine state, was founded in 1430 and flourished between the fifteenth and seventeenth centuries. Its name, Mrauk-U, links it with a story in which Ashoka is an important character. Sometimes the Buddha features in place of Ashoka, but the contours of the story remain broadly similar. The tale goes back to a time when Ashoka is said to have visited Rakhine and met a monkey-queen there. She had coupled with a peacock-king and produced two eggs. Ashoka is supposed to have then predicted that a great city would arise right there and be named Myauk (monkey) U (egg), or modern Mrauk-U.[11] The tale circulated in a time when the court had strong ties with Sri Lanka, with missions from the island bringing holy texts and Rakhine's monks venturing to Sri Lanka. Ashoka predicting the future creation of a city was, all the same, an indigenous invention to invest the city with ancient prestige and links with similar Buddhist legends – the Buddha himself is said to have predicted that Pataliputra would become a great city in the time of Ashoka. In Mrauk-U, Ashoka sometimes manages to displace Sakyamuni himself.

If the Bagan kings have a presence in the Mahamuni shrine via the Bodawpaya epigraphs, so does Rakhine: the golden Buddha in that immense shrine is said to have been brought there by the

---

[11] Fraser-Lu and Stadtner (2015): 327.

very same king. The colossal statue was originally in Rakhine, apparently, and connected with a defining myth of Rakhine: the Buddha is said to have converted a king of Rakhine called Chandrasuriya. This converted monarch received permission – from the Buddha himself – to cast a metal likeness of the Buddha. The statue's height was some 12 ft, 7 in, this being exactly as tall as the living Buddha, the Great Sage having specified when giving permission that the "image of me . . . shall not vary from the actual size of my body even by the breadth of a hair."[12] This myth goes back at least to the sixteenth century; an Arakanese manuscript called the *Sappadanapakarna* recorded the legend, and the image of the statue was for long seen as a symbol of the Rakhine realm.[13] King Bodawpaya, after he conquered Rakhine in 1784, brought it back with him, along with booty and thousands of prisoners of war. A vivid description of the event tells us that "the image [i.e. the metal replica] was dragged over the mountains by Burmese soldiers, and was accompanied by numerous captives of war, who afterwards settled in Mandalay."[14] The size of this Buddha meant, according to the legend, that it had to be cut into pieces before being lugged across, and then put together again after it reached its resting place. This seems a tall tale: the likelihood of a giant Buddha cut to size by a Buddhist king and then stuck together again with some variety of fevicol strikes me as more than slightly implausible.

It was probably heard sceptically as well by the artists who painted the statue's travel in large paintings that decorate long galleries in the temple complex of Mahamuni. These illustrations depict the temple's Buddha arriving undismembered by a river route. The ship on which it came, its reception by King Bodawpaya who went into the waters to guide it, and the enshrining

---

[12] Kaung (2013): 110.
[13] Fraser-Lu and Stadtner (2015): 15.
[14] *The Imperial Gazetteer of India XVII* (1908–31): 1.41.

of the image are painted on a huge scale. It has been suggested that the caption beneath the painting showing riverine transport says it was brought "back" to Burma – which is either a rather strange way of describing political loot or a way of suggesting that it was not loot at all because it was being restored to an originary location.[15]

At some distance from all these controversies, the Mahamuni Buddha continues to look calm and composed, oblivious of his own trials and tribulations and contested history.

It takes a little over three hours to reach Bagan from Mandalay by an expressway that is featureless, as most such roads are. The dazzling destination, though, makes up for the journey. Bagan, I knew, has a couple of thousand monuments in an area a little over five thousand hectares, but I was still unprepared for a skyline filled with spires. It was just before sunset when we landed in the midst of its stupas and shrines and watched the atmosphere change from evening light to dense dusk. This skyline is best viewed from temples whose layered terraces reminded me of Borobudur in Indonesia. I don't remember much about the temple to the middle terrace of which we climbed, except that the terrific strain was well worth the effort: the view, as the luminous orange orb sank slowly behind stupas and temples, their fringes enveloped by ground mist, was breathtaking.

Elements of the ancient and modern converge in amazing ways at Bagan. Ancient India can be spotted in the Mahabodhi Paya of the early-thirteenth century CE which is modelled after the temple bearing that name in Bihar – the one where Ashoka presented a throne ("vajrasana") in remembrance of the Buddha's enlightenment (Figs 6.2 and 6.3). A more contemporary and mundane connection was equally visible in wads of cur-

---

[15] Schober (1997): 277–8.

Fig. 6.2: The Mahabodhi temple in Bagan

rency notes which had been "demonetised" by the Indian prime minister in November 2016, seriously inconveniencing virtually every Indian for no good reason and impoverishing many such as Bagan's tourist guides who were in no position to use what

Fig. 6.3: View of the "shikhara" of the Mahabodhi temple in Bagan

they had earned in rupees. A happier connection here was the presence of India's Archaeological Survey, which has helped in conservation work. At the Ananda temple – among the most important historic Buddhist temple complexes of the territory –

Indian archaeologists had helped restore several parts of it. One of these restorers, Amalesh Roy, was steeped in Myanmar and its archaeology. A Bengali-speaking archaeologist who also spoke Burmese and wore a local lungi, he had recently retired from the Survey and, fortunately for us, was back in Bagan as a consultant. Our sense of the architectural landscape of Bagan, a boat ride on the Irrawaddy, and the views we had of Bagan's shrines and museums all owe much to his sense of delight when sharing with us his deep knowledge of them.

In one of the temples on the edge of Bagan, in Mybinkaba, I ran unexpectedly into Ashoka. The twelfth-century Kubyauk-Gyi temple is, unlike the larger Buddhist pagodas and temples, a relatively small shrine to the south of the main archaeological complex in Bagan. Its small size does not prepare you for a magnificent interior. Stories featuring the Buddha and his life, his previous lives, kings, and more ordinary people are all told through wall paintings, with labels in the old Mon language which explain what is depicted. This language was used in epigraphs in south Myanmar and parts of central and northern Thailand. "Dhammasok" is how Ashoka is mentioned in the labels. I had only known the Myanmarese Ashoka from the epigraphs of Bagan-based kings; now he suddenly appeared more physically in several frescoes within the shrine.

The long history of contacts between South East Asia and South Asia antedates knowledge of Ashoka in the Irrawaddy basin: Buddhism is noted here in various Pali inscriptions from the fifth century CE onwards, the various formulae and verses in them most often given in their Theravadin recensions.[16] Archaeology supports the existence of such contacts with other parts of Myanmar, as at the walled settlement of Beikthano where a Buddha image and a terracotta seal with the Brahmi script were found in contexts which go back to between the second

---

[16] Skilling (1997): 94–6.

and fourth centuries CE.[17] Large bulbous stupas in Sri Ksetra in the south-central plains are made in a Sinhalese or Sri Lankan style.[18] The *Dipavamsa* and *Mahavamsa* became major sources of artistic inspiration in twelfth-century Bagan, so that at the exquisite Kubyauk-Gyi temple Ashoka figures in various murals and their decorative textual glosses (Fig. 6.4). This temple's interiors have more than five hundred murals and, when I first heard of Ashoka rendered within them, my immediate reaction was to think of them as Indian-inspired. I was mistaken: their source of inspiration is entirely the Sri Lankan chronicles. The Bagan–Sri Lanka relationship also included Anawrahta's help in Vijayabahu's resistance to the Cholas of South India, and in the monks sent from Bagan to Sri Lanka.[19] Why the chronicles came to be so dramatically used at this particular temple, though, has to do more specifically with a Bagan prince, Rajakumar, who

Fig. 6.4: The Kubyauk-Gyi temple

[17] Miksic and Goh (2017): 196.
[18] Ibid.: 198.
[19] For relations between Pagan and Sri Lanka through Buddhist monks, see Than Tun (2002).

was the son of King Kyanzittha – to whose artistic activities we will soon turn.[20]

The subjects depicted in the temple are Buddhist, ranging from the Jataka tales to scenes from the life of the Buddha and incidents relating to many historical kings; in these Ashoka figures rather prominently in his Buddhist avatar. The northern wall of the entrance archway to the shrine contains four panels centring on incidents from his life, with the top tier on the northern wall showing a gloss: "This is king Kala, king of the Nagas. He creates a likeness of the Buddha and shows it to king Dhammasok (Asoka)." The allusion is to a section in the *Mahavamsa* where Ashoka sends for the Naga king Mahakala, who has beheld four Buddhas and then created the "beauteous figure of the Buddha, endowed with the thirty-two great signs and brilliant with the eighty lesser signs."[21] Another epigraph says, "This is when king Dhammasok takes the relics"; a third speaks of a monastic dedication by the emperor: "This is when Dhammasok dedicates the monastery to . . ." – an allusion to the *Mahavamsa*'s description of Ashoka building the Ashokarama himself while exhorting all kings to build viharas.[22] There are also label epigraphs on Ashoka's engagement with the king of the "island of Singhal". This reference is to the Sinhala monarch Devanampiya Tissa, described as a friend of the Indian ruler, who sent him the ornaments of sovereignty.[23] Another panel concerns the time when Dhammasoka sent the relic of the tree with Theri Sanghamitta to the island of "Singhal".

Ashoka's engagement with the Samgha is captured in the representation of "Tisapagut" – a reference to Mogaliputta Tissa – and "King Dhammasok" discussing the broadening of their religion.[24] The Third Buddhist Council is mentioned in

[20] Luce, Shin, and Oo (1970): 158.
[21] Geiger (1912), V. 87–92: 33–4.
[22] Ibid.: V. 79–80: 32–3.
[23] Luce, Shin, and Oo (1970): 158.
[24] Luce and Shin (1969): 379.

inscriptions, and Ashoka therefore inevitably figures in them. Mogaliputta Tissa performs miracles for Ashoka in one, and in another Ashoka gets his ministers to tell the monks to hold the Uposatha festival (Figs 6.5 and 6.6.).

In the painting where Mogaliputta Tissa figures, he is dominant while Ashoka seems to be there by the way, alongside a

Fig. 6.5: Mogaliputta Tissa performing miracles for Ashoka, shown with a crown to his right. *Courtesy* Amalesh Roy

Fig. 6.6: Ashoka requesting monks to hold the Uposatha festival, Mogaliputta at the centre. *Courtesy* Amalesh Roy

whole lot of others. These paintings are part of a small set on the Buddhist Councils. In one of them we see King Ajatshatru who called the First Council, and in another King Kalasoka in whose time the Second Council was supposed to have been held. All three Councils are recorded in the Pali chronicles of Sri Lanka.

These frescoes featuring Ashoka are unlike anything that I had seen in South Asia. Why had the Bagan rulers chosen to represent him and South Asian Buddhism? Understanding this requires a short historical excursion. Bagan had become the region's political capital in the middle of the eleventh century with King Anawrahta. Some decades later, after the rule of Anawrahta's son Man Lulan, there came the third ruler in this line, Kyanzittha. To accede, Kyanzittha needed the support of the Mons and forged a union with them by marrying his daughter to a Mon prince and promising that his own heir would be none other than their offspring. This deprived Rajakumar, Kyanzittha's own son, of his inheritance – along the general lines of Bhishma when he is ruled out as a future king in the Mahabharata. Rajakumar, being artistically inclined and in need of something to do now that he was never going to be ruling the kingdom, busied himself with temple murals, the result being the temple masterpieces commemorating Ashoka and Buddhism.

Rajakumar in fact mastered the full range of Theravada literature, cosmology, and history, and put his knowledge spectacularly on display in his temple. His intent, as far as I could tell, was to use paint and accompanying explanatory gloss to provide the worldview of the textual tradition to Buddhists of his time. Rajakumar also does what many scholars do: he engages with the text, dropping the bits that do not interest him and adding others that make the story more personal. He brings the story of Buddhism's spread up to the time of the Anawrahta, whom his father had served as a general. The Sinhalese king Vijayabahu, who died around time this temple was being built, is imaged here as well.

Rajakumar's art patronage immortalises him far more comprehensively than the ordinary wielding of power would have done had he become king. I could not help wondering how his narration of the Buddhist past might have differed had he not relied on the Sri Lankan chronicles. Thoughts of this kind crossed my mind because, searching for the historically authenticated Ashoka, I was instead constantly confronted with a Buddhist avatar – and this meant yet another localised transformation of Ashoka into a figure that did not match the monarch in his own Indian records.

Some six hundred years after Rajakumar, Ashoka comes alive once more in Myanmar, this time within a memorialisation of Anawrahta. By this point in time the descriptions in Burmese texts had added much flesh to this Bagan king and, in many ways, changed him.

The historian Geok Yian Goh, in her history of the transformation of the image of Anawrahta across the centuries, has described this process in fascinating detail.[25] Anawrahta was based in Bagan but widely seen as the first major empire-builder of Myanmar. The paradox was that while he had a long reign of some thirty-three years, the contemporary sources do not seem particularly impressed by his achievements. A few temples were attributed to his reign, as were many sealings – or votive tablets as they are more commonly described. These tablets have been seen as indicating the geographical extent of Anawrahta's kingdom, having been found from Katha in northern Myanmar to Thaton near the coast. These miniature religious artefacts are very similar to those made and used across the Bay of Bengal, in large parts of South Asia and South East Asia.[26]

It was in a now-famous chronicle completed in 1724, known as the *Mahayazawingyi* (MYG), that an attempt was made by its author, U Kala, to present a history "not only of kings and religion, but a distinct nation." In presenting the origin of Myanmar and its evolution, a larger world is fleshed out within this first

---

[25] Yian Goh (2015).
[26] Ghosh (2014): 189–201.

national chronicle of Burma, and the unifying characteristic of this author's universe is Buddhism. U Kala was both a collector and a producer of texts. His parents' wealth made a career of private scholarship possible for him. He wrote three chronicles, devoting himself to an exploration of three concepts – the world, the law, and the monarch ("loka", "dhamma", and "yaza/raja").[27] And in so writing of these themes, the similarities he sets up in the lives of Anawrahta and Ashoka are deliberate and striking.

In line with the Ashoka in the Sri Lankan *Mahavamsa*, the Myanmar king is shown as having been converted to Buddhism by monks – Nigrodha converts Ashoka, and Shin Arahan converts Anawrahta. Yian Goh's summation of this in MYG is worth quoting:

> The MYG describes a hunter bringing Shin Arahan to see King Anawrahta, and Anawrahta, like Asoka, discerns from the monk's deportment that he is a holy person. Shin Arahan when asked to take a seat befitting his status, goes right up to the throne and sits there, establishing therefore in the action his moral superiority to the king. Symbolically the act asserts the higher status of *arhatship* over secular kingship . . . he asks the latter (Shin Arahan) to preach to him the doctrine of the Lord Buddha. Shin Arahan also preaches sermons to Anawrahta starting with the *Appamada* which Nigrodha gave to King Asoka.[28]

At this juncture in the text, Yian Goh shows U Kala linking the two teachers and kings: Shin Arahan preaches the Appamada, which Nigrodha had preached to King Siridhammasoka (Asoka).[29]

Other similarities appear in their reconstructed lives. On the prophecy by the Buddha regarding the birth of future kings, U Kala's text appears to follow the *Ashokavadana* – which had shown the Buddha receiving the gift of dirt from Ashoka in an

---

[27] Yian Goh (2015): 90.
[28] Ibid.: 107–8.
[29] Cited in ibid.: 108.

earlier life and predicting that he, Ashoka, would be reborn as a king. The MYG, for its part, shows the Buddha prophesying that His law will be established in Bagan during Anawrahta's reign, the reason for this being that in Anawrahta's former life he was an elephant that made offerings to the Buddha.[30] A trope common to the very ancient and less ancient texts relates to the purging of heretics: the *Mahavamsa* had described the expulsion of Samgha heretics by Ashoka, and in the U Kala book Anawrahta is shown as expelling heretic Ari monks. All kings who were "dhammarajas", or guardians of the law of the Buddha, had to take it upon themselves to keep their religions clean, and in this the Indian and Myanmarese emperors are similar. And yet, as Goh shows, there are important differences in the Burmese chronicle's images of Ashoka and Anawrahta. Ashoka's killing of his brothers is depicted as remorseless, whereas the Bagan king, traumatised at having killed his brother, repents. In this repentance it could be surmised he is reminiscent of post-Kalinga Ashoka; the surmise would be misplaced because the MYG's author cannot, in his depiction of Anawrahta's contrition, be alluding to post-Kalinga Ashoka, the simple reason being that the Ashokan edicts were discovered and translated more than a century after U Kala's chronicle. In suggesting the charisma of Anawrahta as a nation-builder of a large Buddhist polity, Buddhist textual accounts were the chief or perhaps even sole sources available to U Kala.

The Ashokan ideal in the MYG expanded into the model of kingship within other Burmese chronicles and texts.[31] And in these their kings as well as those of Sri Lanka were portrayed in line with the prototypical moral king of India: the template of the beneficent South East Asian king was firmly set to show a religious preceptor who had rid the Samgha of corruption.

[30] Ibid.: 111.
[31] Pranke (2004), for instance, points to the Vamsadipani ("Treatise on the Lineage of Elders") whose author simply lifted much material from U Kala's history.

The world I encountered in Myanmar encompassed India and Sri Lanka; it was a far more global Buddhist universe in these countries than anything I had seen in India. I was struck by the range of rulers and exploits in temples and art here, their coexistence spanning a geography and temporality unseen in Indian textual sources of antique times. In the vanished world of thousands of years ago within India, our writers had not engaged with – and not even revealed knowledge of – contemporary cultures and distinct traditions that flourished beyond South Asia.

Insularity, I remember telling myself, is not only the hallmark of island nations.

Ashokas in Thailand

IT SAYS IN THE BIBLE that "there is nothing hidden which will not be revealed, nor has anything been kept secret but that it should come to light."[1] When Jesus is asked by his following why he speaks in parables, he replies that his meaning is never unclear to those who have the eyes to see. This particular nugget of wisdom is bound to strike a chord in every historian of the ancient world, because the past speaks to the present through images that can go unnoticed or remain uninterpreted unless the eye is peeled to ferret out what the multitude is likely to miss. My eye, or more truly both my eyes, were continuously wide open for every sign of Ashoka. I was inclined to spot him in even the faintest glimmer of anything Buddhist that may have originated in the India of his time. As seen at the start of this book, I had found that he can be encountered in all kinds of unlikely places in Thailand – one had merely to be strongly predisposed to look for him – a confirmed case of "seek and ye shall find".

[1] Bible, New King James Version, Mark 4: 22.

Ordinary folk in this country, Thailand, naturally, don't know much about the Indian ruler, and not remotely in the way that they know the Buddha, who is revered in practically every corner. (Mahatma Gandhi comes a distant second, and only because Indian currency notes, on which he is invariably seen smiling, are not as valueless in Thailand as in the West.) Setting off in my Ashoka-besotted frame of mind, I caught his name on a street called Soi Asoke which ran in one of Bangkok's business districts. Next, I heard of sundry Asoke temples scattered across Thailand, many of these being related to the vegetarian Santi Asoke ("peaceful Ashoka") group which participated in anti-government protests that led to the storming of the Bangkok international airport in 2008. Chamlong Srimuang, a former army general and key leader of that protest, was a follower of this sect. In 2016, when I began researching Ashoka's presence by looking at such allusions, I knew little of the history of Thailand or its overseas connections. So it was such names that I started noticing, an interest that in retrospect appears embarrassingly simplistic. I soon learnt that the street called Soi Asoke, now known as Asoke Montri Road, was named after Phra Asoke Montri, whose land donation had made possible its construction. Of course it is far from impossible that Asoke Montri was named after my emperor, so I consoled myself I was on to something even if the connection wasn't direct. Ashoka would moreover have approved of Santi Asoke's emphasis on reducing meat consumption and capitalist wealth accumulation, even if the Thai adherents of this sect were not inspired by his morality: these were among the precepts, they believe, that had been stipulated by the Buddha.

What of relics with an Ashokan aura? At Chiang Mai, in north Thailand, a standing pillar bearing a wheel had survived. Numerous friends and websites had pointed towards what was said to be a thirteenth-century specimen that imitated an Ashokan pillar in the forested Buddhist establishment of Wat Umong

("Wat" means temple complex) in the foothills of Chiang Mai, where I proceeded in the summer of 2016. The idea of a looking through a historic city was attractive, regardless of the Ashokan possibility.

Photographs of the pillar, hemmed in by railing and crowned with four lions back to back bearing a dharmachakra, made it look remarkably similar to Ashoka's handiwork at Sarnath. Since Wat Umong was thought to have been built in the thirteenth century, it was assumed by many that the pillar was put up during the time of King Mangrai of the Lanna dynasty (1238–1311). This raised a question. Mangrai was a restless conqueror and builder whose wars and constructions consistently figure in texts. Why do these never mention him putting up a pillar at Wat Umong? And if Mangrai did in fact set up this pillar in the vicinity of a monastic complex, how was such a faithful reproduction made of the one in Sarnath? It seems far-fetched to think of detailed illustrations being made of a pillar several thousand kilometres away, brought here, and then meticulously followed. So did a local Thai architect travel with monks to Sarnath to size up the monolith there, and what was the technology used for producing such a masterly copy? The thought that some answers would be forthcoming in Chiang Mai was exciting.

On reaching Wat Umong the balloon that was my excitement was instantaneously deflated. The pillar was certainly a reproduction of the Sarnath Ashokan column, but a modern version. It could neither be dated to medieval times nor had any connection with a king of the Lanna line. It was a cement-and-concrete replica set up some decades ago at the initiative of the Buddhist monastic community and its patrons at Wat Umong. They had also had copies made of sundry sculpted panels from Buddhist sites in India. Several of these can be seen in a building very close to the pillar, others are scattered around the temple grounds. These Buddhists were people with a penchant for pillars, several of their reproductions being of Indian reliefs that record pillar worship. The making and instituting of replicas is an old tradition in Thailand, as in many parts of Asia, and its popularity persists.

The Ashokan signs at Chiang Mai made me wonder about older links, so I decided to look deeper and read up Thailand's history to explore other invocations of Ashoka and the outward expansion of images associated with him in the country.

A web of material connections between Thailand and India was writ large. The earliest imprint took me as far back as the second or first century BCE, to the east coast of the upper Thai–Malay peninsula, to a place called Khao Sam Kaeo where the remains of an urban settlement have been excavated.[2] The links of the materials and technologies here suggest trade with India, other parts of South East Asia, and China. The artefacts unearthed underline the importance of traders and craftspeople in networking these areas. Khao Sam Kaeo flourished at the juncture of all these connections a century or more after the reign of Ashoka. The fly in the ointment from my perspective is that nothing in its artefactual repertoire even remotely suggests either a Buddhist or Ashokan connection. The dominant connection is an impressive glass bead industry that used Indian techniques and appears in a full-blown and well-developed form in the settlement's earliest occupation levels. This degree of perfection in the craftsmanship would be unlikely if it had evolved locally. Other goods associated with South Asia found here include Indian rouletted and knobbed ware, and ornaments with auspicious symbols described as triratna, svastika, and nandipada. Occasionally, owners' names appear inscribed in Brahmi characters and in the Prakrit language on seals. The excavators argue that, because of

---

[2] I have depended on Bellina, *et al.* (2014) for the South Thailand–India connections.

the high level of expertise required for the production of glass ornaments, South Asian craftspeople lived here. They "may have been welcomed by local elites to set up industries that played a role in the economic and political strategies of the South China Sea early trading polities."[3]

The peregrinations of such traders extended from the Andaman coast of south Thailand to an entrepôt called Phu Khao Thong.[4] Hard stone ornaments here show designs such as the nandipada and the lion. Fine Indian pottery has also been found here, one piece showing three letters in Tamil-Brahmi dating to the second century CE. The letters were tentatively identified by a group of scholars as "*tu Ra o..*", which could be the Tamil word *turavon* or *turavor*, i.e. an ascetic – but not a Buddhist, because Buddhist monks were described as bhikshus. A different reading has proposed *turavam*, which was a common black plum, or alternatively *turavu*, signifying the receptacle of such a plum. Notwithstanding the storm in this particular ancient teacup over whether the letters signify an ascetic or a plum, the tornado cools to show agreement over the fact that it is a Tamil-Brahmi inscription, perhaps the earliest Tamil epigraph in South East Asia. It appears to be earlier than a third- or fourth-century CE inscription on a touchstone from Khan Luk Pat in Krabi province. Another site called Bang Kluai Nok yielded a Brahmi epigraph, *c.* second to fourth centuries CE, on the reverse of a golden seal. In Sanskritised Prakrit, surrounding a representation of an auspicious throne-like seat, the inscription says, "Of the sailor captain Brahaspatisharma".

Ancient Thai artefacts and articles of trade have not caught the eye during digs in India, not because there was no reciprocal trade but because those familiar with the archaeology of Thailand have not looked at Indian collections while keeping in mind

[3] Ibid.: 78.
[4] This is based on Chaisuwan (2011): 83–111.

the Biblical injunction of having the eye to see what may seem hidden to others. Names like "suvarnabhumi" (golden land) and "suvarnadvipa" (golden island) occur in Jataka stories and have been thought of when reconstructing early contact. The Mahajanaka Jataka and the Suparaga Jataka describe maritime journeys to Suvarnabhumi, but since the vessels in them suffered mishaps, where exactly they were headed is not at all clear; we surmise they were sailing towards a land to the east of the Indian subcontinent. Suvarnabhumi was probably a generic name that included lower Myanmar, central Thailand, the Mekong delta, and the Malay peninsula.[5] Various polities in South East Asia identify themselves with Suvarnabhumi for nationalist reasons: the word comes in handy as ancient proof of theirs as the "golden land", the first Buddhist state of the region.[6]

Either way, trading nodes in Thailand brought Indian artefacts into South East Asia. These networks did not, to begin with, have much to do with religion per se, they were mainly convenient channels for the penetration of religious imagery and ideas into a new region. Brahmanism and Buddhism were subsequent arrivals. There is much wisdom in the assumption that this lag "of several centuries between early contact and cultural transmission indicates . . . that mere contact is insufficient to enable cultural traits to be transferred."[7] It is unlikely that there was anything specifically Buddhist or Ashokan before the fourth or fifth century CE in Thailand.

A distinctly Ashokan flavour begins seeping into the region in the shape of fabulously crafted dharmachakras from the sixth century. Thailand is proof that the Indian "wheel of law" dharmachakra, like the image of the scales of justice that moved from the West to the East, was an internationally attractive notion.

[5] Revire (2018): 168.
[6] Ibid.: 170.
[7] Miksic and Yian Goh (2017): 169.

I first saw these wheels on visits to the Bangkok National Museum, which has many in its display collection, some placed in a hall showing the masterpieces of the museum (Fig. 7.1).[8] These

Fig. 7.1: Dharmachakra with a couchant deer in front in the Bangkok National Museum

[8] Yupho (1965).

dharmachakras are made of stone, beautifully carved, and often show crouching deer; some of them surmount pillars. The need to replicate something resembling the Sarnath pillar seems to have been first understood in 1963 at a place called Chedi 11 in U Thong where a chakra, along with a pillar and a supporting socle, were found together and which, when reassembled, fitted perfectly.[9] The ensemble of the wheel of law on a pillar alongside deer is, even if not specifically Sarnath-inspired, in a general way Indian-inspired. The elements of Sarnath all exist in the image: the Buddha turned the wheel of law and preached his first sermon to a clutch of five disciples at a deer park. The connections had been kept alive by the Ashokan pillar at Sarnath. It was impossible to see the luminous sculpted orbs in Bangkok without thinking of the Indian prototype. I imagined visitors and pilgrims from Thai shores seeing them at Sarnath and other Buddhist sites from Amaravati to Sanchi, and replicating them in their own country.[10]

Many of the dharmachakras in the Bangkok museum were procured from Nakhon Pathom in central Thailand – about 50 km west of Bangkok – the originary fount of the proliferation of this form in the region. "Nakhon Pathom" derives from

---

[9] Brown (1996): 72–3.

[10] The Sanchi representations of chakra-topped pillars have been mentioned in the chapter on Sanchi. Several reliefs showing dharmachakra stambhas at Amaravati can be seen in Burgess (1886). The epigraphs associated with them, unlike the Dvaravati dharmachakras, were mainly donative. What has been said of the Dvaravati dharmachakras by Brown was stated by Skilling in relation to Buddhism: "Perhaps because of the absence of indigenous information – of contemporary chronicles or histories – the Buddhism of early South-east Asia is all too often portrayed as an inanimate cultural package that was passively received from abroad. All the evidence, however, is against this. The Buddhism of the Chao Phraya plain was not a simple copy from Ceylon or India: from the time of the very first evidence, it already has a unique face, implying an earlier evolution for which no record remain." Skilling (1997): 103.

the Pali word for "first city", "nagarapathama", and is said to have become officially so only in the early part of the twentieth century.[11] The city was part of the Dvaravati culture, the name Dvaravati ("which had gates") deriving from Dwaraka, the ancient Yadava capital mentioned in the Mahabharata. Why this was the chosen appellation for a Thai polity remains elusive, but as a political entity it existed from the sixth century and ended around the ninth century. A ruling group using the name Dvaravati is alluded to by Xuanzang and I'tsing, and three diplomatic missions from Dvaravati are known to have gone to China.[12] Numismatic confirmation of this name comes from two medals found during excavations of a stupa at Nern Hin – not far from the Phra Pathom Chedi stupa, Thailand's tallest – at Nakhon Pathom, which says "sri-dvaravati-shvarapunya" or "meritorious deeds of the ruler of Dvaravati".[13] A third was found at the city of U Thong with the same inscription. All are stamped in Sanskrit.

Over forty Dvaravati sites are known in central Thailand and elements of its material culture can be seen at the Phra Pathom Chedi, a large stupa with a long history. I was struck by its small Phrapathomchedi Museum, which displays an eclectic collection of pottery beads and terracotta plaques, Buddha statues and heads, and some beautiful stone dharmachakras (Fig. 7.2). In his study of these Dvaravati dharmachakras the art historian Robert L. Brown says the significance of the dharmachakra was both religious and political: the ruler maintained his power through military means but also by using symbolism and religion. Dharmachakras therefore may well be an allusion to Chakravartin, the universal emperor or divine Buddhist king. The Thai dharmachakras are in this sense an echo of the symbolism of the Ashokan.[14]

[11] Revire (2018): 177.
[12] Murphy (2010): 45.
[13] Brown (1996): xxii.
[14] For a discussion of Ashoka and the idea of the Chakravartin, Strong (1989): 49–56.

Fig. 7.2: Dharmachakra in the Phrapathomchedi Museum, Nakhon Pathom

The duration of the integration of this symbolism within Dvaravati culture suggests it flourished roughly around the fifth century CE, the time of the Gupta dynasty in India. The mechanisms of the adoption and integration by Dvaravati elites remain mysterious,[15] but their manipulation and modification are superbly outlined in Brown's analysis of how an "Indian form is adopted but given a specific Dvaravati significance".[16] The modifications are several. Unlike the Dvaravati pillars, Indian pillars shun a socle. The Thai practice of providing this kind of base for the columnar structure above it is likely to have been adopted from early Khmer lintels.[17] And while deer frequently occur flanking a chakra in relief carvings in both India and Dvaravati, Indian art shows no three-dimensional stone deer positioned near the central wheel. Also, the three dimensional dharmachakras in Thailand are prolific: Brown analyses more than forty chakras whereas India has only four or five, the most complete of which at Amaravati reveals features much simpler than the ornately decorated wheels of Thailand.[18]

Ashoka's pillar at Sarnath includes an epigraph, whereas the Thai chakras show inscriptions on the spokes and the hubs. The placement of epigraphs on these Dvaravati dharmachakras was carefully thought through for functionality, the turning of the wheel being associated with the parts of the texts that had been recited. Chakra 5 from Phra Pathom has words evoking the four noble truths of Buddhism, appropriate since these were first taught by the Buddha at Sarnath. Chakra 6, originally from Si Thep and now in the Newark Museum collection, shows inscriptions relating to the Buddha's first sermon between spokes on both sides of the wheel. A similar epigraph in Pali from Sarnath of the second–third century – carved on a stone umbrella

[15] Assavavirulhakarn (2010): 22–3.
[16] Brown (1996): 70.
[17] Ibid.: 76.
[18] Ibid.: 162–3. To the dharmachakras in India mentioned by Brown, one may add the Phanigiri octagonal pillar whose epigraph records the donation of a chakra in the eighteenth year of the first known Ikshavaku king Rudrapurushadatta. The chakra has not been found but was likely to have originally crowned the pillar. Baums, Griffiths, Strauch, and Tournier (2016): 369–72.

and not a dharmachakra[19] – mentions the same first sermon. The only dharmachakra that we have from Sarnath exists on a pillar whose epigraph reveals a third-century BCE monarch opposed to divisions among monks and nuns – quite evidently Ashoka. The dharmachakras of Dvaravati never mention rulers. The connections between them and India lie more in the broader transmission and subsequent variant translations of Buddhism from India to South East Asia.

My early assumption of an Ashoka-inspired artistic phenomenon is reflected in Brown's admission that he too was soon disabused of this notion:

> [T]he fact that three-dimensional dharmacakrastambhas occur only in India and Dvaravati was one reason I chose to study these monuments, thinking that some direct relationship can be traced. Not only, however, does there turn out to be almost no relationship between the Indian and Dvaravati cakras in terms of patterns, design organization, and structure, but with only four Indian examples, even an analysis of Indian three-dimensional cakras becomes impossible.[20]

In short, while pillars mounted with dharmachakras were known in India much before South East Asia, and while Buddhism is the religious context shared between South and South East Asia in the first millenniun CE, the more elaborate Dvaravati chakras are remarkably different from those in India. Brown is quite right to marvel that the "mystery is how can something be different from Indian art in all its parts (like the *cakras*), yet be at the same time so completely Indian."[21]

Chiang Mai is more than 600 km north of the core area of the Dvaravati culture at Nakhon Pathom. It is located in a moun-

[19] Sahni (1914): 230.
[20] Brown (1996): 160.
[21] Ibid.: 182.

tainous region with no access to the sea, quite unlike the heart of the Dvaravati which occupies an alluvial river plain not far from the Gulf of Thailand. Within the mountains, the key plains area is the Chiang Mai–Lamphun basin. Here, chronicles came to be written in the second millennium CE with names of kings and lines of dynastic succession – some of them Indian. This makes this northern region entirely unlike Dvaravati, where no equivalent texts and no lineages similar to those in the north's chronicles are discernible.

The earliest of these Thai mountain chronicles were written in the fifteenth and sixteenth centuries against the backdrop of a developing political unity in the north.[22] This was a new phenomenon which needed to be explained by chroniclers, and which, through the process of historical recording, fostered a sense of awareness of the past.[23] The chronicles have been described as a "mix of religion, fact, and folklore", not always "strict records of historical fact".[24] Some of them, such as the *Jinakalamalipakaranam*, have a strongly religious content linking north Thailand and Sri Lanka. India and Indian kings are mentioned in them fairly regularly, one reason being the centrality of Buddhism within the chronicles, which include a general history of Buddhism beginning with the Buddha in India, before moving on to a chronological account of local kings and dynasties.

The *Jinakalamalipakaranam*, translated as "The Sheaf of Garlands of the Epochs of the Conqueror", was written in Pali by Ratanapanna Thera of Chiang Mai. Its first part, located in

---

[22] In the chronicle tradition of Thailand, the character of the past changes around the thirteenth century. Wyatt (1982): 31 says this with clarity in relation to the Tai world: "Whereas most of their chronicles up to that time are simply lists of kings or collections of legends, usually undated, in the thirteenth and fourteenth centuries they become annals of states, replete with detailed accounts of religious events and wars, of dynastic conflicts and popular movements."

[23] Ongsakul (2005): 2.

[24] Ibid.: 1.

India, has a long chronology and recounts the details of all the Buddha's lives and incarnations.[25] The narrative moves from a biography of Siddhartha Gautama and his transformation into the "Perfectly Enlightened One" to rulers like Ajatasattu and Bimbisara, the Nandas, and eventually the "Moriya clan". In this the text relies on the *Mahavamsa* to provide its own more summary account, including how the Maurya dynasty ascended the throne at Pataliputra:

> Canakka slayed the ninth, Dhanananda, and consecrated Candagutta born of the Moriya clan, as king of the entire Jambudipa. He too, reigned for twenty-four years in Pupphapura which bears the name, city of Pataliputra. His son Bindusara reigned for twenty-eight years. And Bindusara had one hundred and one sons. Among them Asoka, son of Queen Sudhamma born of the Moriya clan, killed ninety-nine leaving his uterine brother Tissa and reigned for thirty-seven years. He indeed reigned for four years even without being consecrated ruler and, on the expiry of four years, the 218th year after the passing away of the Teacher in perfect Nibbana. And again, in the third year after his consecration the Elder Nigrodha established the King together with his followers in the Dispensation with faith unwavering.[26]

Ratanapanna then offers a long description of Ashoka's patronage to Buddhism: in the very year he became a Buddhist, on the day of the lunar eclipse, he began "building 84,000 monasteries in 84,000 townships throughout Jambudipa". Soon thereafter he had his son Mahinda, then twenty years old, and Sanghamitta who was eighteen, admitted into the monastic order. Then follows the establishment of Buddhism in Sri Lanka with Ashoka sending Devanampiya Tissa "the requisites for a consecration".

---

[25] Jayawickrama (1968).
[26] Ibid.: 60–1.

The text provides information on Sri Lanka and its kings. This makes sense: the Mahavihara interpretation of Theravada Buddhism was brought to this region of Thailand by a Sinhalese forest-dwelling monastic lineage, and a monastery called Wat Suan Dok (Flower Garden Monastery) was set up outside Chiang Mai.[27] Eventually, the chronicle moves on to Haripunjaya in north Thailand and thence to an account of rulers and dynasties and the region's temples.

Ashoka resurfaces in the chronicle when it reaches the reign of a king called Adicca who ruled Haripunjaya, and the account here is amusingly coprophilic: apparently the king when in the privy was bespattered on his head and mouth by a crow. A child who had learned the crow language questioned one of the summoned crows and explained the omen. It transpired that at the very place where the privy stood the Buddha had, aeons earlier, proclaimed that in the reign of Adicca there would appear a relic. Paying heed to the crow's momentous disclosure, the king "had the privy removed, the place levelled, fumigated with frankincense and transformed into a clean place." Thereafter, upon his supplication to the heavens, a golden casket containing a relic "which was caused to have been made by the righteous monarch Asoka, emerged, by the power of the deities."[28] The chronicle attempts to historicise this event by giving it a precise chronology: "during whatsoever year the righteous monarch made the dispersal of the relics throughout the entire Jambudipa . . . in the 1383rd year after that [and] in the sixteenth year of the consecration of King Adicca, the Great Relic manifested itself in Haripunjaya."

The region's links with Sri Lanka and Sinhala monks are also emphasised in this part of the text. In the time of King Tiloka, a Bodhi tree propagated from a seed of the southern branch of the

[27] Veidlinger (2007): 3.
[28] These quotations are from Jayawickrama (1968): 106–7.

one in Sri Lanka is described as brought and planted there, and consequently, as "the Great Bodhi was planted there, the place came to be known as the Monastery of the Great Bodhi" – this being the Wat Cedi Cet Yod in Chiang Mai.

The chronicle is one which, in short, traverses India and Sri Lanka before settling into a history of north Thailand. Its genealogy, linking the Indian Ashoka and the Bodhi tree and a Sri Lankan king with Thai rulers, parallels and seems to derive from the genealogies constructed in the Pali chronicles of Sri Lanka, the intent in all cases being to establish the heaven-sanctioned rule of a regional dynasty.

There is one other chronicle of significance within the ancient history of this region, namely the Chiang Mai Chronicle. This is yet another example of the chronicle genre, though what it recounts is both similar and different from the account in the *Jinakalamalipakaranam*.

The Chiang Mai Chronicle is named after the city that was founded at the end of the thirteenth century and became a recognised site of Buddhist scholarship. The chronicle itself, like the city, was a composite work, growing over the centuries with successive authors modifying earlier texts. The manuscript that I read in translation dates to 1828, although one compilation of the text was written in the fifteenth century, shortly after the reign of King Tilokrat, who ruled from there.[29] David Wyatt and Aroonrut Wichienkeeo allude to a large number of extant versions, which reveals the popularity of this chronicle: there "are probably fewer than a dozen different versions of the royal chronicles of Siam known to scholars; but there are considerably more than a hundred versions of the Chiang Mai Chronicle which have come down to us."[30]

---

[29] Wyatt and Wichienkeeo (1998): xxxix.

[30] Ibid.: xxxi. The particular one that they used for producing an edition and translation was one that Dr Hans Penth of the Social Research Institute in Chiang Mai – after investigating seven or eight manuscripts – had considered the most complete and legible.

As with the *Jinakalamalipakaranam*, its opening pages go back to India, to a king before the Buddha attained nirvana. This was a ruler in Benares named Mahasamantaraja, who was suffused with "merit, with wisdom and physical and moral perfection".[31] Between his reign and the birth of the Buddha we are asked to believe there were a few lakh rulers. Siddhartha, we are told, was born two years before Bimbisara. His life and enlightenment are summarised in a paragraph, starting from the time he "took form in the womb of Lady Srimahamaya" to his passing away on a full moon day of the eighth month, with the funeral pyre being ignited on a Sunday.[32] Shortly after, the "Moraya" line starts with "Candagutta" (Chandragupta) and Bindusara. Ashoka Dhammaraja is the eldest of the hundred sons of Bindusara, and thus it was that he "became the *cakkavati*-king-subduing-the-Jambu-Continent". Ashoka's Buddhist son Mahinda-thera is alluded to, and shortly thereafter the description of the lineages of India ends, the India part of the chronicle being far more of a summary than the *Jinakalamalipakaranam*; in translation it takes up only a little over three pages of a text of more than two hundred pages. India is inserted more as a pretext for the author to suggest he knows the world of Buddhism, as his references to Mithila and Rajagaha, Benares and Kapilavatthu – and of course Ashoka – make clear. The author is in fact a bit of an ignoramus and a bit of an inventor: he shows no knowledge of the Maurya capital Pataliputra, he declares Ashoka the oldest son of Bindusara, and he ignores Ashoka's daughter Sanghamitta entirely, though, as seen in the Pali chronicles, she was prominent both in the Buddhist Samgha and in propagating her religion. The chronicle's interest is on the local history of dynastic succession, and soon we are with Queen Camadevi of Haripunjaya who began ruling from Lamphun in the tenth century.

In the town of Lamphun, which was once the capital of her

[31] Ibid.: 1–2.
[32] Ibid.: 3.

state, something relating to Camadevi reminded me of Ashoka. The reason I went to Lamphun was that one of my students had spent much of her working life looking at India's women rulers, and the idea of learning about a comparable Thai queen was for me sufficient motivation.[33] Apparently, when establishing her authority, Queen Camadevi had to fight off all kinds of attacks, and her success depended in no small measure on the valour of her war elephant. One of Camadevi's enemies, upon seeing the sun's rays on the tips of the tusks of this white elephant, was so frightened that he fled the battlefield. When the elephant died – if he was a white elephant he may have died of disuse – the queen built a commemorative stupa on the outskirts of Lamphun where she had his tusks buried. A stupa which stands there attracts much worship. The regular offerings to it of sugarcane and bananas are so plentiful that the dead elephant's spirit must feel it is in clover. I remember being overcome by a sense that in her solicitude for the elephant the queen shows herself more Ashokan than Ashoka. Compassion to animals was taken to a new level by the institutional worship of her white elephant. The chronicle, I felt, does not do justice to her reign, given that she ruled fifty years and died at the age of ninety-two. The chronicle's male authorship is obvious also from its interest in male rulers such as King Mangrai who, with his fourfold army, attacked and conquered many lands. Mangrai subdued large areas of northern Thailand and made Chiang Mai a major political and religious centre, which seems to me pretty standard and vastly less interesting than an idiosyncratic queen who was no doubt the only woman ruler in the known universe to have deified a white elephant.

But of all the rulers and lineages in the Chiang Mai Chronicle, the king who invokes Ashoka most clearly is a fifteenth-century

---

[33] Devika Rangachari is her name. She is the author of historical works and historical fiction, much of which centres around women.

ruler, Tilokrat. The context for his invocation of Ashoka relates to his political ambitions. A Burmese ascetic from Bagan called Mang Lung Lwang, who had come to live in Chiang Mai, is the chief protagonist here, giving advice to Tilokrat. The people who the king sent to interrogate the monk asked him if there were "ceremonies which could be performed that would make our life longer and more happy and complete".[34] In his reply the Bagan monk cites Ashoka's as a long and successful life:

> The magical arts which conduce to the flourishing of the country, and cause the Great Lord/ who rules the country to have majesty and power to subdue all the Jambu Continent, are verily like those of King Asoka, who had a long and happy life, and I have studied them fully. Those life-extending techniques are difficult of attainment. If/ the Great King really wants them, he can attain them. We will explain them all, in every detail. If they are too difficult for him, then tell me and I will not so teach him.[35]

The magic of longevity and improved rule are best exemplified by Ashoka. The monk then asks the king to build new quarters and raze parts of old Chiang Mai. The city wall which King Mangrai had built is razed and the moat filled up and levelled; the king has labourers "cut down the banyan tree which was the glory of the city of Chiang Mai,/ with its wide and beautiful shaded canopy, from its crown down to its roots", flattening the area. The monk's interest in this is to enable the construction of a palace; in fact a whole city called Si Phum is built and in it the king is consecrated "to have the royal power to subdue continents, like King Ashoka".[36]

The twist in the tale comes almost immediately when there is considerable disarray rather than glory as a consequence of the building of Si Phum. Chiang Mai is defiled and sullied by all

[34] Wyatt and Wichienkeeo (1998): 98.
[35] Ibid.: 98.
[36] Ibid.: 99.

kinds of excreta, and the country as a whole is soon in a pretty pickle. Eventually, intercepting two agents of the ruler of the South, Borommaracha, Tilokrat learns that the Burmese ascetic was no holy man but an imposter who had been paid a thousand units of gold by Borommaracha to destroy the tree which was the glory of Chiang Mai and supplant chaos in its stead. The story ends with Tilokrat having the imposter monk thrown into a river, the moral of the tale being that kings seeking longevity and power can be fooled by poseurs who bandy the names of immortal kings such as Ashoka. Shakespeare, as always, can be relied on to supply a line that sums it all up poetically: "he that is so yoked by a fool,/ Methinks, should not be chronicled for wise."[37]

Tilokrat may have been made an ass of by a Burmese imposter, but he was otherwise far from being an ass – he built a fine temple in Chiang Mai modelled on the Mahabodhi temple of Bagan which, in turn, was said to be a copy of one in India. The Wat Cedi Cet Yod in Chiang Mai is architecturally impressive, but its resemblance to the Mahabodhi temple in India is pretty faint (Fig. 7.3.). Still, Tilokart may perhaps have known that an early temple built by Ashoka had been copied in Bagan and was worth replicating in his own territory – the architectural copying of an earlier great king's work being a regular strategy in the repertoire of later kings wanting to enhance the credibility of their rule. One great scholar of South and South East Asia has pointed out that the Buddhist conception of kingship and polity here was premised on the image of Ashoka as the "great precedent and model for some of the emergent polities of South and Southeast Asia."[38]

The most spectacular integration and modification of the historical Ashoka I found was, however, in south Thailand. A whole dynasty of rulers chronicled there bore his name from the twelfth

---

[37] *The Two Gentlemen of Verona*, I.i.42–3.
[38] Tambiah (1976): 5.

Fig. 7.3: Wat Cedi Cet Yod in Chiang Mai,
apparently modelled on the Mahabodhi temple in Bihar

century till the end of the thirteenth century.[39] These kings were known collectively as Sri Thammasokarat (Sri Dharrma Ashoka Raja) and their base was centred in Nakhon Si Thammarat – meaning the city of Dharrmaraja (Fig. 7.4) – the city with which this book began.

This town's present avatar is very different from its past geocultural significance. In the early part of the second millennium CE

---

[39] The manuscripts of the chronicles were likely to be of the nineteenth century but contained earlier material. For instance, an inscription from Vat Hua Vian in Jaiya mentioned a King Shri Dharmaraja whose personal name is Chandrabhanu – he is also mentioned within the Nakhon chronicles. The same Chandrabhanu figures in the mid-thirteenth century in evidence from Sri Lanka. See Wyatt (1975): 39 and 47.

Fig. 7.4: Modern statue of Ashoka Dhamma-raja in Nakhon Si Thammarat

a number of political entities here had names like Lankasuka (probably in the Patani region), Takkola (in the present-day Kedah area), and Tambralinga (in the vicinity of Nakhon Si Thammarat).[40] Dan-ma-lin (or Tambralinga) continued to be

[40] Ibid.: 1.

used in Chinese accounts of the fourteenth century, even after the name Nakhon Si Thammarat had become more popular in the late twelfth century.

The story linking India and Nakhon as it exists in two versions of a local chronicle was published by an American historian, David Wyatt, as *The Crystal Sands* (1975). Wyatt tells us that, as perceived by its local chroniclers, the earliest history of Nagara Sri Dharrmaraja had no direct link with the classical states of South East Asia such as Angkorian Cambodia, or Srivijaya, or even Bagan. What gave these chroniclers a categorical sense of continuity – bridging numerous abandonments of the principality – was their strong sense that Nagara Sri Dharrmaraja was special because it had been blessed with the sacred presence of the corporeal relics of the Buddha.[41] Maps show that, for a long time, the sandy coastal peninsula stretching from Sankhla to Nagara Sri Dharrmaraja was called the "Tooth Peninsula (Dantahlem)". This holy presence of relics, and local identity wrapped around them, is the starting point of how this state saw itself constituted and fitted into its local environment.

The relics were described as being originally in India, their location in the subcontinent being alternatively called "Dantapuri" and "Nagarpuri". In this location, two children of the ruler, Kosharaja, and his queen, Mahadevi, were attacked by another ruler, Ankusraja. One of the children was a daughter called Hemjala, and the other was a younger son called Dandakumar.[42] The children had been attacked by the rival king because they were in possession of the holy tooth relic. To escape their attackers, Dandakumar and Hemjala boarded a boat and left for Sri Lanka (Fig. 7.5), Hemjala having wrapped the relics into her hair.

Their boat capsized, the two lost their way, they struggled through a forest, and finally they found themselves at a crystalline

[41] Ibid.: 65.
[42] The summary of the story as contained in the two versions of the chronicle is based on ibid.

Fig. 7.5: Modern statues of Dandakumar and Hemjala

beach surrounded by the sea, where they buried the sacred relics. A little later, on the advice of a local Mahathera, they unearthed the relics and attempted taking them to Sri Lanka, but the boat was stranded in the doldrums and its crew, believing that the brother and sister were the cause of the stymie, tried to kill them. However, they were saved by the same Mahathera, the boat managed to sail on, and the relics ultimately reached Sri Lanka. There the ruler got four Brahmanas and the two in possession of the relics to again sail away, with one part of the relics arriving again at the crystalline beach, and another part going back to Dandapuri.

The Thailand part of this rather shaggy dog story is the crystalline beach; subsequent political events, in which the various Dharrmasokarajas figure, unfold off this beach. It is here that the local kings build cities, create the chedi (stupa), renovate it, and so on and so forth. Today, it is the great stupa at Wat Mahathat that dominates Nakhon, its dome and square base surrounded by statues of elephants and showing the strong influence of medieval Sri Lankan art.

The Nakhon chronicles are naturally interested in the political significance of the relics. They present the first ruler of this dynasty establishing himself here after escaping from an epidemic at Hongsawadi (Pegu) in Myanmar. This first ruler was Dharrmasokaraja and he wished to found a city at the Beach of the Crystal Sand. But he was thwarted by yet another epidemic, so he decided to build on a hill, which was how Nakhon was founded in around the twelfth century. A chedi was constructed for the relics – none of the different versions of the chronicles mention how the relics were found.

Till this point the story seems to echo Ashokan elements that connect with the obsession of rulers with Buddhist relics and the construction of stupas. The legend of the Indian Ashoka having built 84,000 stupas here I have already mentioned; the chronicled versions, however, speak only of the building of one stupa. In conclusion, the chronicles take the amazing turn discussed at the start of this book, where the Indian Ashoka becomes a supplicant vis-à-vis the Dhammasokaraja of Nagara Sri Dharmmaraja – a tale that I do not need to retell in detail here, but which does in sum show Ashoka as, once again, the vital link between the Buddhism of Nakhon's kings and the ideal template for governance. A later king, Thammasok II, is shown arranging for the "erection of a great reliquary like that which Sri Dharrmasokaraja had made earlier", and planting Bodhi trees.[43] And yet another king, Thammasok V, is recorded as restoring the region's great stupa.

What underlies these local chronicles is the need for a new dynasty to present itself as antique. This it does by looking back and binding the region and its kings with a larger geography of relics around South Asia, around the Buddha, and around Ashoka. The interesting twist in the story, where Ashoka becomes a supplicant, is done by chroniclers who were perhaps eager to curry favour with their rulers by showing them as the custodians of a power so sacred that even the great Indian king sought it from them.

What the chronicles highlight and what exists on the ground in Nakhon Si Thammarat differs in other ways as well. Situated in the isthmian tract between two oceans, the area has had the openness of an island to trade and cultural influences. Within the Nakhon area are five places which have yielded Dong Song bronze drums of Vietnamese inspiration.[44] There are also lots of Chinese ceramics in the area south of Nakhon city dating from the mid- to late-thirteenth century.[45] There are Vishnu images too: in fact, the area shows the highest density in all of South East Asia of images referred to as "the conch shell on the hip type" – where a conch is held in the god's hand next to his hip. Many of these go as far back as the fifth century CE.[46] Siva lingas have surfaced in the region, many of them on display in the Nakhon National Museum. Three yonis, or the base on which the linga is placed, have been discovered. An archaeologist, Preecha Noonsuk, is

---

[43] This and the following lines are based on Munro-Hay (2001), ch. 5.
[44] Noonsuk (2013): 69.
[45] Ibid.: 194.
[46] Ibid.: 90.

probably right in assuming that the Great Reliquary was established on formerly Hindu sacred space, for stone fragments and sculptures of Hindu shrines can still be seen.[47] Yet nothing of the ancient Hindu kind really figures in the chronicles, which are only concerned with tales around Buddhist relics and the Thai namesakes of Ashoka. Theravada Buddhism became predominant here, with Sri Lanka central in a network of exchanges of monks and images and in the borrowing and refashioning of legends.

The world beyond Ashoka's time in Thailand, it became clear to me, was peopled by cultures that did not simply regurgitate old and familiar histories. They walked their own paths, cherry-picking symbols and beliefs, constructing chronicles and compendia. In relation to Ashoka, new myths sprang up from old ones. They had little to do with the historical emperor and everything to do with new ways of creating cultural identities and framing political lineages.

[47] Ibid.: 209–10.

Fabricating Remembrance

Having stopped in my tracks at Nakhon Si Thammarat, where this book began, I looked back at my travels in search of Ashoka and the question I asked was – what emerges from the several imprints of the emperor that I saw?

I certainly encountered much variety in historical memory. Sanchi was where he had delivered a stern message to the Samgha, and later, it seemed to me, the Buddhist community there had struck back. Instead of showcasing his power as an emperor, it had memorialised the limits of his influence. At Junagadh the Maurya monarch had positioned edicts but not thought it necessary to record his renovations to the Sudarshana Lake: his work there was only remembered many centuries later by the king of another dynasty. What Kanaganahalli displayed was an almost incidental insertion of Ashoka within a litany of Satavahana kings on a magnificent stupa. Ironically, this was where his ideas had been made visible within his own lifetime; now, the king had been given a face and a name. At Barabar Ashoka, and the Ajivikas whom he and his family had patronised, had either been scrubbed out or simply forgotten. In Sri Lanka, Ashoka's remembrance was more the remembrance of his children. From the shores of Sri Lanka, stories of Ashoka, alongside the chronicles that speak of him, had travelled to Myanmar and Thailand, where he seemed to have become the ideal Buddhist king worthy of emulation. New ways of visualising the emperor had emerged: he was now an inveterate stupa builder in some locations and elsewhere a petitioner pleading relics from a namesake.

Various threads, as far as I could see, bound these diverse artistic and literary remembrances – in sculpture and in paintings, in chronicles and in epigraphs. Looking at the whole lot as a single composition or imagined frieze on an imagined stupa entrance made me ask whether a single historical core was identifiable within these diverse remembrances. Or whether in fact it made more sense to see each remembrance as so individual, discrete, and distant from the historically recorded king that every remembrance was a purposive distortion verging on a deliberate forgetting.

The truth is that both ways of seeing Ashoka's afterlife are possible: the diversity in images of him is substantial, but the derivation of each is recognisably from a core. And if I were allowed no more than a single sentence to define that core, it would be that Ashoka never stopped being remembered as the exemplary Buddhist king.

Going backwards in time, his own stoneware is the first template for those who later wished to recall him. And the most widely circulating image on stone is the re-rendering of the Sarnath pillar with its magnificent lion capital. Sculptors in far-flung locations at Buddhist sites – from Mathura and Bharhut to Sanchi, Amaravati, and Kanaganahalli – chiselled stone slabs to arrive at copies showing a dharmachakra aloft a pillar.

It all began soon after the disappearance of the Maurya dynasty and continued into the early centuries CE. The sculpting of large dharmachakras crowning pillar capitals could only have happened if those who prepared the designs had either seen the Sarnath pillar or were provided detailed sketches of it. Sometimes they made changes, as for instance when the lions were replaced by elephants. In Sanchi the sculptors may well have thought that the elephant, associated so intimately with the birth of the Buddha, was as good an animal to put on top of a pillar as glowering lions. The dharmachakras of Thailand also show a play of basic similarity and superimposed difference: dharmachakras on pillars stay unchanged from the Indian prototype, but the intricate carvings and inscriptions on the Thai versions of the wheels of law introduce a locally preferred variation. The historical original is remembered but not exactly replicated. Some features are retained and others axed in the act of refashioning.

Ashoka's Sarnath pillar seems to have become *the* signifier of the Buddha's first sermon. Whether it also expanded into becoming an emblem of Ashoka remains an open question. As a human figure, Ashoka could not be anchored around a historical template. Imperial representations of him were not fashioned in his time because the tradition of imaging a king on coins and paintings and sculpture had not yet begun in North India. There is therefore simply no way of knowing what the emperor looked like. So the question of interest is how they put a face on him later and what elements they chose to represent his life with.

At both Sanchi and Kanaganahalli Ashoka is almost always represented with people. He is either with one of his wives and female companions, or accompanied by an army, or a crowd of worshippers. Ashoka at Kanaganahalli looks young and slim in comparison with the older, slightly pot-bellied emperor at Sanchi – it does help explain the queen of the Kanaganahalli Ashoka casting that very female gaze in his direction. But the contrasts in Ashoka's representation at the two locations are equally interesting. At Kanaganahalli the holy thread across his chest makes him appear a Brahman, which was not how he was remembered elsewhere, nor at Sanchi. The caste symbol is perhaps explicable as an insertion by local social compulsions or the sculptor's personal background. Perhaps both.

No such mystifying reason attaches to Ashoka's imagining in relation to the Bodhi tree and his queen. His Eighth Rock Edict mentions Sambodhi (Mahabodhi) as a place to which he journeyed in the tenth year of his consecration. His queen does not seem to have accompanied him and he proclaims the visit as life-changing for his own self. It seems plausible that this was Ashoka's way of connecting himself with the Buddha, whose enlightenment had arrived under the Bodhi tree. The underlying idea is a transformation via epiphany in both cases. And the transformation, though initially a solitary occurrence, subsequently involved the multitudes, for Ashoka's dealings with his subjects changed after this trip to the tree. Pleasure tours became tours of morality and these "dharma-yatras" involved gifts to Brahmans and Shramanas as well as support to the aged – "supporting (them) with gold, visiting the people of the country, instructing (them) in morality, and questioning (them) about morality..."[1]

The royal metamorphosis, coming from the horse's mouth, should really have been eye candy for artists and sculptors commissioned to re-represent the most monumental conversion to Buddhism known in history. And yet it does not seem to have been seen this way among those who hired subsequent sculptors. Instead, it was either a grief-stricken king, as at Sanchi – bemoaning Queen Tishyarakshita having almost succeeded in killing off the precious tree – or a king who comes with his (presumably) repentant queen. Kanaganahalli shows Ashoka in the same mould, as a royal devotee of the tree. This later fascination with rendering a pilgrim king worshipping the Bodhi tree is remote from what Ashoka himself provided. Sculptural tableaux

---

[1] This is from the Girnar version of the Eighth Rock Edict in Hultzsch (1924): 14–15.

tell tame stories, as against the compelling messaging of Ashoka himself who saw his visit to Mahabodhi as greatly transforming the nature of his kingship. He, rather than the Bodhi tree, is the centre of his own story.

As Constantine is in Europe in relation to Christianity, the spread of the religion, and the Nicene Creed, so Ashoka is in relation to Buddhism, the outward expansion of his faith, and the Third Buddhist Council. It would thus seem logical for memorialisations of him in lands far removed from his own to have strengthened the association between the location of the Buddha's enlightenment and the Great Sage's most famous kingly convert. What in fact happens is that Ashoka's personal life is relegated in favour of his achievement as the great Buddhist proselytiser and builder of shrines. It has been shown that the importance attached to the Mahabodhi temple is palpable in Myanmar from epigraphs, representations in temple models, and depictions on seals and plaques.[2] At Bagan in Myanmar and at Chiang Mai in Thailand temples were built in imitation of the Mahabodhi shrine. South East Asian rulers also sent "repair" missions to Mahabodhi, epigraphs pertaining to them showing Ashoka prominently. A thirteenth-century epigraph from Bodh Gaya, written in the Burmese language and script, recording a repair mission by a King Dhammaraja from Burma, implicitly honours the building of the original temple there by Ashoka: "When 218 years of the Buddha's dispensation had elapsed, one of the 84,000 *caityas* built by Siri Dhammasoka (i.e. the Maurya emperor Asoka), king of Jambudvipa, at the place where the milk rice offering had been made [a reference to Sujata's offering of "payasa" to Siddhartha at Bodh Gaya] fell into ruin due to the stress of age and time."[3] A similar association was made more

---

[2] Singh (2014): 48–52.

[3] This is what is suggested in the relevant part of the inscription as presented by Singh (2014): 49 from the translation offered by Gordon H. Luce. For an early translation of this inscription, Sein Ko (1911–12): 119.

than five hundred years later when, in 1875, Mindon, king of Burma, sought permission to renovate the Mahabodhi complex: he too invoked Ashoka. Two millennia had passed, with many phases of renovation since, and yet the Burmese king wanted to undertake the "repair of the sacred chaitya built by King Dharmasoka over the site of the Aparajita throne."[4]

Beyond all this, what is the geography of India imaged in the retelling of the life and times of Ashoka?

The emperor himself provided glimpses of Mahabodhi and other Buddhist sacred places, all in the Nepal terai. We meet him at Nigali Sagar (or Niglihawa) where, some four years after his Mahabodhi visit, he expanded and rebuilt a stupa dedicated to the Buddha Konakamana (or Kanakmuni) and put up a pillar. At Lumbini, the birthplace of the Buddha, we see him putting up a commemorative pillar and reducing agricultural taxes on the village of Lumbini. At Gotihawa, he embeds one more pillar.

Beyond this pilgrim circuit, a surprisingly large political universe is evident in Ashoka's words. His edicts allude to kings and regions located across three continents, from Greece to Egypt to Tamraparni. Considering South East Asia's later interest in Ashoka, it would have seemed retrospectively reciprocal for him to have shown some consciousness of the world to his east, but there is no evidence of his having sent emissaries or missions in that direction, as he seems to have done southwards.

Two other aspects of voyages in search of Ashoka interest me as I conclude this account of my own. The first is what I see as Ashoka's own voyage in search of what, after the Kalinga war, he had come to consider his deepest spiritual self – which is

---

[4] This figured in the text of the proposals sent by the foreign minister of the Government of Burma when he wrote to the governor general. Mentioned by Ahir (1994): 86.

presented as his pilgrimage with Upagupta, a Buddhist monk from Mathura, accompanying whom he is shown in search of residual signs of the Buddha. This pilgrimage is described in the *Ashokavadana*. It was no improvised or ordinary travel, we learn, but a pilgrimage of the greatest seriousness and sanctity as Ashoka wanted to "honour the places where the Blessed One lived". In such sites he also wanted to position his own presence in the form of shrines to his deity. The king and the monk were accompanied by a fourfold army and "perfumes, garlands and flowers" which would have required a retinue of carriers and caretakers.[5] No details are provided about the technology of travel, nor how many days were spent on the road. The account centres on the king's emotions as he is taken around by Upagupta.

The manner in which his pilgrimage is presented makes it seem that Ashoka apparently knew very little about the life of the Buddha until the instruction he received from Upagupta. At Lumbini he conversed with the spirit of the tree whose branch the Buddha's mother had grasped while giving birth to him. On hearing this account of the birth of the Blessed One, he offered 100,000 pieces of gold at Lumbini and built a chaitya there. Accounts that he hears of the Buddha at Kapilavastu, at the Bodhi tree, at Rishipatana (Sarnath), and at Kushinagari are followed by similar giftings of gold and construction of a chaitya. Nowhere do pillars – the most visible and abiding markers of Ashoka now – figure in this account. In fact Ashoka's construction of pillars, which are so central to our own understanding of Ashoka's Buddhism, is ignored in the *Ashokavadana*.

This was not because the pillars had disappeared: some centuries later they featured prominently in the accounts of Chinese Buddhist pilgrims to India. And this brings me to the second point of concluding interest – the travels of devout pilgrims who, even if they were not in explicit search of Ashoka, did notice

---

[5] Strong (1989): 244.

his persistence in Indian Buddhist contexts. Faxian, the first of them, came with a group of monks in the fifth century CE. This man's original name was Kung, but he assumed the religious title by which he is known to us, and also called himself Shih, or Sakyaputra, meaning the disciple or son of Sakya (the Buddha).[6] Faxian is known to have become a novice (sramanera) in a monastery at the age of three. The start of his travelogue gives the reason for his travel: "Fa-hian, when formerly residing at Ch'ang-an, regretted the imperfect condition of the *Vinaya pitaka*."[7] Thus, he resolved to go to India for "the purpose of seeking the rules and regulations (of the *Vinaya*)." When the Buddhist priests at Jetavana heard that these monks had come from "the land of Han" they exclaimed: "to think that men from the frontiers of the earth should come so far as this from a desire to search for the law." Faxian and his companions were the first Chinamen they had seen. Faxian, and these ancient pilgrims generally, were far more indefatigable in search of the Buddha than their counterparts in our time, evident from the fact that Faxian took some fourteen years to get back to China, where he composed the history of his travels, passing away at the age of eighty-six.

Faxian's travels were a variant on anthropological fieldwork, a kind of ethnographic documentation of what he noticed, ranging from the topography of the lands through which he passed to the sorts of clothes that people wore, the festivals and tales around places and people, the nature of shrines (Buddhist and Brahmanic) and monasteries, and a great deal else. Kings are invariably mentioned in his account – Ajatshatru, Bimbisara, Ashoka, and Kanishka, for instance – as well as many unnamed monarchs. Ashoka's visibility across the Buddhist landscape is conspicuous in Faxian, who mentions many Ashokan pillars and the legends woven around them that he heard. An example of

[6] Beal (1906): xi.
[7] Ibid.: xxiii.

this is the pillar at Sankisa (now in Uttar Pradesh). In legends, this was where the Buddha descended from the Trayastrimasa heaven (a world inhabited by "devas") to preach the law, his descent being by a three-tiered ladder. Once he was down, the tiers disappeared, except for seven steps that remained visible. Apparently

> Ashoka, wishing to discover the utmost depths to which these ladders went, employed men to dig down and examine it. They went on digging till they came to the yellow spring (the earth's foundation), but yet had not come to the bottom. The king, deriving from this an increase of faith and reverence, forthwith built over the ladders a *vihara*, and facing the middle flight he placed a standing figure (of Buddha) sixteen feet high. Behind the *vihara* he erected a stone pillar thirty cubits high and on the top placed the figure of a lion. Within the pillar on the four sides are figures of the Buddha; both within and without it shining and bright as glass.[8]

The Ashokan lion became central in Faxian's account of the settling of a dispute between monks and heretics over whether this specific place belonged to one or the other. Both parties agreed that if the vihara area belonged to the Buddhists, there would be some "supernatural proof" thereof. The proof emanated from the stone lion on the Ashokan pillar when it "uttered a loud roar". The ensuing shock and awe ensured that the heretics meekly withdrew their dispute.

Some two hundred years later Xuanzang, an even more famous Chinese pilgrim, travelled from Kashmir and Punjab to Bihar, Assam, and the peninsula. He was born Chen Hui around 600 CE and ordained around the age of twenty. His interest in Indian Buddhist sites was to procure original works and learn the doctrines directly from teachers in the originating country.[9] After a fifteen-year sojourn he returned to China, twenty horses

---

[8] Ibid.: xl–xli.
[9] Sen (2006): 29. Also see Deeg (2018) and Brose (2021).

trotting along saddled with the manuscripts and relics he had collected.[10] His observations take in monasteries, ruined cities, stupas, the myths surrounding them, and Ashokan pillars and stupas. He found the Lumbini pillar broken in the middle – apparently it had on it the figure of a horse which had at some point "by the contrivance of a wicked dragon" sundered in the middle and fallen to the ground.[11] He found the monolith at Sarnath glistening and as bright as jade, "and all those who pray frequently before it see from time to time, according to their petitions, figures with good or bad signs."[12] His description of the stone pillar at Vaishali holds good even today for it still has the figure of a lion as its apex. These Chinese texts document a variety of remembrance wholly missing in the *Ashokavadana*.

Retracing the footsteps of the Chinese pilgrims, Alexander Cunningham relied on them in the nineteenth century as infallible guides when identifying the places they had visited, seeing the features he encountered on the ground through signposts in their accounts. Xuanzang he found the most reliable of ancient travellers: in Bodh Gaya, "several of the objects enumerated by the Chinese pilgrim I have been able to identify from their exact correspondence with his description."[13] Cunningham's correlation of the Chinese texts with residual material traces helped solidify the modern image of ancient India which had taken a decisive direction with James Prinsep's deciphering of Brahmi and Kharoshthi, the revelations contained in the scripts being in effect the discovery of the historical Ashoka.

Ironically, while much of the epigraphic, architectural, and "concrete" evidence of Ashoka is in Indian locations, his textual future was ensured in the Buddhist literature outside India, Buddhism having largely been marginalised in the domain of its

[10] Singhal (1984): 73.
[11] Beal (1884): 24.
[12] Ibid.: 45.
[13] Cunningham (1871): 5.

origins and having to migrate over the Himalaya, as well as to the far south and far east of the subcontinent. The basic import of the chronicles of Sri Lanka and South East Asia is well expressed by the French scholar François Lagirarde in his description of the range of holy and kingly protagonists and their archetypal actions in Buddhist narratives of north Thailand. In these the Buddha, unsurprisingly, occupies pole position, but Ashoka frequently appears too, and the Frenchman's description of this in the north Thai chronicles works as a pithy conclusion of how, over my travels, I too found him remembered:

> the reference here is the character called *thammikarat* (Dhammikaraja), understood as a king, or kings, followers of the Dharma, pious Buddhist kings highly respected as keepers of (social) justice. Many *tamnan* give accounts of King Asoka without details about his biography, as we may know it. However, he is frequently depicted, similar to the Buddha, as a great traveller who eventually visited Lanna by himself (for instance in the *Tamnan Cho Phrae* or the *Tamnan Sela That Laem*). However, Ashoka is taken as an ideal which many local *thammikarat* will defend: these righteous kings are both mythical and historical. As an official title, "dhammikaraja" has been known in the pre-Lanna period (in Hariphunchai at the beginning of the twelfth century) and was used in all later Thai/Tai kingdoms, including Lanna.[14]

Given what Lagirarde says about a realm so distant from India, you would expect Buddhist kings in India to recall Ashoka in similar ways and even more fondly. But, though I searched for Ashoka in the epigraphic imprints of the Kushana rulers of north-west India and the Pala rulers of the east and among the Maitrakas of Gujarat and even the Odisha dynasts such as the Bhaumakaras, I did not find him among any of them. The only memorialisation of him that I have seen in words within the country are those recorded on the instructions of Rudradaman in

---

[14] Lagirarde (2012): 86.

Fig. 8.1: Nehru with Burmese premier U Nu at Sanchi when Buddhist relics were returned by the UK. U Nu's autobiography calls Nehru the reincarnation of Ashoka

Junagadh. The proper, worthy, and much-needed memorialisation of Ashoka as a ruler by an Indian ruler happens only in the twentieth century with the erudite Jawaharlal Nehru.

Resembling Ashoka as a ruler, Nehru was for two decades after 1947 the unquestioned head of an Indian state roughly similar in size to the Ashokan empire; and, like the ancient king, Nehru was his own "sutradhara" (narrator). He invoked Ashoka on crucial public occasions, most notably when a resolution in the Constituent Assembly about India's flag was moved in 1947. The Ashokan wheel in the Indian flag, he said, was something "which all of us have seen, the one at the top of the capital of the Asokan column and in many other places. That wheel is a symbol of India's ancient culture; it is a symbol of the many things that India has stood for in the ages." The Ashokan wheel made Nehru feel "exceedingly happy that in this sense indirectly we have associated with this flag of ours not only this emblem but in the sense the name of Asoka, one of the most magnificent names not only in India's history but in world history."[15]

The wheel on top of the pillar could not in fact have been seen in its entirety by Nehru or any other Indian because only a few of its fragments had been recovered. More important, however, than the material reality of the wheel was its symbolism: as a symbol it was associated via Ashoka's Sarnath pillar with the Buddhist faith and had now been made the national emblem of a new country's civilisational heritage. Some years later one historian provided a historical anchor to Nehru's idea by showing that the dharmachakra on the top of the lion capital at Sarnath was "not a sectarian concept but was the fruit of a number of religious, philosophic and cult motifs which received universal approval for thousands of years in the accumulated tradition of the Indian people."[16]

With such dramatic appropriations of antiquity are the identities and emblems of nation-states forged and communities imagined. If you look, as I have tried to do in this book, at how a variety of rulers and institutions harnessed Ashoka and reconstructed his image in relation to their own political and religious aspirations, an ancient artificer, a medieval chronicler, and a modern prime minister appear in the same mould. Collectively, they show us that this is how it really is: this is how the past is remembered and public memory given shape. It is done by twisting, warping, distorting, beautifying, prettifying, resculpting, reimagining, and reshaping. For all history is, in the end, the malleable handmaid of those in pursuit of political power.

---

[15] For this and other elements which made Ashoka a major figure in Nehru's quest as a political leader, Vajpeyi (2012): 194–200.

[16] Agrawala (1964): ii.

Bibliography

Agrawala, Vasudeva. S. 1964. *The Wheel Flag of India – Chakra-Dhvaja*. Varanasi: Prithivi Prakashan.

Amar, Abhishek. 2012. "Buddhist Responses to Brahmana Challenges in Medieval India: Bodhgaya and Gaya". *Journal of the Royal Asiatic Society* 22 (1): 155–85.

Assavavirulhakarn. 2010. *The Ascendancy of Theravada Buddhism in Southeast Asia*. Chiang Mai: Silkworm Books.

Amin, Shahid. 1988. "Gandhi as Mahatma: Gorakhpur District, Eastern U.P. 1921–22", in Ranajit Guha and Gayatri Chakravorty Spivak, eds, *Selected Subaltern Studies*. New Delhi: Oxford University Press.

Bailey, Greg, and Richard Gombrich, ed. and trans. 2005. *Love Lyrics by Amaru, Bhartrhari, and by Bilhana*. New York: New York University Press.

Bakker, Hans. 2010. "Royal Patronage and Religious Tolerance: The Formative Period of Gupta-Vakataka Culture". *Journal of the Royal Asiatic Society* 20 (4): 461–75.

Basham, A.L. 1951 (rpntd 2009). *History and Doctrines of the Ajivikas – A Vanished Indian Religion*. Delhi: Motilal Banarsidass.

Baums, Stephan, Arlo Griffiths, Ingo Strauch, and Vincent Tournier. 2016. "Early Inscriptions of Andhra Desa: Results of Fieldwork in January and February 2016". *Bulletin de l'Ecole Fracaise d'Extreme-Orient*, 102: 355–98.

Beal, Samuel. 1906. *Buddhist Records of the Western World*, volume 1. London: Kegan Paul, Trench, Trubner & Co.

Beglar, J.D., and A. Cunningham. 1878 (rpntd 2000). *Report of a Tour Through the Bengal Provinces*, Archaeological Survey of India Volume VIII. New Delhi: Archaeological Survey of India.

Begley, Vimala. 1988. "Rouletted Ware at Arikamedu: A New Approach". *American Journal of Archaeology*, 92 (3): 427–40.

Begum, Sultan Jahan. 1922 & 1927. *An Account of My Life*, vols II and III. Bombay: The Times Press.

Bellina, Berenice, *et al.* 2014. "The Development of Coastal Polities in the Upper-Thai-Malay Peninsula", in Nicolas Revire and Stephen A. Murphy, ed., *Before Siam – Essays in Art and Archaeology*. Bangkok: River Books & The Siam Society, 68–89.

Bhandarkar, Devadatta Ramkrishna (revised by), Bahadurchand Chhabra and Govind Swamirao Gai, ed. 1981. *Inscriptions of the Early Gupta Kings: Corpus Inscriptionum Indicarum III*. New Delhi: Archaeological Survey of India.

Bhandarkar, Ramkrishna Gopal. 1928 (3rd edn). *Early History of the Dekkan Down to the Mahomedan Conquest*. Calcutta: Chuckervertty, Chatterjee & Co., Ltd.

Brose, Benjamin. 2021. *Xuanzang – China's Legendary Pilgrim and Translator*. Colorado: Shambhala Publications, Inc.

Brown, Robert L. 1996. *The Dvaravati Wheels of the Law and the Indianization of South East Asia*. Leiden, New York, Koln: E.J. Brill.

Burgess, J.A.S. 1886 (rpntd 1996). *The Buddhist Stupas of Amaravati and Jaggayyapeta in the Krishna District, Madras Presidency*. New Delhi: Archaeological Survey of India.

Chattopadhyay, Rupendra Kumar. 2014. "The Satavahanas and Their Successors", in Dilip K. Chakrabarti and Makkhan Lal, ed., *History of Ancient India Volume IV*. New Delhi: Vivekananda International Foundation and Aryan Books International, 71–95.

Chhabra, B. Ch. 1949–50. "Intwa Clay Sealing". *Epigraphia Indica*, XXVIII: 174–5.

Chaisuwan, Boonyarit. 2011. "Early Contacts Between India and the Andaman Coast in Thailand from the Second Century BCE to Eleventh Century CE", in Pierre-Yves Manguin, A. Mani, and Geoff Wade, ed., *Early Interactions Between South and Southeast Asia – Reflections on Cross-Cultural Exchange*. Singapore and New Delhi: Institute of Southeast Asian Studies and Manohar, 83–111.

Coningham, Robin A.E. 1995. "Monks, Caves and Kings: A Reassessment of the Nature of Early Buddhism in Sri Lanka". *World Archaeology*, 27 (2): 222–42.

Cornwall, Owen T.A. 2020. "Alexander and the Astrolabe in Persianate India: Imagining Empire in the Delhi Sultanate". *The Indian Economic and Social History Review*, 57 (2): 1–31.

Cousens, Henry. 1891. "Report on the Boria or Lakha Medi Stupa Near Junagadh". *Journal of the Royal Asiatic Society of Bengal*, 17–23.

Cunningham, A. 1871 (rpntd 2000). *Four Reports Made During the Years 1862-63-64-65*, Archaeological Survey of India Volume I. New Delhi: Archaeological Survey of India.

———. 1854 (rpntd 1997). *The Bhilsa Topes*. New Delhi: Munshiram Manoharlal Publishers Pvt. Ltd.

Das, G.K. 1977. *E.M. Forster's India*. London: Macmillan.

Deeg, Max, 2018. "The Historical Turn: How Chinese Buddhist Travelogues Changed Western Perception of Buddhism". *Hualin International Journal of Buddhist Studies* 1.1: 43–75.

Dehejia, Vidya. 1997 (rpntd 2005). *Discourse in Early Buddhist Art – Visual Narratives of India*. New Delhi: Munshiram Manoharlal Publishers Pvt. Ltd.

Dharamsey, Virchand. 2012. *Bhagwanlal Indraji – The First Indian Archaeologist*. Vadodara: Darshak Itihas Nidhi.

Durosielle, Chas. 1921. *Archaeological Survey of Burma: A List of Inscriptions Found in Burma – Part I – The List of Inscriptions Arranged in the Order of Their Dates*. Rangoon: Superintendent of Government Printing.

Edde, Anne-Marie. 2011. *Saladin*. Massachusetts and London: The Belknap Press of Harvard University Press.

Falk, Harry. 2006. *Ashokan Sites and Artefacts: A Source-book with Bibliography*. Mainz am Rhein: Verlag Philipp von Zabern.

Fell, Edward. 1834. "Description of an Ancient and Remarkable Monument Near Bhilsa". *Journal of the Asiatic Society of Bengal*, III: 490–4.

Fleet, John Faithfull. 1998. *Corpus Inscriptionum Indicarum Volume III: Inscriptions of the Early Gupta Kings and Their Successors*. Calcutta: Superintendent of Government Printing.

Forster, E.M. 1924 (rpntd 2005). *A Passage to India*. London: Penguin.

Fraser-Lu, Sylvia, and Donald M. Stadtner. 2015. *Buddhist Art of Myanmar*. New Haven and London: Asia Society Museum in association with Yale University Press.

Fynes, R.C.C. 1995. "The Religious Patronage of the Satavahana Dynasty". *South Asian Studies*, 11: 43–50.

Geiger, Wilhelm. 1912 (1964 edn). *The Mahavamsa or The Great Chronicle of Ceylon*. London: Luzac & Company Ltd.

Ghosh, Suchandra. 2014. "Viewing Our Shared Past through Buddhist Votive Tables Across Eastern India, Bangladesh and Peninsular India", in Upinder Singh and Parul Pandya Dhar, ed., *Asian Encounters – Exploring Connected Histories*. New Delhi: Oxford University Press, 189–201.

Godakumbura, C. 1968. "Kantarodai". *The Journal of the Ceylon Branch of the Royal Asiatic Society*, 67–85.

Gokhale, 2004. "Sri Lanka in Early Indian Inscriptions". *Annals of the Bhandarkar Oriental Research Institute*, 85: 135–9.

Guha, Sumit. 2019. *History & Collective Memory in South Asia*. Ranikhet: Permanent Black.

Gupta, Ekta, M.B. Rajani, and Srikumar Menon. 2019. "Remote Sensing Investigation of the Buddhist Archaeological Landscape Around Sannati, India". *Journal of Archaeological Science Reports*, 25: 294–307.

Gupta, S.P. (1980). *The Roots of Indian Art*. Delhi: B.R. Publishing Corporation.

Guruge, A.W.P. 1993. *Asoka, the Righteous: A Definitive Biography*. Colombo: The Central Cultural Fund.

Hazra, Kanai Lal. 1986 (rpntd 2002). *The Buddhist Annals and Chronicles of South-East Asia*. New Delhi: Munshiram Manoharlal Publishers Pvt. Ltd.

Hnuber, O.V. 2018. "Some Buddhst Donors and Their Families". *Indo-Iranian Journal* 61: 353–68.

Hultzsch, E. 1924 (rpntd 1991). *Corpus Inscriptionum Indicarum Volume I: Inscriptions of Ashoka*. New Delhi: Archaeological Survey of India.

Imperial Gazetteer of India XVII, The, 1908–31.

Indian Archaeology – A Review 2003–04. New Delhi: Archaeological Survey of India.

Indraji, Bhagwanlal, and Georg Buhler. 1878. "The Inscriptions of Rudradaman at Junagadh". *The Indian Antiquary*, VII: 257–63.

Jamsedjee, Ardeseer. 1890–4. "The Sudarshana or Lake Beautiful of the Girnar Inscriptions, BC 300–AD 450, With an Introduction by O. Codrington". *Journal of the Bombay Branch of the Royal Asiatic Society*, LVIII: 47–55.

Kaung, U. Thaw. 2013. *Myanmar Wonderland – Places of Historical Interest and Scenic Beauty*. Yangon: Today Publishing Ltd.

Khunsong, Saritpong, Phasook Indrawooth, and Surapol Natapintu. 2011. "Excavation of a pre-Dvaravati Site at Hor-Ek in Ancient Nakhon Pathom". *Journal of the Siam Society* (99): 150–70.

Kielhorn, F. 1905-6. "Junagadh Rock Inscription of Rudradaman; The Year 72". *Epigraphia Indica*, VIII: 36–49.

Lagirarde, François. 2012. "Narratives as Ritual Histories: The Case of the Northern-Thai Buddhist Chronicles", in Peter Skilling and Justin McDaniel, eds, *Buddhist Narrative in Asia and Beyond*, vol. 1. Bangkok: Institute of Thai Studies, Chulalaongkorn University, 83–96.

Lahiri, Nayanjot. 2019. "How Did Mahatma Gandhi End Up Joining Gods on a Gopuram of a Vishnu Temple in Sri Lanka?" *Scroll. in*, March 30th.

———. 2017. *Monuments Matter – India's Archaeological Heritage since Independence*. Mumbai: Marg Foundation.

———. 2015. *Ashoka in Ancient India*. Ranikhet and Cambridge: Permanent Black and Harvard University Press.

———. 2012a. *Marshalling the Past – Ancient India and its Modern Histories*. Ranikhet: Permanent Black.

———. 2012b. "Hold Fast to the Past". *Hindustan Times*, October 26: 12.

———. 2011. "Revisiting the Cultural Landscape of Junagadh in the Time of the Mauryas". *Puratattva* 41: 115–30.

Luce, G.H., B.B. Shin, and U.T. Oo. 1970. "Old Burma: Early Pagan". *Artibus Asiae Supplementum*, 25.

Ma Mu, Khin Ma. 2018. "Terracotta Votive Tablets from Catubhummika Hngak Twin Monastery, Thaton". *SPAFA Journal* (2), 1–29.

Majumdar, Susmita Basu. 2017. *Barabar-Nagarjuni Hills – A Biography of the Twin Sites*. Patna: Kashi Prasad Jayaswal Research Institute.

———. Soumya Ghosh, and Shoumita Chatterjee. 2019. "Separate Rock Edicts of Asoka: A Critical Appraisal". *Pratna Samiksha*, 10: 53–73.

Manuel, J. 2006. "The Dilemma of the Archaeological Conservator: Examples from Buddhist Sites in Madhya Pradesh". *Puratan*, 14: 54–60.

Marshall, J., A. Foucher, and N.G. Majumdar. 1940 (rpntd 1983). *The Monuments of Sanchi*, 3 volumes. Delhi: Swati Publications.

Miksic, John N., and Geok Yian Goh. 2017. *Ancient Southeast Asia*. Routledge: London and New York.

Mishra, Phani Kanta. 2001. "Deorkothar Stups: New Light on Early Buddhism". *Marg*, 52 (1): 64–74.

Mitra, Debala. 1957. (7th edn 2001). *Sanchi*. New Delhi: Archaeological Survey of India.

Munro-Hay, Stuart. 2001. *Nakhon Sri Thammarat – The Archaeology, History and Legends of a Southern Thai Town*. Bangkok: White Lotus Press.

Murphy, Charlennen, Alison Weisskopf, Wijeratthne Bohingamuwa, Gamini Adikari, Nimal Perera, James Blinkhorn, Mark Horton, Dorian Q. Fuller, and Nicole Boivin. 2018. "Early Agriculture in Sri Lanka: New Archaeobotanical Analyses and Radiocarbon Dates from the Early Historic Sites of Kirinda and Kanttharodai (Kandarodai)". *Archaeological Research in Asia* (16): 88–102.

Noonsuk, Wannasarn. 2013. *Tambralinga and Nakhon Si Thammarat: Early Kingdoms of the Isthmus of Southeast Asia*. Nakhon Si Thammarat: Nakhon Si Thammarat Rajabhat University.

Oldenberg, Hermann. 1879 (rpntd 1982). *The Dipavamsa – An Ancient Buddhist Historical Record*. New Delhi: Asian Educational Services.

Ongsakul, Sarassawadee. 2005 (English translation by Chitaporn Tanratanakul). *History of Lanna*. Bangkok: Silkworm Books.

Paranavitana, S. 1970. *Inscriptions of Ceylon Volume I. Early Brahmi Inscriptions*. Ceylon: Department of Archaeology.

Pichard, Pierre, and François Lagirarde. 2013. *The Buddhist Monastery – A Cross-Cultural Survey*. Chiang Mai: Silkworm Books.

Pieris, Anoma. 2019. *Sovereignty, Space and Civil War in Sri Lanka*. London and New York: Routledge.

Pieris, P.E. 1917. "Nagadipa and Buddhist Remains in Jaffna". *The Journal of the Ceylon Branch of the Royal Asiatic Society of Great Britain and Ireland*, 26 (70, 1): 11–30.

Poonacha, K.P. 2011. *Excavations at Kanaganahalli (Sannati)*. New Delhi: Archaeological Survey of India.

Pramanaik, Shubhra. 2004–5. "Significant Discoveries Around Sudarshan Lake, Junagadh". *Puratattva*, 35: 179–81.

Pranke, Patrick Arthur. 2004. "The 'Treatise on the Lineage of the Elders' (*Vamsadipani*): Monastic Reform and the Writing of Buddhist History in Eighteenth-Century Burma". Dissertation, University of Michgan.

Raghupathy, Ponnampalam. 1987. *Early Settlements in Jaffna – An Archaeological Survey*. Madras: Thillimalar Raghupathy.

Rajan, K. 2011. "Emergence of Early Historic Trade in Peninsular India", in Pierre-Yves Manguin, A. Mani, and Geoff Wade, ed., *Early Interactions Between South and Southeast Asia – Reflections on Cross-Cultural Exchange*. Singapore and New Delhi: Institute of Southeast Asian Studies and Manohar, 177–96.

———. 2012. *Rediscovering India – An Exhibition of Important Archaeological Finds: 1961–2011*. New Delhi: Archaeological Survey of India.

Rajyagor, S.B. 1975. *Gujarat State Gazetteers Junagadh District*. Ahmedabad: Government of Gujarat.

Revire, Nicolas. 2018. "Facts and Fiction: The Myth of Suvannabhumi Through the Thai and Burmese Looking Glass". *Trans-Regional and -National Studies of Southeast Asia*, 6 (2): 167–205.

Romm, James, ed. 2012. *The Landmark Arrian: The Campaigns of Alexander*. New York: Anchor Books.

Sahni, Daya Ram. 1914. *Catalogue of the Museum of Archaeology at Sarnath*. Calcutta: Superintendent of Government Printing.

Salomon, Richard. 1998. *Indian Epigraphy – A Guide to the Study of Inscriptions in Sanskrit, Prakrit, and the Other Indo-Aryan Languages*. New Delhi: Munshiram Manoharlal Publishers Pvt. Ltd.

Sarma, I.K., and J.V. Rao. 1993. *Early Brahmi Inscriptions from Sannati*. New Delhi: Harman Publishing House.

Schalk, Peter. 1996. "The Vallipuram Buddha Image 'Rediscovered'", in *Symposium on Religious Art, Dance and Music, Held at Åbo, Finland, on the 16th–18th August 1994*. Abo: The Donner Institute, pp. 295–312.

Schober, J. 1997. "Trajectories in Buddhist Sacred Biography", in J. Schober, ed., *Sacred Biography in the Buddhist Traditions of South and Southeast Asia*. Honolulu: University of Hawai'i Press, 1–15.

Sen, Tansen. 2006. "The Travel Records of Chinese Pilgrims Faxian, Xuanzang, and Yijing". *Education about Asia*, 11 (3): 24–33.

Seshadri, M. 1972. "Buddhist Monuments in Mysore". *Artibus Asiae,* 34 (2/3): 169–82.

Silva, Roland. 2006. *Architecture and Town Planning in Sri Lanka During the Early and Medieval Periods – Environment, Town, Village and Monastic Planning.* Sri Lanka: Department of Archaeology.

Singh, Upinder. 2021. *The World of India's First Archaeologist – Letters from Alexander Cunningham to J.D.M. Beglar.* New Delhi: Oxford University Press.

———. 2016. "Sanchi: The History of the Patronage of an Ancient Buddhist Establishment". *Indian Economic and Social History Review,* 33: 1–35.

———. 2014. "Gifts from Other Lands: Southeast Asian Religious Endowments in India", in Upinder Singh and Parul Pandya Dhar, ed., *Asian Encounters – Exploring Connected Histories.* New Delhi: Oxford University Press, 44–61.

———. 2004. *The Discovery Ancient India – Early Archaeologists and the Beginnings of Archaeology.* Delhi: Permanent Black.

Singhal, D.P. 1984. *Buddhism in East Asia.* New Delhi: Books & Books.

Sircar, D.C. 2000. *Asokan Studies.* Calcutta: Indian Museum.

Sivasundaram, Sujit. 2007. "Buddhist Kingship, British Archaeology and Historical Narratives in Sri Lanka". *Past & Present* (197): 111–42.

Skilling, Peter. 1997. "The Advent of Theravada Buddhism in Mainland South-east Asia". *Journal of the International Association of Buddhist Studies,* 20 (1): 93-1-8.

Spate, O.H.K., and A.T.A. Learmouth. 1967 (Indian edn 1984). *India and Pakistan: A General and Regional Geography.* New Delhi: Munshiram Manoharlal Publishers Pvt. Ltd.

Spooner, D.B. 1910. Letter dated 6th April, Spooner Papers, Stanford: Stanford University Libraries.

———. 1908–9 (rpntd 1990). "Excavations at Shah-ji-Dheri". *Archaeological Survey of India Annual Report 1908–09.* Delhi: Swati Publications.

Strong, John S. 1989 (rpntd 2008). *The Legend of King Asoka: A Study and Translation of the Asokavadana.* Delhi: Motilal Banarsidass.

Sykes, W.H. 1837. "Inscriptions from the Boodh Caves, Near Joonur. Communicated in a Letter to Sir John Malcolm, G.C.B., President of the Literary Society, Bombay'. *Journal of the Royal Asiatic Society of Great Britain & Ireland*, 4 (8): 287–91.

Tambiah, S.J. 1976. *World Conqueror and World Renouncer – A Study of Buddhism and Polity in Thailand against a Historical Background*. Cambridge: Cambridge University Press.

Tod, James. 1839 (rpntd 1971). *Travels in Western India Embracing a Visit to the Sacred Mounts of the Jains and the Most Celebrated Shrines of Hindu Faith Between Rajpootana and the Indus; With an Account of the Ancient City of Nehrwalla*. Delhi: Oriental Publishers.

Thaplyal, K.K. 1985. *Inscriptions of the Maukharis, Later Guptas, Puspabhutis and Yasovarman of Kanauj*. New Delhi: Indian Council of Historical Research.

Than Tun, Win. 2002. "Myanmar Buddhism of the Pagan Period (AD 1000–1300)". PhD thesis. Singapore: National University of Singapore.

Thwin, Michael Aung. 1979. "The Role of Sasana Reform in Burmese History: Economic Dimensions of a Religious Purification". *Journal of Asian Studies*, 38 (4): 671–88.

Tyldesley, Joyce. 2008. *Cleopatra – Last Queen of Egypt*. Basic Books: New York.

Vajpeyi, Ananya. 2012. *Righteous Republic – The Political Foundation of Modern India*. Cambridge and London: Harvard University Press.

Veidlinger, Daniel M. 2007. *Spreading the Dhamma – Writing, Orality, and Textual Transmission in Buddhist North Thailand*. Honolulu: University of Hawai'i Press.

Veluppillai, A. 1981. "Tamil in Ancient Jaffna and Vallipuram Gold Plate". *Journal of Tamil Studies*, 1–14.

Veluthat, I. 2000. "The Sannathi Inscriptions and the Questions They Raise'. *Proceedings of the Indian History Congress*, Golden Jubilee Session 1999, Calicut, 1081–6.

Weerakkody, D.P.M. 1997. *Taprobane – Ancient Sri Lanka as Known to Greeks and Romans*. Brepols: Turnhout.

Wijeyeratne, Roshan de Silva. 2007. "Buddhism, the Asokan Persona, and the Galactic Polity: Rethinking Sri Lanka's Constitutional Present". *Social Analysis: The International Journal of Anthropology*, 1: 156–70.

Williams, Joanna. 1973. "Recut Asokan Capital and the Gupta Attitude Towards the Past". *Artibus Asiae*, 35 (3): 225–40.

Woodward, Mark R. 1988. "When One Wheel Stops: Theravada Buddhism and the British Raj in Upper Burma'. *Crossroads: An Interdisciplinary Journal of Southeast Asian Studies*, 4 (1): 57–90.

Wyatt, David K. 2001. "Relics, Oaths and Politics in Thirteenth-Century Siam". *Journal of Southeast Asian Studies*, 32 (1): 3–65.

———. 1982 (rpntd 2004). *Thailand – A Short History*. Chiang Mai: Silkworm Books.

———. 1975. *The Crystal Sands – The Chronicles of Nagara Sri Dharmaraja*, Data Paper Number 98. Ithaca and New York: Cornell University.

———, and Aroonrut Wichienkeeo. 1998. *The Chiang Mai Chronicle*. Chiang Mai: Silkworm Books.

Yi, Ma Yi. 1965. "Burmese Sources for the History of the Konbaung Period 1752–1885". *Journal of Southeast Asian History*, 6 (1): 48–66.

Yian Goh, Geok. 2015. *The Wheel-Turner and His House*. Illinois: Northern Illinois University Press.

Yupho, D. 1965 (rpntd 1990). *Dharmacakra or the Wheel of Law*. Bangkok: The Fine Arts Department.

Zin, Monika. 2019. "The Techniques of the Narrative Representations in Old India", in Elisabeth Wagner-Durand, *et al.*, ed., *Image – Narration – Context: Visual Narratives in the Cultures and Societies of the Old World*. Heidelberg: Propylaeum, Freiburger Studien zur Archäologie & Visuellen Kultur, I, 137–56.

———. 2018a. *The Kanaganahalli Stupa – An Analysis of the 60 Massive Slabs Covering the Dome*. New Delhi: Aryan Books International.

———. 2018b. "Kanaganahalli in Satavahana Art and Buddhism: King Asoka in Front of the Bodhi Tree". *Journal of the International Association of Buddhist Studies*, 41: 537–68.

Index

Adhaloka Chaitya (ancient name of Kanaganahalli stupa complex) 62; *also see* Kanaganahalli
Adicca, King 191
Adityana 87
Afghanistan 4, 10, 60
Africa 120
Ajatshatru, King 45, 171, 190, 211
Ajayata 68
Ajivika 102, 104–5, 111–14, 116, 118, 204
Alaungsithu, King 159–61
Allahabad inscription of Samudragupta 95
Amarapura 152
Amaravati, Andhra 48, 68, 184, 187, 205
Ambatthala 135
Ananda temple 166
Anantavarman 110, 115–16, 118
  conversion of caves in Barabar and Nagarjuni hills 116
Anawrahta, King 158–9, 161, 168, 172–5
ancient India 1, 3, 6, 8, 21, 68, 83, 95, 115, 137, 143, 147, 164, 213
Andhra 60, 62–3, 65, 68
Angkorian Cambodia 199

animals 13–14, 17, 31, 36, 41, 59, 61, 76, 90, 194, 206
  carving 41
  castration 14
  compassion for 194
  depiction of 41
  killing 41
  pack 14
  slaughter of 14
Annaikoddai 132
Anula, Queen 124, 134
Anuradhapura 122–3, 127, 134–5, 137–40, 146–7
  temple complex at 147
  Mahavihara 123, 138
Arabian Sea 83
archaeological
  digs and discoveries 27, 85
  history 133
  mound 131
  remains 131
  remnants 84, 86, 96
  sites 51, 53, 97
Archaeological Survey of India (ASI) 26–8, 53, 55, 57–8, 79, 85, 117, 153, 155–6, 166
archaeology 53, 61, 63, 133, 139–40, 167, 181
  Indian 53, 63
  Thailand's 181
architecture 54, 58, 109, 111, 131

227

228　INDEX

Ashoka's visibility in 58
stupa 54
temple 131
art 5, 23, 48, 71, 74, 77, 172, 176, 185, 187–8, 201
  ancient 71
  Indian 187–8
  old 74
  palimpsest techniques in 71
  Sri Lankan (in south Thailand) 201
artefacts and antiquities 1, 3, 7, 12, 22, 26–8, 34, 58–9, 62, 82, 87–8, 92, 99, 105, 112, 119, 162, 173, 180–2
artisans 68, 111
artists 5, 31, 41, 71, 74, 77, 163, 207
ascetics 102–4, 109, 111–12, 114, 116
Ashoka (emperor)
  admonitory 33
  after Kalinga 9
  afterlife 75, 205
  avatar 40, 47, 79
  Buddha 49
  Buddhist pontiff 15
  builder of stupas 161
  commemoration of 7
  communicator 11
  conquest of Kalinga 91
  construction of pillars 210
  conversion to Buddhism 10
  defeated 12
  dhammic zeal 19
  factions and 15
  first sermon 30, 40–1, 184, 187–8, 206
  guardian of animals 14
  ideas, ideals, innovations 8, 11, 13
  Kanaganahalli slab 77
  major rock edicts 17, 60
  military victory 18
  Nakhon Si Thammarat 2
  pilgrim 15, 74
  power of 48
  provincial capital 59
  reign of 29, 87, 180
  representations of 57, 69, 71, 74–5
  Sarnath pillar 7
  sculptural rendering of 71
  stories of 43, 45, 48, 149, 205
  visit to Ramagrama stupa 43–5
  visit to the Bodhi tree 45–6, 73, 75
Ashokan
  carved architrave 110
  caves 113
  edicts 11, 16, 52, 77, 79, 91, 95–6, 119, 148, 151, 175
  epigraphs 29, 52, 59, 95–6, 109, 111
  pillar(s) 7, 31–2, 41, 57, 178, 184, 211–13
  renovation of dam 97
  stupas 7, 35, 64
  wheel in flag 215
Ashoka in Ancient India 3, 6
Ashokarama 148, 169
Ashokavadana 4, 43, 45, 113, 174, 210, 213
Asia 1, 4, 7, 12, 19, 120, 123, 127, 151, 154–5, 162, 167, 172–3, 176, 180–2, 184, 188, 196, 199, 202, 209, 214
Asoke Montri, Phra 178
Asoke temples, Thailand 178

Atavikas 18, 151
Aung San (general) 154
Ayubbid dynasty 5

Babina 20–2
Bagan 158–68, 172–3, 175,
  195–6, 199, 208
  architectural landscape of 167
  shrines and museums 167
  twelfth-century 168
Bagan–Sri Lanka relationship 168
Bairat edicts, Rajasthan 15, 82
Bakker, Hans 143
Bang Kluai Nok 181
Bangkok 178, 183, 184
Bangkok National Museum 183–4
Barabar 101–4, 113, 116–17, 204
Bay of Bengal 1, 129, 173
Bayon temple, Cambodia 84
Beach of the Crystal Sand,
  Thailand 201
Begum, Sultan Jahan 26–7, 93–4
  An Account of My Life 93
Beikthano 167
Benares 193
Bhaddasala (*also* Bhadrasala) 125,
  139
Bhaduka 125
Bharhut 142, 205
Bhaumakaras 214
Bhavnath 99–100
Bhikkuni (Buddhist nun) 124,
  126, 135
Bhikkus/Bhikshus 148–50, 181
  demoted 149
  unworthy 149–50
Bhikshu Samgha 99
Bhilsa 25
Bhopal 20, 22, 24, 26–8
Bhor Devi temple 98–100

Bhutapati 116
Bibi Kamal Sahiba 101–2
Bihar 1, 7, 28, 30, 101–2, 104–5,
  111, 115–17, 164, 197, 212
  caves in 111
Bilhana 67
Bindusara, king 30, 113, 190, 193,
  211
birds 14, 17, 41, 112
Bodawpaya, King 159–63
  epigraphs 162
Bodh Gaya 73, 126, 208, 213
Bodhimula 115
Bodhisattvas 2
Bodhi tree 30, 43, 45, 48, 53,
  73–5, 124–8, 134–5, 138,
  147, 191–2, 207–8, 210
Bombay (Mumbai) 97, 119
Borobudur 164
Borommaracha 196
Bota-Sriparvatta 27
Brahmanas 13, 17, 90–1, 201
Brahmans 17, 71–2, 145, 206–7
  disrespect of 17
  support to 72
Brahmi epigraph/inscription 28,
  141, 181
Britain 155, 156
British India 53, 155
  ASI reports 53
  excavations in 155
British Raj 26, 155
British rule 153, 155
Buddha
  bones of 155–7
  departure from Kapilavastu 43
  enlightenment 164, 208
  first sermon at Sarnath 40–1,
    187, 206
  funeral pyre 30

immanence of the 150
incarnations of 138
Jaya gifts earth to 48
principal disciples 36
prophecy 47
relics of 3, 30, 138, 154–5, 199
Buddha Konakamana 15, 209
Buddha's relics 147, 153–4
Buddha's relics, Mandalay 154
Buddha's remains 36, 156
Buddhism 7, 10, 14, 30–1, 34, 42, 63, 69, 72–3, 77, 79, 88, 118, 122–5, 127, 132–3, 138, 140, 143–6, 148, 155, 167, 172, 174, 182, 184, 187–91, 193, 202–3, 207–8, 210, 213
  archaeological evidence of 140
  establishment of 140, 190
  in the Indian South 72
  Mahayana form of 123
Buddhist 34, 37, 50, 71–2, 88, 100, 102, 120, 130, 134, 148, 172, 179, 212
  caves 99
  chronicles 30, 122, 143
  community 25, 61, 204
  devotees 128
  establishments 35, 140, 142, 178
  faith 150, 155, 216
  images 130
  literature 34, 47, 213
  monastic community 40, 179
  monastic set-up 99
  relics 3, 53, 150, 154, 157, 201, 203, 215
  Samgha/Sangha 17, 49, 160, 193
  sanctuaries 68
  Shramanas 15

shrines 54, 158
sites 64, 132–3, 140, 179, 184, 205, 212
Burma (Myanmar) 7, 119, 152–8, 160–2, 164, 167, 173–4, 176, 182, 201, 205, 208–9
Burmese royal dynasty 152

Calcutta (Kolkata) 81, 119, 156
Camadevi, Queen 193–4
  Theri Sanghamitta 121, 134, 169
Central India 7, 15, 22, 35, 59
chaityas/chetiyas 27, 130, 137–8, 140 209–10
chakra 74, 184, 187–8
  Thai 187
Chakravartin 185
Chamunda 87
Chandragupta (*also* Candagutta), first monarch of the Maurya dynasty 86–7, 92, 94, 97, 143, 190, 193
Chandragupta II 143
Chandralamba temple, Sannathi 52–3, 77–8
Ch'ang-an 211
Chao Phraya 184
Chedi 184, 201
Chen Hui 212
Chhimukha (*also* Simukha) Satavahana 65–6, 71
Chiang Mai 7, 10, 178–80, 188–9, 191–2, 194–7, 208
  Ashokan signs at 180
  Sarnath pillar at 10
Chiang Mai Chronicle 192, 194
China 1, 3, 7, 180–1, 185, 211–12
  in Ashoka stupas 7
Chitradurga 50

Cholas 125, 168
Christianity 5, 72, 84, 208
chronicles 2, 30, 46, 122, 127,
    143, 145–8, 150–1, 162,
    168, 171–2, 174–5, 184, 189,
    192–3, 197, 201–3, 205, 214
  Burmese 175
  Lankan 46, 148, 150–1, 168,
    172
  medieval 2
  Nakhon (Thailand) 197, 201
  Pali 122, 145, 150–1, 171,
    192–3
Cleopatra, Egyptian queen 5, 39
coins 28, 64–5, 98–9, 131, 154,
    206
  gold 154
  Pandyan 131
  silver 131
Colombo National Museum 129
Colonial Burma 153
consecration 8, 18, 115, 125,
    190–1, 207
Constantine 208
conversion 10, 116, 133, 140, 207
converts 43, 174
copper 28, 98, 120
  coins 28
coral and lapis lazuli 59
culture 5, 12, 19, 58, 132, 134,
    176, 185–6, 188, 203, 215
  contemporary 176
  diversity of 19
  Dvaravati 185–6, 188
  material 185
  megalithic 132
  public 12
Cyrene 4

Dalai Lama 156

Dambulla caves 147
Damilas 151
Dandakumar 199–200
Dandapuri 201
Dan-ma-lin 198
Dantahlem 199
Dantapuri 199
Daridra kantara 114
Dasharatha 116
Datar Hill 97
Deccan plateau 20, 50, 64
dedications 68, 111, 158
deer 67, 76, 91, 183–4, 187
  crouching 184
  park 184
deities 2, 15, 37–8, 53, 72, 77–8,
    105, 108, 114, 117, 158, 191,
    210
  Brahmanical 108
  female 53
  image of 77–8
Department of Archaeology, Sri
    Lanka 131
Deur Kuthar, Rewa, Madhya
    Pradesh 34–5
Devanampiya, King 124, 143–4,
    169, 190
Devanampiyatissa 124
Devanampiya Tissa ("DT"),
    Sinhala monarch 124–6,
    134–5, 137–8, 143–4, 150,
    169, 190
Devaraj, Balamurugan 104–5
Devi, spouse of Emperor Ashoka
    22, 30, 32, 38–9, 43, 98,
    121
dhamma (*also* dharma) 13, 16–17,
    90, 93, 124, 127, 137, 150,
    174
  message of 16, 90

practice of 17
protection of 150
state based on 93
yatras 13, 18
Dhammaraja, King 208
Dhammasok 167, 169
Dhammasokaraja 201
Dhammasoka, Siri 124, 126, 159, 169, 208
Dhammikaraja 214
Dhanananda 190
Dharagir gate 97
Dharamsey, Virchand 64, 82
Dharmacakrastambhas 188
dharmachakras 31, 40, 56, 73, 179, 182–8, 205–6, 216
  Dvaravati 184–5, 187
  significance of 185
  Thai 185
Dharmarajikas 47
Dharmasoka, King 38, 209
Dharwar 59
Dhatusena, King 123
Dighasandana 138
Dighasandase-napati-parivena 138
Dipavamsa 120, 122, 146, 161, 168
donations 37–8, 68, 139, 143–4, 178, 187
Dong Song bronze drums 202
donors 37–40, 68–9, 143, 146, 158
  royal 143, 146
Drona stupa 45
Dutthagamani (and Dutugamunu) 123, 151
Dvaravati 184–9
dynasties 1–2, 5–6, 12, 26, 49, 52, 62, 64–5, 68, 86, 95, 152,
  160, 179, 186, 189–92, 196, 201–2, 204–5
  Ayubbid 5
  Burmese royal 152
  Gupta 62, 186
  Konbaung 160
  Kushana 62
  Lanna 179
  Maurya 1, 6, 12, 52, 62, 86, 190, 205
  Satavahana 62

Eastern India 30
Eastern Sri Lanka 144
East India Company 87, 155
edicts 4, 8, 11–18, 29, 33, 48, 50–3, 60, 65, 77–9, 82, 90–2, 94–6, 99, 119, 124–5, 142, 148, 150–1, 175, 204, 207, 209
Egypt 4, 209
elephant 41, 44–5, 76, 109, 115, 135, 175, 194, 201, 206
  design 109
  panel 115
  white 194
Eliot, T.S. 22
  Waste Land, The 22
emperors/kings/rulers
  Bagan 173, 175
  Buddhist 48, 69, 72, 124, 127, 149, 151, 163, 185, 205, 214
  Burmese 209
  Damila 151
  Hindu 72
  Indian 1–4, 26, 125, 140, 169, 178, 189, 202, 215
  Kanva 65
  Maukhari 115

Mauryan 72
Mughal 96
Myanmarese 175
Pala 214
Roman 72
Satavahana 64–5, 67, 69–72, 77, 204
Sinhala 123
South East Asian 175
Sri Lankan 149, 192
Thai 192
England 112, 155, 160
epigraphs 6–7, 27, 29, 32, 36, 39, 43, 52, 59, 64–6, 68, 71, 79, 82–4, 92–6, 98, 109–11, 114–15, 120, 130, 140–5, 147, 158–62, 167, 169, 181, 184, 187–8, 205, 208
Erragudi 13, 17–18, 125
Europe 127, 208
excavations 27, 53, 61, 132, 155–6, 185
    in 1970 132
    in British India 155
    Kanaganahalli 61
    Kanishka stupa 155
    Nern Hin 185
    Shah-ji-ki Dheri 156

faiths 15, 44, 69, 72, 102, 114, 116, 125, 130, 134, 150, 155, 190, 208, 212, 216
    Buddhist 150, 155, 216
    display of 69
    personal 72
    religious 102
    Vaishnava 116
Faxian 211–12
"Fifty Stanzas of a Thief" 67

forests 14, 18, 24, 86–7, 97, 99–100, 114, 151, 191, 199
    dwellers in 18, 151
Forster, E.M. 103–4, 112, 116–17
    A Passage to India 103, 112, 116
    "Caves" 103

Gandhara 38, 125
Gandhi, Mahatma 5–6, 105, 131, 178
Gangetic
    plains 15, 20
    region 34
gateways 24–8, 39–40, 43, 45, 48, 55, 73, 111
    carved 39, 43, 48, 55, 111
    epigraphs on 39
    narrative 45
    pillar 45
gifts 13–14, 37, 39, 48, 68, 73, 123, 125, 137, 174, 207
Girinagara 94
Girnar 13, 81–2, 85–91, 94–100, 207
    inscriptions 82
    mountain (and hills) 87, 88
    "parikrama" 99
    Reserve Sanctuary 97
    rock 81–2, 88–9, 91, 95–7, 100
    seven-peaked 87
    Tod's response to 90
gold 13, 59, 98, 129, 133, 154, 156, 158, 196, 207, 210
    coins 154
    control and regulation of 59
    objects 59
    workings 59
Golden Buddha 162
Golden land 182
Gonatas, Antigonus II 4

INDEX

Goraknath peak 85
Goths 12
Gotihawa 7, 209
  broken pillar at 7
governance 6, 11–12, 17–18, 148, 151, 202
  Ashokan element of 148
  by consensus 148
  ideas of 11, 151
  ideology of 6
  novel modes of 12
Greece 209
Gujarat 60, 81, 85–6, 214
Gulbarga 51
Gulf of Thailand 189
Guptas 83, 95, 115, 143, 186
  dynasty 186
  epigraph 95
  monarch 83, 143

Hariphunchai 214
Haripunjaya 191, 193
Hasnapur Dam 99
Hatthalhaka-vihara 135
Hemis monastery, Ladakh 157
Hemjala 199–200
Henry VIII 160
hills 50, 82–3, 85, 87–8, 98–9, 101–5, 109, 112, 115–16, 118
Hindu 2, 38, 41, 58, 72, 79, 88, 100, 105, 108, 116, 118, 203
  deities 2, 38
  fanatics 41
  gods and goddesses 105
  Hinduism 64, 79
  sacred space 203
  shrines 203
  temples 58

historical
  forgetting 7
  memory 7, 204
  remembrance 6
history 2, 4, 6–7, 12, 21, 25, 27, 49, 53, 58, 62–3, 80, 94–5, 101–2, 104–5, 118, 121–2, 131, 133, 146–7, 150, 164, 167, 172–3, 175, 178, 180, 185, 189, 192–3, 199, 207, 211, 216
Hongsawadi (Pegu) 201
Hospet 51–2
Huns 12, 80

Idika 144
images 5, 7–8, 12, 22–3, 105–8, 130, 139, 175, 177, 180, 202–3, 205
Imperial Gazetteer of India XVII, The 163
Indonesia 164
Indraji, Bhagvanlal 64, 81–2, 89, 99
Inle lake 159–61
inscriptions 27–8, 33, 37, 39, 51, 60, 63–4, 81–4, 90, 95–7, 99, 103, 111, 139–40, 142–6, 158–60, 167, 170, 181, 185, 187, 197, 206, 208
  Brahmi 28, 142, 181
  dedicatory 143
  first-century CE 139
  of 1196 CE 160
  rock 51
  Satavahana 63
  seal 99
  sixteenth-century 96
  Tamil-Brahmi 181

INDEX 235

Intawa 99–100
  excavated in 1949 99
Irrawaddy 158, 160, 167
Israel 151
Issarasamanarama 134
I'tsing 185
Itthiya 125, 139, 144

Jaffna 121–2, 124, 127–34
  Buddhist sites in 133
  Public Library 121
  Tamils 133
Jahanabad (*also* Jehanabad), Bihar 7, 101–2, 104–5
Jahanara Begum 101
Jahangir, Mughal emperor 96
Jain 88, 100, 102
Jambudipa/Jambudvipa 137, 190–1, 208
Jambukola Patuna 124, 127–9, 134
Jamsedjee, Khan Bahadur Ardeseer 96–7
Jataka stories/tales 64, 169, 182
Jatinga-Rameshwara 50
Jaya Sri Maha Bodhi 47–8, 139
Jerusalem 5
Jetavana 211
Jhansi 20, 21
Jina Baba ki Madi 99–100
Jinakalamalipakaranam 189, 192–3
Jogiana Hill 97
Johnson, Captain 26
Journal of the Asiatic Society of Bengal 25
Junagadh, Gujarat 81–8, 92, 94–7, 99–100, 204, 215

Kakanava/Kakanaya/Kakanada 27

Kakudha pond 138
Kala, king of the Nagas 169
Kalinga 9, 10, 12, 18, 29, 48, 60, 68, 71, 91, 175, 209
Kalsi 12–13
Kamboja 38
Kanaganahalli, Karnataka 7, 49, 51–5, 57–9, 61–2, 64–5, 69, 71, 73, 75–8, 80, 204–7
  edict stone 78
  depiction of Ashoka at 64, 73
  portraits at 71
  sculptural programme at 69
  stupa 52, 61, 69
Kanakmuni 209
Kandy-Matale 145
Kanishka, King 63, 154–5, 211
Kanishka stupa 155
Kanithatissaka, king 130
Kannauj 115
Kantarodai 131–3
Kanthakacetiya (*also* Kanthaka Cetiya) 140, 144
Kanyakumari 129
Kapilavastu (*also* Kapilavatthu) 43, 193, 210
Karna Chaupad (*also* Karna Chaupar) 111, 114
Karnataka 4, 7, 50–1, 53, 58–62, 65, 69, 73, 75
Karunashankar, Haridatt 82
Karuvaki 12
Kashmir 67, 125, 212
Kathiawad gazetteer 82
Kausambi (*also* Kaushambi) 15, 148
Kedah 198
Khajuraho temples 41
Khan, Genghis 12
Khan Luk Pat 181

Khao Sam Kaeo 180
kingship 11–12, 47, 124, 127, 161, 174–5, 196, 208
Klesha kantara 114
Konakamuni 15
Konbaung dynasty 160
Koppal District 50
Kosharaja 199
Krabi province 181
Krishna Rao, Kapatral 52–3
Kshatriya 115
Kubyauk-Gyi temple 167–8
Kushana 62–3, 214
Kushinagara (*also* Kushinagari) 30, 210
Kyanzittha, king 169, 172

Ladakh 157
Lady Srimahamaya 193
Lakha Medi stupa 97–8
Lamphun 189, 193–4
languages and scripts
  Ashokan Brahmi 24, 81
  Brahmi 24, 28, 81, 90, 132, 140–2, 167, 180–1, 213
  Burmese 167, 208
  crow 191
  decipherment of 63
  Devanagari 24
  Kharoshthi 213
  Mon 167
  Pali 3, 120, 122–3, 145, 150–51, 167, 171, 185, 187, 189, 192–3
  Prakrit 129, 180–1
  Roman 24
  Sanskrit 4, 30, 81–2, 185
  Tamil-Brahmi 181
Lankasuka 198

Lanna dynasty 179, 214
Liberation Tigers of Tamil Eelam 121
Lingasugur 52
Lion capital, Sarnath 61, 205, 216
Lion pillar 73
lions and bulls 31, 40–1, 56, 76, 86, 179, 206
  Asiatic 86
  carved 40
  remnants of 61
  winged 56, 76
Lohapasada 138
Lomasha Rishi cave 109–11, 114–16
Lower Chindwin 160
Lumbini pillar 213
Lumbini 15, 209–10, 213

Macbeth 91–2, 113
Macedon 4
Maddock, T.H. 26
Madhya Pradesh 25, 34
Magadha 51, 86, 102, 115
Magas 4
Mahabharata 151, 172, 185
Mahabodhi 74, 111, 164–6, 196–7, 207–9
Mahabodhi temple, Bagan 165–6, 196
Mahabodhi temple, Bihar 197
Mahadevi, Queen 199
Mahajanaka Jataka 182
Mahakala, King 169
Mahallanaga, King 130
Mahamahinda-thera 121
Mahamegha-vana 137, 140
Mahamuni (Great Sage) temple 158, 162–4

INDEX

Mahanama 122, 124
Maharashtra 62, 68, 82
Mahasamantaraja 193
Mahasitthu, Twinthin Taikwun 161
Maha-thera (*also* Mahathera) 120, 121, 200–1
Mahavamsa 113, 122–7, 130, 132–5, 137–40, 144, 146, 148, 150–1, 161, 168–9, 174–5, 190
Mahavira 102
Mahayana 123
Mahayazawingyi (MYG) 173–5
Mahida (*also* Mahida-tera, Mahinda, Mahinda-thera) 30, 39, 120–1, 123–6, 128, 135, 137–9, 144–5, 190, 193
Mahishmati 37
Mahmud of Ghazni 58
Maitrakas 214
Malay peninsula 2, 180, 182
Malwa 22, 38
Mandalay, Myanmar 152–5, 157–8, 160, 163–4
Mang Lung Lwang 195
Mangrai, king 179, 194–5
Man Lulan 172
Mantai 131
Marabar caves 103, 112
Mara, the Evil One 43
Marcus Aurelius 9
Marshall, John 26–7, 31, 34, 53
Maski 52, 59–60, 71
Matalaka 66
Mathura 62–3, 154, 205, 210
Maudgalyayana 36
Maurya 1, 6, 12, 34, 52, 58–9, 61–2, 86, 94–5, 190, 193, 204–5, 208
megaliths 58, 130, 134
  burial tradition 132
Mekong delta 182
memorialisation 7–8, 80, 173, 208, 214–15
memorials 21, 85, 134–5
memories 4–5, 7, 17–19, 21, 26, 51, 69, 113, 154, 204, 216
  collective 7
  controlling 7
  food 21
  historical 7, 204
  human 5
  local 26
  modes of 7
  political 4
  public 216
  structuring 7
Mendarda 87
Mihindu Seya 139
Mihintale 135–41, 143–4
Mindon, king of Burma 152, 209
Minto, Lord 156
Missaka mountain, Mihintale 135–6, 139
Mithila 193
Mogaliputta 125, 149, 169–71
Mohanty, Gopinath 24
monasteries 29–31, 40, 99, 123–4, 134, 140, 148, 153, 157, 160, 169, 190–1, 211, 213
Monastery of the Great Bodhi 192
monks and heretics 3, 15, 29–31, 33, 36–7, 40, 43, 66, 68–9, 120, 122, 125, 134–6, 138, 144, 146, 149, 153–4, 157, 161–2, 168, 170–1, 174–5,

238 INDEX

179, 181, 188, 191, 195–6, 203, 210–12
Mrauk-U (Arakan) 162
Myanmarese Ashoka 167
Mybinkaba 167

Nagadata 38
Nagadipa ghara 130
Naganika 65
Nagarapathama 185
Nagara Sri Dharmmaraja (*also* Nagara Sri Dharrmaraja) 199, 201
Nagaraya 65
Nagarjunakonda 48
Nagarjuni hills 116
Nagarpuri 199
Nagas 38, 44–5, 65, 75–6, 123, 145, 169
Nagasena 38
Nakhon National Museum 202
Nakhon Pathom 184–6, 188
Nakhon Si Thammarat 1–4, 7, 79, 184–6, 188, 197–9, 201–2, 204
Nalanda inscription 39
Nanaghat 63–4
Nasik (Maharashtra) 68
National Archives of India, New Delhi 27
National Museum, New Delhi 80
Nauriyal, Kishan 85
Nehru, Jawaharlal 6, 215–16
Nepal 7, 10, 15, 209
  Ashokan pillars in 7
  Buddhist sacred places in 15
Nern Hin excavations 185
Newark Museum 187
New Chronicle 161

Ngalengouk 160
Nibbana 190
Nicene Creed 208
Nigali Sagar 15, 209
Niglihawa 209
Nigrodha 174, 190
Noonsuk, Preecha 202
Norse sagas 151
North Black Polished Ware 59
Northern Myanmar 173
Northern Sri Lanka 132
North India 3, 20, 35, 59, 206
North Thailand 167, 178, 189, 191–2, 194, 214
North West Frontier Province 155
nuns 15, 29, 33, 37–8, 40, 43, 68, 120, 124, 134–5, 188

Occappukallu 145
Old Testament 151
Orissa 60

Pacina Rajha Naga 145
pagodas 159–61, 167
paintings 127, 147, 154, 160, 163–4, 167, 170–1, 205–6
Pakangayi 160
Pakistan 10, 34, 157
Palkigundu 50
Palk Straits 129, 131
Pandyan coins 131
Pandyas 125
Panguraria epigraph 29
Parakramabahu, King 149–50
Paranavitana, S. 142–6
Pataliputra, Maurya capital 22, 29, 43, 47, 51, 90, 161–2, 190, 193
pearls 125, 161

INDEX

Persia 5
Peshawar 153, 156–8
Phlebas 23
Phra Pathom Chedi 185, 187
Phrapathomchedi Museum,
  Nakhon Pathom 185–6
Phra Pathom Chedi stupa 185
Phu Khao Thong 181
Phuteshwar Mahadeva 7
Pillar Edicts 8, 96
pillars 7, 9–10, 13–15, 18, 25, 29,
  31–2, 35, 38, 40–1, 43, 45,
  48–9, 55–7, 61, 65, 73, 78,
  95, 138, 148, 155, 178–80,
  184, 187–8, 205–6, 209–13,
  216
Piyadasina 114
Piyanguka 129
Piyapasika 39
Poonacha, K.P. 53–4, 61, 67–8
Pramanaik, Shubhra 99
Prinsep, James 81, 90, 213
Priyadarshi 39
Priyadarshika 39
Ptolemaic Egypt 4
Ptolemy 119, 120
Pulumayi, king 67–8
punch-marked silver coins 131
Punjab 212
Pushkara in Rajasthan 37
Pushyagupta, Vaishya 94
Pusyamitra, first Sunga king 34

Queen's Edict 12
Quested, Adela 103–4, 112

Raghupathy, P. 130–2
Rajagaha 193
Rajagala 144–6
Rajagriha 47, 51

Rajakumar 168, 172–3
  art patronage 172
Rajapaksa, Mahinda 128
Rajapaksa, Shiranthi
  Wickramasinghe 127
Rajasinha, Kirti Sri, king of Kandy
  147
Raja Siri Chhimukha Sadavahano
  Nagaraya Sakhavapi 65
Rajasthan 15, 37, 82, 87
Rajha Abaya 145
Rajha Shiva 145
Rajkot 85
Rajno Chchimukha Satavahana 65
Rakhine 162–3
Ramagrama stupa 43–4, 48, 75–6
Ramayana, the 135, 151
Ranamandala, Sannathi 53, 61
Rani of Jhansi 21
Ratanapanna 189–90
Rawalpindi, Pakistan 34
relic(s) 3–4, 6, 21, 26, 30–1, 33,
  36–7, 44–5, 47–48, 51, 53,
  62, 87, 97–9, 129, 138–9,
  144, 147, 150, 152–8, 162,
  169, 178, 191, 199–203, 205,
  213, 215
reliquaries 3, 154
remembrance 1, 5–6, 8, 21, 49, 95,
  164, 204–5, 213
restoration 26, 57, 93
  expenses 93
  work 26, 57
Rishipatana (Sarnath) 210
rivers 21, 37, 43, 52, 82–3, 88, 94,
  97, 109, 125, 158, 160, 163,
  189, 196
  Bhima 52
  Ganga 30, 125
  Irrawaddy 158, 160

240 INDEX

Narmada 37
Niranjana 43
Palasini 83, 94
Phalgu 109
Sonarekha (*also* Suvarnarekha) 88, 94, 97
Suvarnasikata 94
Rock Edicts 13–14, 17–18, 48, 60, 92
   major 14, 60
rocks 4, 10–14, 17–18, 21, 48, 51–52, 60–1, 81–2, 84–5, 88–93, 95–8, 100, 102, 105, 108–09, 111, 113–14, 117–18, 138–40, 142, 146
   carving 114
   edicts 14, 48, 60, 92
   engraved 52
   formations 84
   granite 89, 102, 112, 117
   inscribed 61
   inscriptions 51
   slabs 84
   surfaces 10, 113
Roman empire 72
Rudradaman 84, 94–7, 214
   epigraph 94–5
   inscription 84, 95–8
   reign of 97
Rudrapurushadatta, Ikshavaku King 187
Rudrasena, Maharaja 99
Rupani, Parimal 96, 97
Ruwanweli stupa 138

Saas bahu ka bitha 26
Saka Kshatrapa 84
Sakka 138
Sakyamuni 33, 162
Sakyaputra 211
Sakya (the Buddha) 211
Saladin, Sultan 5
Salipabbatam 130
Samanera, Sumana 125
Sambala 125
Samgha (*also* Sangha) 15, 17, 32–3, 37–8, 47, 49, 99, 144, 148–9, 160–1, 169, 175, 193, 204
   proactive 37
   purification of the 148–9, 161
Samghabheda 15, 33, 148
Samudragupta 63, 95
Sanchi 7, 9, 15, 20–36, 38–41, 43–9, 55, 61, 64, 73, 75, 93, 148, 155, 184, 204–7, 215
   Stupa 2, 28, 36, 40–1
Sanchi gateways and railings 27, 39, 45, 55, 73
   stories on 45
Sanghamitta 30, 39, 120–2, 124–9, 134, 135, 138, 169, 190, 193
   arrival in Jaffna 129
   sacred Bodhi tree 30
   statues of 127
   tale of 135
Sankhla 199
Sankisa pillar 212
Sannathi 51–3, 58–60, 77
Santi Asoke ("peaceful Ashoka") group 178
Sappadanapakarna 163
Sariputra 36
Sarnath 7, 9–10, 15, 29–31, 40–1, 57, 73, 148, 179, 184, 187–8, 205–6, 210, 213, 216

Sarnath pillar 7, 9–10, 40–1, 184, 205–6, 216
  at Chiang Mai 10
  at Sanchi 9, 41
Satakarni, Gautamiputra 64–7
Satakarni I, king 65–6
Satakarni, Sundara, king 67
Satavahana 61–72, 77, 204
  dynasty 62
  inscriptions 63
  political presence 61
  reign 62
  rulers 64–5, 77
Saurashtra 83, 86, 89
Scandinavia 151
sculptors 28, 41, 67, 72, 206–7
sculptures 27–8, 43, 54, 56, 65, 68, 71, 73, 80, 108, 203, 205–6
  beads and fragments of 28
  cracked 56
seals 134, 180, 208
  inscription 99
Seleucid kingdom 4
Selliah, Krishnarajah 131
Seneviratne, Sudharshan 121
Seventh Pillar Edict, Delhi-Topra pillar 18
Shah-ji-ki Dheri 155–6
  excavations 156
Shardulavarman 115
Shin Arahan 174
Shramanas 13, 15, 17, 90–1, 207
shrines 29, 34, 37, 53–4, 68, 76–8, 101, 106, 108, 116, 130, 152–3, 158, 160, 162, 164, 167, 169, 203, 208, 210–11
Shunga (*also* Sunga) kings 34–5
Shwegu Dhamatha pagoda 160
Shwe-in-dein pagoda 159

Siam (Thailand) 130, 192
Siddeshwarnath temple 106–7, 109, 117
Siddhartha Gautama 124, 190, 193, 208
Silakuta 135
Sila peak 135
silver 98, 131
Sinhala-Buddhist 133
Si Phum 195
Siridhammasoka, king 160, 174
sites 7–8, 35, 40–1, 50–3, 55, 57–9, 61, 64, 77, 82, 97, 99, 108, 118, 130, 132–3, 137, 140, 143–4, 155, 179, 181, 184–5, 192, 205, 209–10, 212
  archaeological 51, 52, 53, 97
  bombed-out 58
  Dvaravati 185
  historic 8, 58–9, 99
  monastic 99
  monumental 35
  protected 57
  religious 64
  sacred 77
Si Thammsok 2
Si Thep 187
Sithu I 159
Sixth Rock Edict, Erragudi 13
Skandagupta, King 82–4, 95
Soi Asoke 178
Sopara edicts 82
South Bihar 101, 115
South China Sea 1, 181
South East Asia 4, 7, 19, 151, 154, 162, 167, 173, 175, 180–2, 188, 196, 199, 202, 208–9, 214
  religious establishments in 154
  Tamil epigraph in 181

South India 131, 168
South Myanmar 167
South Thailand 1, 181, 196
Spooner, D.B. 156–7
Sri Dharmasokaraja, ruler of "Madhyadesha" 2, 202
Sri-dvaravati-shvarapunya 185
Sri Ksetra 168
Sri Lanka (Ceylon) 7, 30, 119–25, 127, 130–2, 134–5, 137–8, 140, 142–51, 161–2, 168, 171, 175–6, 184, 189–92, 197, 199–201, 203, 205, 214
  Brahmi inscriptions of 142
  Buddhist kings in 149
  chronicles 30, 46, 150, 151, 168, 172
  historic spots in 140
Srimuang, Chamlong 178
Sri Thammasokarat 197
Srivijaya 199
stone pillar, Vaishali 213
stones 6, 8, 11, 16, 29, 31, 35–40, 43, 47–8, 52–3, 57, 59–60, 64, 72, 77–9, 84, 86–7, 93, 95, 97–8, 104–6, 109, 130, 158, 181, 184–5, 187, 203, 205, 212–13
  artefacts 87
  carvings 57
  coffer 98
  deities 105
  disc 59
  edicts 60
  hero 86
  mining 104
  ornaments 181
  pedestal 79
  pillar 31, 43, 212, 213

precious 98
reliefs 64
semi-precious 59
tablets 84
Sudama cave 109–10, 113–15
Sudarshana 82, 86, 93–4, 96, 204
Sudarshana Lake 82, 86, 93, 96, 204
Sujata 43, 208
Sultan Jahan Begum, ruler of Bhopal 26
Suparaga Jataka 182
Surajkund 99
Susrman, Kanva king 65
Suvarnabhumi 182
Suvarnadvipa 182
Suvarnagiri 59
Sykes, Colonel W.H. 63–4
symbolism 185–6, 216

Takkola 198
Talala 87
Tamba 120
Tambapanni (*also* Tamrapanni and Tamraparni) 119–20, 124–5, 209
Tambiah, S. 148, 196
Tambralinga 198
Tamil-Brahmi inscription 181
Tamil diaspora 133
Tamil Nadu 134
Tamils 123, 133, 151
Tamnan Cho Phrae 214
Tamnan Sela That Laem 214
Tamralipti 124
Tangyi pagoda, Bagan 159
Taprobane 119–20
temples and gardens 2, 12, 28, 41, 45, 52–3, 77–8, 88, 84,

98, 106–9, 117–18, 129–32,
  147, 158, 163–9, 172–3, 176,
  178–9, 191, 196–7, 208
 architecture 131
 Buddhist 108
 murals 172
 precincts 106
Ten Commandments of Moses 84
Thailand and India connections 2,
  180
Thai–Malay peninsula 180
Thai/Thailand 1–4, 7, 130, 167,
  177–8, 180–2, 184–5, 187,
  189, 191–2, 194, 196, 201,
  203, 205–6, 208, 214
 artefacts 181
 chakras 187
 dharmachakras 185
 dynasties 2
 mountain chronicles 189
 political history 2
 trading nodes in 182
Thammasok, King 202
Thammikarat (Dhammikaraja) 214
theras 37, 125, 137–9, 144, 148–9,
  189
Theravada 122–3, 150, 161, 172,
  191, 203
Theravada Buddhism 122, 191
 Mahavihara interpretation of
  191
Thibaw, King 156
Third Buddhist Council 148, 169,
  208
Third Rock Edict, Erragudi 13
Thirteenth Rock Edict 12, 18, 92,
  124
 at Erragudi 18
 at Kalsi 12
Thwin 161

Tibet 3, 133, 156
Tiloka, King 191
Tilokrat, King 192, 195–6
Timur 12
Tisapagut 169
Tishyarakshita, Queen 45, 207
Tissa 124, 130, 137, 143, 169–70,
  190
Tissamaharama 131
Tiss-aya 145
Tod, Colonel James 82, 87, 89–90
 Annals and Antiquities of Rajasthan 87
Tranakayira, Maharathi 65
Tushaspha, Yavana king 94
Twelfth Rock Edict, Girnar 13

Udayagiri 143
Ujjayini 22, 30, 38, 67
U Kala 173–5
U-Khanti monastery 153–4
University of Jaffna 131
U Nu, Burmese premier 215
Upagupta 210
Uparkot 87, 99
Upasikavihara 134
Uposatha 148, 170–1
Uposatha festival, Mogaliputta
  149, 170–1
Upunita-vihara 29
Urajayat (mountain) 82, 83, 94
U Thong 184, 185
Uttarakhand 60
Uttar Pradesh 30, 115, 212
Uttiya 125, 139, 144

Vaishali, Bihar 29–30, 73, 213
Vajjis 30
Vajrasana 111, 164
Vallipuram 129–33

Vamsadipani 175
Vamsatthappakasini 113
Varaha and Narayana panels 143
Varanasi 30
Varunadatta 144
Vedisa 30
Vedisagiri vihara 30
Vessagiriya 140–1
Vibhajja-doctrine 149
Vidisha 22–3, 30–1, 38, 43, 61, 143
Vietnam 58
Vijaya 120, 133
Vijayabahu 161, 168, 172
Vikatatungashiva 114
Vinaya pitaka 211
Vinhnumita 38
Vipulasrimitra 39
   Nalanda inscription of 39
Visavadar 87
Vishnumitra 38
Vishnu temple 129–32
Vishwa Jhompri cave 109, 114
Voharika Tissa, king 130

Wat Cedi Cet Yod, Chiang Mai 192, 196–7
Wat Mahathat 201
Wat Suan Dok 191
Wat Umong 178–79

Weerakkody 120
Western India 64, 87
wheel 48, 178, 182, 184, 187, 215–16
wheels of law 31, 40, 206
   Thai versions of 206
Wichienkeeo, Aroonrut 192
women 22, 26–7, 31, 37, 39, 45, 65, 67, 73, 88, 93, 101, 103, 125, 194
   Buddhist 31
   courtiers 65
   emancipation 27, 93
   Japanese 88
   peasant 39
   royal 101
   rulers 26, 194
   Sri Lankan 125
   Sufi 101
Wyatt, David 189, 192, 195, 197, 199

Xuanzang 108–9, 185, 212–13

Yakshas 38, 123
Yakshis 37, 76
Yavana 94, 125
Yian Goh, Geok 168, 173–5, 182

Zin, Monika 57, 65, 73

www.ingramcontent.com/pod-product-compliance
Lightning Source LLC
Chambersburg PA
CBHW030537230426
43665CB00010B/930